Luminos is the Open Access monograph publishing program from UC Press. Luminos provides a framework for preserving and reinvigorating monograph publishing for the future and increases the reach and visibility of important scholarly work. Titles published in the UC Press Luminos model are published with the same high standards for selection, peer review, production, and marketing as those in our traditional program. www.luminosoa.org

This book is part of a project that has received funding from
the European Research Council (ERC) under the
European Union's Horizon 2020 research and innovation program
(grant agreement no. 862367).

European Research Council

Established by the European Commission

Atmospheric Knowledge

Atmospheric Knowledge

Environmentality, Latency, and Sonic Multimodality

Birgit Abels and Patrick Eisenlohr

UNIVERSITY OF CALIFORNIA PRESS

University of California Press
Oakland, California

Suggested citation: Abels, B. and Eisenlohr, P. *Atmospheric Knowledge: Environmentality, Latency, and Sonic Multimodality*. Oakland: University of California Press, 2025. DOI: https://doi.org/10.1525/luminos.244

Library of Congress Cataloging-in-Publication Data

Names: Abels, Birgit, author | Eisenlohr, Patrick, author
Title: Atmospheric knowledge : environmentality, latency, and sonic
    multimodality / Birgit Abels and Patrick Eisenlohr.
Description: Oakland, California : University of California Press, [2025] |
    Includes bibliographical references and index.
Identifiers: LCCN 2025002767 (print) | LCCN 2025002768 (ebook) |
    ISBN 9780520423190 cloth | ISBN 9780520417328 paperback |
    ISBN 9780520417342 ebook
Subjects: LCSH: Music—Environmental aspects—Islands of the Pacific |
    Music—Environmental aspects—Islands of the Indian Ocean |
    Island people—Islands of the Pacific—Music—History and criticism |
    Island people—Islands of the Indian Ocean—Music—History and
    criticism | Atmosphere—Philosophy | Sound—Islands of the Pacific |
    Sound—Islands of the Indian Ocean | Islands of the Pacific—Social
    life and customs | Islands of the Indian Ocean—Social life and customs
Classification: LCC ML3916 .A14 2025 (print) | LCC ML3916 (ebook) |
    DDC 780.916—dc23/eng/20250527

LC record available at https://lccn.loc.gov/2025002767
LC ebook record available at https://lccn.loc.gov/2025002768

GPSR Authorized Representative: Easy Access System Europe,
Mustamäe tee 50, 10621 Tallinn, Estonia, gpsr.requests@easproject.com

34   33   32   31   30   29   28   27   26   25
10   9   8   7   6   5   4   3   2   1

To our loved ones

CONTENTS

FIGURES

AUDIO CLIPS

ACKNOWLEDGMENTS

Birgit's research for this book was made possible by a European Research Council Consolidator Grant, while Patrick's research in Mauritius and Mumbai was funded by a Vidi grant from the Netherlands Organization for Scientific Research. Birgit is indebted to Barbara B. Smith, Simeon Adelbai, Kiblas Soaladaob, and numerous friends in Palau for supporting her research in invaluable ways, while Patrick thanks Enayet Hossen Edun, Rehana Edun and their family in Mauritius, the staff of World Islamic Network and its director Imran Rasool, and Rehana Ghadially in Mumbai for making his research for this book possible.

Patrick presented earlier versions of ideas laid out in this book at Harvard University, Columbia University, the Max Planck Institute for the Study of Religious and Ethnic Diversity in Göttingen, the University of Mainz, the University of Bern, the Cologne University of Music and Dance, the University of Hamburg, the Max Planck Institute for Social Anthropology in Halle, Jamia Millia Islamia, and the Centre for the Study of Developing Societies in Delhi, greatly benefiting from the feedback of these audiences. For their comments he would especially like to thank Lisa Björkman, Julia Byl, Matthew Engelke, Erol Köymen, Vyjayanthi Rao, Kamala Russell, Michael Schnegg, Ravi Sundaram, Jim Sykes, and Peter van der Veer. At the University of California Press, we had the pleasure to work with Kate Marshall and Eric Schmidt as editors, and we would like to thank them for their trust and enthusiasm for this project.

Birgit is the sole author of chapters 3, 6, and 8, while Patrick is the sole author of chapters 2, 4, 5, and 7.

Portions of chapter 2 appeared in an earlier version in Patrick Eisenlohr, "Sonic atmospheres in Mauritian devotional Islam: Sensing transoceanic connections in a Creole society," in *Sounding the Indian Ocean: Musical Circulations in the Afro-Asiatic Seascape*, ed. Jim Sykes and Julia Byl, 145–57 (Oakland: University of California Press, 2023). An earlier version of parts of chapter 3 was previously published as Birgit Abels, "Sound ties, 'rising from the depths of brine and regions of fire deeper still': Knowing through popular music in the Western Pacific Island world," *Journal of World Popular Music* 8, no. 2 (2021): 1–19. Portions of chapter 4 were previously published in a different form as Patrick Eisenlohr, "Atmospheric citizenship: Sonic movement and public religion in Shiʻi Mumbai," *Public Culture* 33, no. 3 (2021): 371–92. Sections of chapter 5 appeared in an earlier version in Patrick Eisenlohr, "Atmospheres: The multisensoriality of spatially extended emotions," *Ethos* 52, no. 1 (2024): 37–50. The "Obil ngesur" chant at the heart of chapter 8 is also discussed in Birgit Abels, "'It's only the water and the rocks that own the land': Sound knowledge and environmental change in Palau, Western Micronesia," *Asian-European Music Research Journal* 2 (2018): 21–32.

Introducing Atmospheric Knowledge

The bright sunlight reflected off the quiet Pacific Ocean's surface on this hot, cloudless day in late March 2007. Malakal, a small island port just off Palau's capital, Koror, had been bustling with preparations for hours. Today the *Hōkūleʻa* and *Alingano Maisu* were going to make a port call here. The *Hōkūleʻa* is a *waʻa kaulua*, a double-hulled voyaging canoe built by the Polynesian Voyaging Society in 1975. The mission has been to document and perpetuate traditional Polynesian voyaging wisdom and ethos; the *Hōkūleʻa* continues to be their flagship.[1] That particular voyage in 2007 began in Honolulu, Oʻahu, on January 11; the *Hōkūleʻa* was joined by the *Alingano Maisu*, another traditionally built double-hulled voyaging canoe, a little later. The *Alingano Maisu* was going to be a gift to Satawalese master navigator Pius "Mau" Piailug, who had navigated the *Hōkūleʻa* on its maiden voyage to Papaʻete in 1976 using traditional way-finding techniques. The 2007 voyage served to deliver the Maisu to Satawal, Micronesia, and there were many stops to other island nations on the way. Like every voyage since the first one in the mid-1970s, the 2007 Micronesia voyage was an intense celebration of Pacific lore and deep knowledge of the sea. And so, on this day, Malakal wasn't waiting for any other ship; rather, Malakal was getting ready for a full-blown immersion into the sight, salt on the skin, and sound of embracing Pacific Islanderness and its particular ways of being in the world. Traditional way-faring in the Pacific Island world is an embodied knowledge that requires the ability to "discern directionality by feeling what the rocking, rolling, pitching and swaying of a canoe can reveal about direction" (Diaz, forthcoming).

Traditional Micronesian hospitality has correspondingly visceral qualities—any welcoming ceremony for navigators from across the largest ocean on the planet is intent on making felt the connection the hosts, as fellow Pacific Islanders, have with them. There will be a large crowd, dancers in colorful adornment, the smell of fresh food, and lots of music. Importantly, there will be chanting. Ceremonial chanting is at the heart of pretty much any welcoming protocol in the Pacific Island world. During the exchange of chants, all the hustle and bustle of the surrounding activities stops because it is the sonic event that creates the space for the actual arrival to take place. As the chants resound, the incoming crew is not simply told they're welcome; rather, as their bodies are enveloped in the sonic sensation of the welcoming chant, they literally resonate not with that information but with the *knowledge* that this is so. What's more, there's an underlying shared sense that, in spite of how the modern world may map all those tiny Pacific Island nations as tiny dots in the middle of a huge ocean, Pacific Islanders have always known that they are not remote and that the ocean does not have boundaries like it does for non-Islanders. From this there arises a deep sense of being connected with the water and the sea and, indeed, a deeply felt sense of pride about that connection. It's not the tonal material of the chant or the semantic meaning of the chanter's traditional attire—it's the atmosphere, centrally but not exclusively evoked through the chanting, that gives rise to this knowledge. As chanters from across the breadth of generations of both the welcoming and the visiting parties, from children to seniors, exchange their performances, the sound of their voices not only makes the bond between Pacific Islanders from opposite ends of the Pacific Ocean tangible but transforms it into an atmospheric truth that manifests as intense visceral cognizance.

But how do we know through atmospheres? How can being affected by an atmosphere give rise to knowledge? What role does somatic, nonverbal knowledge play in how we belong to places and in knowing our environments? *Atmospheric Knowledge* takes up these questions through detailed analyses of practices that generate atmospheres and in which knowledge emerges through visceral intermingling with atmospheres. From combined musicological and anthropological perspectives, we investigate atmospheres by way of performative and sonic practices across a range of ethnographic settings. The rich affordances of sonic connections for knowing our environments are at the center of this book.

Oceanic relations and sonic affectedness are the main threads of our investigation of atmospheric knowledge. From the phenomenological perspective we take in this book, atmospheres are feelings poured into space. They can be perceived through visceral encounters and somatic intermingling with the world. *Atmospheric Knowledge* is a joint project of a musicologist and an anthropologist who were both ethnographically guided to the theme of atmospheres, each in their own ways. For Birgit, the musicologist, an interest in a phenomenology of atmospheres emerged from her engagement with Pacific epistemologies as sound knowledge. In her research, principally in the Micronesian island nation of Palau, she found her interlocutors' musical practices to be suffused by Oceanic knowledge that does not take the world of the Pacific as islands separated by a vast sea. Instead, the

Pacific itself is a "sea of islands" whose relationalities are at the same time, in the words of Tongan scholar Epeli Hauʻofa (1993) "passageways of knowing." Musical practices are alternative ways of knowing that make experienceable this world of relatedness to the sea and the relational constitution of island worlds through sonic connection. This kind of Oceanic knowledge, which Birgit's interlocutors actualized in sonic and musical practices, is simultaneously a somatic knowledge of environmental relations. The latter in turn stands in proximity to an analytic of atmospheres, with sonic affectedness being one of its central modalities. Sonic affectedness is more than the result of auditory perception. It is a more comprehensive engagement with the sonic as a "vibrational practice" (Eidsheim 2015) that goes far beyond the sense of hearing, suggesting motion in a more holistic felt-bodily sense that cannot be reduced to a single sensory modality. As Birgit learned in her ethnographic fieldwork in Palau, it is precisely this entanglement among the sonic, bodily motion, its actualization in music and dance, and the suggestion of Oceanic relations through felt motion that make up sonic epistemologies as atmospheric knowledge. In short, for Birgit, atmospheric knowledge was suggested by her learning about and work through Pacific epistemologies.

Patrick, the anthropologist, was first nudged toward an analytic of atmospheres as a result of the conversations he had with his Mauritian Muslim interlocutors when he was trying to learn and make sense of the sonic dimensions of the voice in recitations of a particular Islamic genre of Urdu praise poetry. As a linguistic and media anthropologist, he was originally interested in the discursive dimensions, along with the circulations of text and participant roles enacted in performances of the poetry, while his interlocutors kept on pushing him toward the importance of nondiscursive sonic qualities of voices in ritual recitals. They described what they considered appropriate attributes of such voices and spoke about voices as sonic forces that would grip and energize the persons exposed to them, quite literally transporting them elsewhere. While Patrick's Mauritian Muslim interlocutors often felt that the effects of the reciting voice were ultimately impossible to put into words, the prevalence of referrals to felt movement and the use of metaphors of motion led Patrick to ultimately draw a connection to a phenomenology of atmospheres, where suggestions of motion are the principal working mechanism of atmospheres. In other words, in Patrick's research, too, sonic affectedness of the felt-body brought about atmospheric knowledge, in somatic kinds of knowledge that turned out to be principally qualified as religious.

In another strong parallel to Birgit's musicological research in the Western Pacific, oceanic and transoceanic connections played a large role in the kinds of atmospheric knowledge Patrick learned about through working in Muslim communities in the Indian Ocean world in both sites of his ethnographic fieldwork, Mauritius and the Indian megacity Mumbai. While the Islamic sonic practices he learned about, such as the genre of poetry in honor of the Prophet Muhammad that first prompted his interest in sonic affectedness, are about feeling greater proximity to the divine, they also enact relations to places of religious longing and authority beyond the sea. This is plainly in evidence in the Indian Ocean setting of the Mauritian Muslims, who are of Indian ancestry and whose recitation of Urdu praise poetry connects them to their land of ancestry and its places of religious authority and simultaneously with the Hijaz region of the Arabian peninsula, more particularly Medina, a main theme of the poetry and often taken to be the favorite city of the Prophet Muhammad. The sonic practices among the Twelver Shiʿi Muslims in Mumbai Patrick worked with, too, are not exhausted by their claiming of urban space and belonging in Mumbai. They also reenact Shiʿi transoceanic connections, among them relations to sites of ritual remembrance across the Arabian Sea, in what is today Iraq and Iran. Thus a common theme running through this book combining studies from both Pacific and Indian Ocean worlds are oceanic and transoceanic connections as atmospheric knowledge that sonic practices enact and actualize. On the basis of our combined ethnographic experiences, a main goal of our book is also to draw attention to strong parallels between phenomenological approaches to atmospheres developed in Europe and related bodies of knowledge elsewhere. The lesson we draw from this comparison is that, despite the specificities of their respective contexts of emergence, none of these intellectual traditions are parochial, and placing them in dialogue is a promising way to arrive at a better understanding of environmental knowledge and the felt aspects of social life.

ATMOSPHERES AS KNOWLEDGE

Atmosphere as an analytic has been enjoying a resurgence in recent years. It is an approach that engages with the felt currents of contemporary politics but that is also often overshadowed by the more popular notion of affect. Yet atmospheres, whose perception coincides with the feeling of being a body, avoid several conceptual pitfalls linked to pretensions of autonomy from signification that characterized earlier versions of affect theory (Leys 2011). Following the phenomenologist Hermann Schmitz, who, arguably, played the role of the primary atmospheric theorist, atmospheres can be understood as emotions poured into space that envelop and intermingle with sentient bodies (1969, 98–106).[2] They escape discursive capture and remain at a level of meaningfulness that stops short of the fully qualified and discursively elaborated categories and labels of politics, religion, and identifications linked to them. According to Schmitz, atmospheres can intermingle with and be present to felt-bodies because they are what he calls "half-things" (*Halbdinge*), phenomena that are fleeting and can be interrupted, such as wind, heat, cold, the weather, pain, a voice, or musical figures (1978, 116–39; 2016, 75; see also Griffero 2017). In distinction from bounded things, half-things have no stable location. In contrast to things, they also do not require a causal link, such as a rock's fall leading to a rock causing an injury, to bring about their effects: the presence and effects of half-things are one and the same. More recently, and more familiar to anglophone readers, Gernot Böhme (2017) has drawn attention to atmospheres as something that can be made and planned.[3]

We take atmospheres to be ways of knowing that are at the same time forces intermingling with felt-bodies in ways that exceed any definite sensory impressions.[4] Atmospheres point to the processual and continuously reconstituted nature of our embodied being in the world. The phenomenological distinction between the physical body *(Körper)* and the felt-body *(Leib)* is crucial for an understanding of our embodied being in the world, because entanglement with the world is above all experienced through the latter.[5] In contrast to the physical body, the felt-body has shifting and vague boundaries, going beyond the boundaries of the physical body to include that which is felt to pertain to the body but may also be situated outside the physical body's limits. Atmospheres are one of the primary dimensions of the interface and overlapping of felt-bodies and the world.

This insight is not unique to the phenomenological tradition of thinking atmospheres we draw on in our book. From our combined musicological and anthropological perspectives, we are especially interested in the resonances between atmospheric knowledge as developed in the phenomenology of atmospheres in Europe, especially in Germany, and kindred traditions of knowledge in other parts in the world. In Birgit's research in Micronesia, the juxtaposition of Indigenous Pacific epistemologies of the environment and transoceanic connections as sound knowledge with phenomenological approaches to atmospheres brought out striking parallels between these two bodies of knowledge. In Patrick's research on Muslim devotional performances and sonic dimensions of urban religion in Mauritius and Mumbai, his interlocutors spoke about vocal sound as having an effect on felt-bodily motion in a way strongly reminiscent of the phenomenology of atmospheres, while his interlocutors in Mumbai themselves sometimes used the Urdu equivalent of atmosphere, *mahaul*, when reflecting on the qualities and effects of religious urban processions. Patrick's Muslim interlocutors in Mauritius and Mumbai did not draw links to the long-standing classical and vernacular South Asian aesthetics of *rasa* (literally, "taste," but also translatable as "sentiment" or "essence"); however, the phenomenology of atmospheres to some extent also resonates with this tradition, which in turn plays into the overall context of performative practices throughout South Asia. This aesthetics can also extend to the realms of sound and music (Kaufmann 1965; I. Kaur 2024; Lorea, forthcoming).[6]

Not unlike atmospheres as spatially extended emotions, rasa are aesthetic and emotional qualities, quasi substances that spread and permeate, much like the tactile and savory qualities of food permeate the process of cooking, the food itself, the act of tasting, and eventually the bodies of those eating it.[7] Overcoming the gap between perceiving subject and perceived object, in rasa aesthetics the feeler and the feeling, the taster and the tasted overlap.[8] Other scholars have fruitfully crossed and compared German neophenomenological notions of atmosphere with, for example, Japanese thought about *Ki*, itself developed in dialogue with older Chinese theories of *Qi*. In resonance with phenomenological approaches to atmospheres, this tradition of thought points to theories of sensation and spherical interconnectedness that overcome distinctions between perceiving subject and perceived object as well as feeler and feeling (Hisayama 2014; Marinucci 2019; Wang 2024, 59–70).[9] Even accounting for the long-distance influences working in all these traditions of knowledge, these bodies of thought all unfolded in very specific and historical and regional milieus in very different parts of the world. We highlight the parallels and the intellectual kinship between these far-flung traditions of thought not to claim the timeless universality of phenomenology but to show that all of them, including the phenomenology of atmospheres, are not strictly provincial theories whose claims do not reach beyond a given regional setting.[10]

The decolonizing of knowledge and the provincialization of European thought have become main themes in anthropology and music studies. Our drawing of parallels between the Eurogenic phenomenology of atmospheres and other related and kindred traditions in other parts of the world needs to be contextualized against the imperative of decolonizing knowledge while avoiding falling into the trap of compartmentalizing and ethnologizing knowledge in ways that allow validity claims of particular bodies of knowledge only within the boundaries of certain world regions and power structures. Often the nationalities, descent, and spatial location of thinkers play important roles in assessing what kind of knowledge is in need of decentering and decolonization, but it is also worth considering the substance of their ideas. While Hermann Schmitz was, by virtue of his background and habitus, very much a twentieth-century German, white, and male professor of philosophy, his insistence that European philosophical thought has taken an entirely wrong turn since the days of post-Homeric Greece also makes him a useful source of alternatives to colonial and hegemonic thought that has spread from Europe throughout the world and that proves so hard to decenter, let alone to dislodge.

Like Michel Foucault, whose epistemology of the discursive formation of power-knowledge as a historical a priori, which has underpinned if not dominated much of postcolonial and decolonial studies since the late twentieth century, Schmitz is a European thinker who potentially provides tools to destabilize the hegemony of European intellectual traditions in our postcolonial global world. In particular, his relentless attacks against *introjectionism* (the notion of bounded selves whose souls, emotions, and logos are taken to be interior phenomena, quite literally located "inside" people, coupled with the tendency to geometrically objectify space and the body, which Schmitz traces to the fifth and fourth centuries BCE in Greece) made him marginal in academic philosophy during much of his lifetime. This critique, however, echoed and partially anticipated contemporary anthropological concerns with the deconstruction of European-derived modern notions of subjectivity and personhood. Schmitz's insistence on porous embodied subjectivity that thoroughly intermingles with environments and can also be inhabited by demons and spirits makes him a counter thinker against hegemonic notions of personhood and the nature of emotional life, whose work is now also being taken up in parts of the Global South (e.g., Reinhardt and Corrêa 2024).

TWO KINDS OF ATMOSPHERES
AND THE INDIVIDUATION OF FELT-BODIES

Atmospheres are not only forces that bring about an intermingling of felt-bodies and their environments. We take felt-bodies, the ground for our embodied being in the world, not as given, preconstituted entities but as the outcome of processes of individuation out of a milieu effected to a large extent by atmospheres. In their somatic address, above all through the suggestions of motion proper to them, atmospheres play a key role in creating the feeling of being a body. Their vague meaningfulness and material impact engender the individuation of such felt-bodies out of a less differentiated whole. They are therefore the forces behind the sense of being in the world by virtue of inhabiting a world as a felt-body that is simultaneously interconnected as it is distinct from everything else. It is our contention that the atmospheric encounter brings about individual felt-bodies along with the possibilities for them to have an environment. Studying atmospheres thus goes to the heart of environmentality and the webs of relations the latter comprises. In constantly reproducing the difference between felt-bodies and their environments, they also set the terms on which such environmental relations can unfold. In this way not only do atmospheres prepare the stage for subliminal and somatic forms of appeal, power, and control but they themselves are one of their most central dimensions.

This may sound like an unabashedly universalist, philosophical account of embodied being in the world. However, what makes atmospheres special is their ability to bundle, to bring together broad arrays of memories, including body memories in the shape of enculturated techniques of the body and cultivated sensory dispositions as well as discourses. This kind of bundling effected by atmospheres makes all these disparate dimensions commensurable, imbuing them with an overarching feel that coincides with the feeling of being a body. This means that the work atmospheres do, reproducing the feeling of being a body along with the web of environmental relations that the individuation of felt-bodies makes possible, is always shot through with the sociocultural and the historical. It is precisely the fact that atmospheres thus understood are not precultural and prehistorical forces such as "autonomous" affect in one of affect theory's earlier and most influential formulations (Massumi 2002) that makes them interesting for us from our combined anthropological and musicological perspectives. Avoiding key difficulties of affect theory, atmospheres speak to many of the same issues that the by-now-established affective turn in the humanities and social sciences is concerned with, such as the need to analyze that which evades discursive rendering and to understand the felt currents of contemporary politics and public life. Atmospheres are thoroughly spatial and situational phenomena, and they have a concrete working mechanism, which is suggestions of motion. They are therefore more amenable to ethnographic and other kinds of empirical analyses than moods and affects, to whom such tangible qualities apply to a lesser extent, if at all.

Our approach to atmospheres is inspired by the work of not only Hermann Schmitz but also Gernot Böhme. From our musicological and anthropological perspectives, we seek to show that the felt-body and its environmentality is always-already sociocultural without falling for a kind of discourse-centered sociocultural constructionism that would sideline the diffuse and vague meaningfulness of less qualified forms of signification that atmospheres revolve around. We draw primarily on Schmitz's notion that atmospheres are emotions poured into space that intermingle with felt-bodies—they are "emotions poured out spatially that move the felt (not the material) body" (Schmitz, Müllan, and Slaby 2011, 247; see also Schmitz 1968; 1969, 98–106; 2016). They are thus not a matter of subjective interiority but quasi-objectively "out there" in ways that often escape the agency of human actors affected by them. According to Schmitz, while the perception of atmospheres coincides with the feeling of being a body, it also exceeds single definite sensory impressions reducible to a particular modality of the sensorium. Their primary mechanism of operation is suggestions of motion *(Bewegungssug-gestionen)* (1966, 77; 1967, 170–72, 324–27; 2016, 85). Atmospheres affect sentient bodies through the manipulation of the body's spatial economy. While Schmitz tends to portray atmospheres as unintentional forces not created by anybody in particular, this obviously does not apply to all kinds of atmospheres. We also find Gernot Böhme's aesthetic theory of atmospheres helpful, because Böhme focuses mainly on the agentive production and targeted arrangement of certain kinds of atmospheres, such as in architecture and design (Böhme [1995] 2013, 2017). For Böhme the workings of atmospheres have much in common with the ancient art of stagecraft. In addition his focus on the generation of atmospheres by design also has the advantage of highlighting the specific agentive power of things and objects; indeed, one way to describe atmospheres, according to Böhme, is that they are "ecstasies of the thing" (1993, 110). Our investigation of atmospheric knowledge therefore unfolds in part along the continuum between these two major kinds of atmospheres described by Schmitz and Böhme, respectively.[11]

ATMOSPHERIC KNOWLEDGE
AND ENVIRONMENTALITY

Environmentality and the individuation of bodies that feel as separate and distinct from everything else are two sides of the same coin; they presuppose each other.

Our perspective on felt-bodies as not pregiven but as the continuously achieved result of operations of differentiation out of a larger whole owes much to Gilbert Simondon's writings on individuation as transduction. According to Simondon, new entities in the world do not come about as a combination of matter and immaterial forms but emerge through processes of transduction ([1964] 1992). Transduction is the process out of which new individual entities such as objects, organisms, and even mental and psychic phenomena emerge out of an inchoate, "metastable," preindividual milieu. Simondon's work was a major inspiration for Gilles Deleuze. The latter thinker's distinction between the virtual and the actual closely aligns with Simondon's philosophy of individuation and transduction. In this philosophy actual phenomena are those that have emerged from processes of individuation out of a metastable preindividual milieu. For Deleuze the latter is in proximity to the virtual, the forces of differentiation, and multiplicity that are behind actual phenomena and responsible for their becoming ([1968] 1994).

One of Simondon's basic examples of individuation as transduction is the growth of a crystal out of its mother solution as

> a process . . . in which an activity gradually sets itself in motion, propagating within a given area, through a structuration of the different zones of the area over which it operates. Each region of the structure that is constituted in this way then serves to constitute the next one to such an extent that at the very time this structuration is effected there is a progressive modification taking place in tandem with it. The simplest image of the transductive process is furnished if one thinks of a crystal, beginning as a tiny seed, which grows and extends oneself in all directions in its mother-water. ([1964] 1992, 313)

Applied to felt-bodies and their environments, such a perspective on individuation as transduction suggests that felt-bodies emerge out of a larger, diffuse whole, leading to a difference between felt-bodies and their environment and eventually resulting in environmental relationality. Atmospheric forces with their somatic appeal can be among those forces that set in motion such processes of emergence and reemergence of felt-bodies from a larger whole, in which the latter then becomes environment. For us atmospheres are of great significance not only because they are the felt dimensions of politics and belonging and, indeed, of somatic aspects of sociocultural phenomena in general. They are of such fundamental importance because they hail felt-bodies into being to begin with. More specifically, Hermann Schmitz (1992) has argued that start and shock can be among such forces that provoke felt-bodily contraction or tightness, which Schmitz takes to be the *principium individuationis*. Broadening this perspective to atmospheres as suggestions of motion that intermingle with felt bodies, we argue that atmospheres thus understood also bring about the individuation of felt-bodies, that is the feeling of being and having a body and, as a consequence, the emergence of such bodies' environments at the same time, resulting in a mesh of environmental relations.

Atmospheric knowledge, the knowledge generated by atmospheres' hailing felt-bodies into being and atmospheres' subsequent intermingling with felt-bodies, is environmental in a double way. With environmentality we mean the web of relations between felt-bodies and atmospheric forces that often result in their at least temporary overlap. In distinguishing the following two kinds of environmentality as atmospheric knowledge, we are inspired by Erich Hörl's (2017) recent discussion of the distinction between environmentality as a broad kind of relationality that recalls Martin Heidegger's notion of *Umweltlichkeit* and environmentality as a more recent manifestation of Foucauldian governmentality. First, atmospheric knowledge is environmental not just because atmospheres are environmental forces that intermingle with felt-bodies but also in terms of its all-encompassing relationality in the sense that being in the world is also always a being-with. Ever since Heidegger referred to the latter condition as *Umweltlichkeit*, the relationality of such inescapable enmeshing with an environment has been thought in ever more radical ways, for example through conceiving nonhumans as actors on a par with humans, culminating in the insight that if everything is interconnected, then there are no autonomous entities and beings and everything consists of almost boundless relations ([1927] 2010, 66; Latour 2007). Among the most radical formulations of such a planetary interconnectedness is the Gaia hypothesis (Lovelock 1979) or Gaia connectivity (Latour 2017), which puts in question the very notion of the environment, stating that the "overflowing richness of biological knowledges" can no longer be captured by the notion of "bounded individuals plus contexts, or organisms plus environments" (Haraway 2016, quoted in Latour 2017, 64; see also Clarke 2017; Stengers 2015). Everything that comes about as a distinct, individualized entity in the world constitutes as a node in a vast web of profound interrelatedness. The latter is an encompassing homeostatic system ruling out the possibility that beings have essences and autonomy.

Applied to our investigation of atmospheric knowledge, this take on environmentality as universal relatedness and interconnectivity appears to be in proximity to Hermann Schmitz's approach to atmospheres as environmental and mostly unintentional forces that intermingle with felt-bodies. Moreover, Schmitz's radical dismissal of a subject-object binary through a phenomenology of the felt-body does not take the latter as given but also specifies the conditions leading to its *individuation*, a term also used by Schmitz in this context. Schmitz's atmospheres constitute a kind of environmentality in which the permeability of felt-bodies and the latter's affection by energetic forces that manifest as suggestions of motion are central. In short, this is a kind of environmentality and radical relationality in which atmospheres are a primary dimension of felt-bodies' intermingling with and situatedness in the world.

Atmospheric knowledge is also environmental in another, second sense. According to Foucault (1991), governmentality, a form of power that is grounded in the management of populations, is central to modernity. The regulation of the environment and human relations with their environment is a particular subvariety of such governmentality that has become ever more important in recent decades (Agrawal 2005; Darier 1999). Indeed, some claim that, especially through the becoming environmental of digital media, it is the contemporary form of governmentality (Hörl 2017, 5). Digital media are environmental in this sense because they surround humans and coconstitute their environments. They are networks based on the ubiquitous distribution of mobile devices and sensors that track and generate gigantic amounts of data, fed back into machines and technical devices that execute and adjust actions accordingly. Environmentality thus understood is a manifestation of power that does not target human actors and human populations directly like other forms of governmentality do. Instead, it is a regime of management and control that seizes on the relationality of humans with their environments. As such, environmentality as a mode of control centers on the purposive manipulation and design of environmental relations. If atmospheres and the knowledge they generate are a key dimension of environmentality, then control and regulation of environmental relations also extends to targeted and designed aspects of atmospheres.

Environmentality as governmentality is therefore in proximity to the planned generation of atmospheres in fields such as architecture and design as discussed by Gernot Böhme, who has emphasized the links between atmospheres and power ([1995] 2013, 2017). Environmentality as governmentality is also the paradigm that informs much of the work on *ambiances*, a term that is proximate to atmospheres (Thibaud 2011). For example, Paul Roquet has shown how ambient media in contemporary Japan, including listening to ambient music through such media, is a neoliberal technique of self-care that results in "ambient subjectivation" (2016, 4). Such approaches to ambient atmospheric control are highly sensitive to environmentality as governmentality. They differ from our approach to atmospheric knowledge as environmentality in that they lack the focus on embodiment and the felt-body's intermingling with and becoming world that is central for phenomenological approaches to atmospheres. We contend that the (re)constitution of felt-bodies is the condition of possibility of environment and environmentality for humans and a whole range of other animals and that the power of atmospheres rests on their intermingling with felt-bodies. Therefore we suggest that coming to terms with environmentality as governmentality requires not only paying attention to the purposeful design of certain atmospheres but also understanding how such atmospheres work in and through felt-bodies.

To understand environmentality as governmentality, it is also important to recognize the limits of environmental relationality. If in radical versions of ecological immanentism everything is connected to everything, it can easily lead to the downplaying of meaningful political differences, boundaries, and power differentials. We find Frédéric Neyrat's critique of excessive relationality and "generalized interconnection" along with his reminder that "every relation is founded on a separation" to be a useful warning against an overemphasis on ecological connection that depoliticizes itself. Neyrat's "ecology of separation" that does not deny environmental relationality but qualifies it in an important way can be translated into atmospheric terms by way of Peter Sloterdijk's spatial philosophy of spheres (2017, 101; see also Abels 2013). According to Sloterdijk ([1998] 2011), environmentality can be understood as an aggregate of bubbles, a foamlike whole that consists of interconnected microspheres, a vision that amounts to a "social immunology cast in atmospheric terms" (Boos and Runkel 2018, 264). Environmentality is also about the continuous maintenance of individual entities and collectives. Immunology, with its emphasis on the defense and stabilization of boundaries and differences, is not just an apt metaphor but literally names the processes that enable the perduring of organisms, simultaneously protecting the latter's ability to enter into environmental relations. Thinking through immunology is a reminder of the processual notion of not just individuation but also of the maintenance of individuated entities. Sloterdijk's take on spheres and environmentality as foamlike aggregates of bubbles points to the atmospheric dimensions of such relations through separation. Atmospheres do not just affect the intermingling of that which is normally taken to be separate, such as felt-bodies and their environments, but can also separate and generate boundaries. Taking seriously the atmospheric differences and separation within all-encompassing environmental relationality enables a better understanding of environmentality as governmentality, as the latter is a modality of power that also operates through separation and hierarchization.

THE TEMPORALITY OF ATMOSPHERIC KNOWLEDGE

To sum up our take on atmospheres as epistemology so far, we make a case for atmospheres as primarily nonverbal and somatic modes of knowledge. We also show how such knowledge emerges in sonic performative practices that shape what can be known of the environment.[12] As we see it, our distinct contribution to the question of somatic knowledge emerging in performance is, first, that atmospheric knowledge is inherently multisensory and holistic, going beyond, for example, acoustemologies by addressing the felt-body in its entirety. Second, we argue that atmospheric knowledge also operates through a future-oriented temporality of its own, namely latency. Our notion of atmospheres as epistemology therefore highlights ways of knowing that which is about to manifest, a type of knowing as a "hunch" of that what is about to be. This quasi-inbuilt temporality of atmospheres calls for more explanation.

Atmospheres are of key importance for an understanding of modal time; they are a previously almost unnoticed but decisive element in the puzzle of human temporality. With modal time we mean human experiences of time in the modes of past, present, and future. We propose that the often-remarked power of atmospheres is also at least in part due to its co-constitution of such modal time, which is among the most fundamental dimensions of being in the world, if not its most central dimension tout court. We have already discussed that atmospheres are at the origin of individuation as subject qua *Leib*. Atmospheres are among those forces that set in motion felt-bodies' differentiation from a surrounding milieu, a differentiation that manifests as the feeling of having and being a body. Atmospheres' somatic force contributes to a state of affairs in which there is something and somebody to begin with, perceiving itself as sufficiently separate and distinct for it to enter into environmental relations. In our view such atmospherically induced processes of individuation on a bodily felt level therefore are also at the origin of human modal time in terms of past, present, and future. In the philosophy of time, such human modal time has traditionally been referred to as A-series time, in distinction from nonhuman B-series time, which manifests as relationships of before and after due to sheer causality (McTaggart 1908).[13]

Building on Edmund Husserl's phenomenological account of human modal time, Maurice Merleau-Ponty was, at least in European thought, the first to directly link human time experience in terms of past, present, and future to bodily perception and motion. According to Husserl (1964), the experienced present has no independent existence because it is the product of incessantly intersecting retentions, the already experienced, and protentions, that which is anticipated. Famously drawing on the example of a melody, in which a listener retains the notes just heard and anticipates those about to follow to be able to grasp the melody as a whole, Husserl showed that the present is an operational frame in which retentions and protentions interact. Merleau-Ponty had the key idea to derive the acts of cognition that Husserl called retentions and protentions from perceptions related to bodily motion. Merleau-Ponty thereby grounded the emergence of human modal time in terms of a phenomenology of perception, for which Husserl had already provided the basic terms, in the dynamics of the felt-body.

Building on early twentieth-century neurological research in Germany, Merleau-Ponty takes body memory—in particular "kinetic memory" *(kinetische Erinnerung* or *kinetisches Gedächtnis)* or also kinesthetic memory *(kinästhetische Erinnerung)* (Liepmann 1905, 48, 139, 61)—to be the counterpart of Husserl's retentions ([1945] 1962, 138–39). Husserlian protentions could, according to Merleau-Ponty, in turn be grounded in the felt-body as a "motor project," or projections of motion *(Bewegungsentwurf)* (Liepmann 1905, 70, 84). Based on an understanding of "motility as basic intentionality," Merleau-Ponty reframes retentions and protentions as Husserlian intentional acts as an "intentional arc" grounded in the interplay between kinetic memory and suggestions of motion ([1945] 1962, 137). Making reference to the notion of the intentional arc *(intentionaler Bogen)* taken from Franz Fischer (1930, 250), who adopted the concept from Kurt Beringer (1926, 190), Merleau-Ponty argues that "the life of consciousness—cognitive life, the life of desire or perceptual life—is subtended by an 'intentional arc' which projects round about us our past, our future, our human setting, our physical, ideological and moral situation, or rather which results in our being situated in all these respects. It is the intentional arc which brings about the unity of the senses, or intelligence, or sensibility and motility" ([1945] 1962, 136). In other words, our cognitive, intellectual, and cultural life as humans is generated by such an intentional arc grounded in bodily motion, and this arc comes about through the continuous intersection of embodied kinetic memory with motor projects or suggestions of motion.

This motion-centered intentional arc is also the base for the emergence of human modal time in terms of past, present, and future. The temporal structure of the felt-body as constituted through motion, above all its memory and anticipation, is the ground of human temporality as such. For Merleau-Ponty all cognitive phenomena, including apprehensions of time, can be derived from the structure and the dynamics of motion of the felt-body in a bottom-up fashion (Förster-Beuthan 2012, 170).[14] The perception of the present then coincides with the feeling of being a body. "The felt present of the felt-body *(Leib)* is a necessary condition for perception. . . . The felt-body is *always* present, nevertheless that which is the future (as projections of motion) or that which is past (as body memory) is distinguishable from this kind of presence" (Förster-Beuthan 2012, 176). Merleau-Ponty uses the remarkable formulation of the body's secreting time for the generation of modal time out of the motional dynamics of the body: "In every focusing movement my body unites present, past and future, it secretes time, or rather it becomes that location in nature where, for the first time, events, instead of pushing each other in to the realm of being, project round the present a double horizon of past and future and acquire historical orientation" ([1945] 1962, 239–40). While Merleau-Ponty breaks new ground in deriving cognitive and intentional acts from the dynamics of the felt-body, he takes the felt-body as a given and is less concerned with its individuation. The latter, however, seems indispensable for understanding for what Merleau-Ponty calls the body's secreting of time, and, as we shall see, the vital role of atmospheres in it.

Hermann Schmitz's (1992, 2007) phenomenology of the felt-body is a useful guide for such an exploration of the origin of human modal time through the dynamic of the felt-body. In contrast to Merleau-Ponty, Schmitz addresses how felt-bodies, and with them the ground of any kind of subjectivity felt to be distinct from other phenomena in the world, come about. For Schmitz, what he calls the "vital drive," a motional dynamic of alternation between felt-bodily contraction and dilation, is ultimately responsible for the feeling of being a body. Bodily contraction, such as in start and shock, provokes the felt-body into being, leading to its emergence, its exposure and tearing out of an undifferentiated milieu of a "chaotic-manifold continuum of duration" (1992, 237). This kind of undifferentiated duration, which appears to be equivalent to Henri Bergson's ([1896] 1911) *durée*, is the milieu out of which the individuation of felt-bodies takes place, the confrontation with a force provoking start and thereby felt-bodily contraction brings about what Schmitz calls the "primitive present" (1992, 235).[15] As noted already, contraction or the tightness *(Enge)* of the felt-body is the *principium individuationis*, the origin of identity and difference as well as human modal time out of undifferentiated duration (1992, 237).

Expanding the notion of start or shock as the origin of individuation of felt-bodies, we suggest that atmospheres as suggestions of motion also help to provoke Schmitz's "primitive present." Suggestions of motion are the principal working mechanism of atmospheres; they hail the felt-body, thereby tearing it out of unqualified duration. As projections of motion, they bring in the future, in the same act also establishing the present as the feeling of being a body. This body then becomes differentiated from that which passed, and the latter in turn becomes body memory, more precisely kinetic memory. We also suggest that there is a primacy of futurity as atmospheres qua suggestions or projections of motion in this account of human modal time centered on the dynamic of the felt-body. Atmospheres as suggestion of motion (the future) provoke the feeling of being a body (the experienced present), bundling this feeling with kinetic memory (the past) along with other forms of memory and sociocultural phenomena, such as past discourse. Playing a crucial role in effecting the unfolding of future, present, and the past at the level of the felt-body, atmospheres are the often overlooked foundation for human apprehensions of time. Atmospheres and their knowledge are so undeniably consequential because they operate at this most basic and ineluctable level of human situatedness in the world.

MULTIMODALITY, INFRAMODALITY,
AND SONIC PRIVILEGE

We are currently witnessing a dissatisfaction with the scholarly monopoly of the written word and a consequent a rise in interest in multimodality and multimodal methods across a range of disciplines (e.g., Pink 2011; Westmoreland 2022). Nevertheless, multimodal thinking has been a long-standing intellectual concern. Already Johann Gottfried Herder argues that "all dismembering of sensation . . . are abstractions *[alle Zergliederung der Sensation . . . sind Abstraktionen]*" (1772, 96, cited in Hasse 2014, 57). In this sense synesthesia is the primary mode of sensation, and the limitation to one particular dimension of the sensorium is the result of abstraction after the fact. An analytic of atmospheres such as the one we propose already contains a theory of multimodality. In particular Schmitz has defined atmospheres as comprising "synesthetic characters," holistic gestalten that ultimately present themselves to and intervene in felt-bodies in a manner that cannot be reduced to any particular sensory impression (1968, 51–68). Synesthesia, in this sense, is not to be understood as an interplay of separate senses, nor as a "confusion" of senses as defined in medicine, but as a holistic perception that is prior to the division of particular dimensions of the sensorium and therefore better termed as *inframodal* rather than *multimodal*.

As mentioned earlier, a primary mechanism through which atmospheres manipulate and affect felt-bodies is suggestions of motion. These are felt-bodily stirrings that stand in relations of analogy and qualitative likeness to the holistic atmospheric forces that provoke them. In this book we pay particular attention to the sonic as traveling kinetic energy that not only envelops but also passes through bodies as a particularly salient kind of force exerting suggestions of movement. The sonic as wave phenomena comprises that which can be heard by humans but also ranges far beyond that, activating touch and kinesthetics so it can often be perceived in a cross-modal manner by the entire body. In such a way, the sonic is also a prime candidate for the generation of what Schmitz calls "synesthetic characters," which cannot be broken down to single sensory impressions but emerge as the aggregate effect of such comprehensive engagement with bodies. As a broader energetic flux that manifests in terms of holistic gestalten, the sonic is a particularly illustrative instance of atmospheric forces that operate through suggestion of motion in synesthetic ways. Therefore, while certainly not reducing the atmospheric to the sonic, we suggest that the sonic entertains a particularly proximate relationship with the atmospheric due to its inbuilt cross-modal and inframodal affordances. There is no denying that different practices and relationships with the environment offer possibilities of intervention into felt-bodily economies of space to different degrees. As it appears to us, the circumstance that sonic motion and felt-bodily motion can fall together, fusing into one, suggests that the sonic has a unique place in the study of atmospheres.

In positing the primacy of the manipulation of the felt-body's spatiality along with synesthetic characters for atmospheric sensation and knowledge, our approach partially aligns with but also differs from sensory anthropology. Sensory anthropology, multisensory anthropology, and the anthropology of the senses all start from the assumption that the "senses are made, not given," arguing that the senses and sensory perception are culturally constructed in the most far-reaching ways, following "the imperative to approach each culture on its own sensory terms" (Howes 2019, 17, 18; Classen 1993; Stoller 1989). Our position is that this great sociocultural diversity is obviously important and real, manifesting in, for example, cultural, social, and religious discourses about sensory perception and learned techniques of the body and acoustemologies (Feld 1996). Nevertheless, we suggest that atmospheric intermingling with felt-bodies is upstream from such more qualified cultural renderings of the sensory.

Atmospheres work through the bundling of such socioculturally diverse sensory dispositions with other discourses and memories, along with enculturated emotions, fusing them with the feeling of being a body. This means that atmospheres by virtue of being upstream from particular culturally qualified sensory regimes cannot be fully reduced to the particular sensory terms of the sociocultural contexts in question. Nonetheless, they also include and cannot exist independently from such enculturated sensation, because they could not operate without the bundling of such sociocultural sensory regimes together with discourses and memories into an overarching feel. In other words, we argue for a continuum between what, following phenomenological usage, we call the felt-body as a notion that names the condition of possibility for human situatedness in the world, and its myriad renderings and sociocultural modifications that result in different modulations of embodiment and sensation. This continuum is also at the same time a continuum of meaningfulness between, on one hand, the vague meaningfulness of atmospheric suggestions of motion that can be qualified in very different directions, and more specific sociocultural renderings of sensory modalities, their interconnections, and their consequences. Atmospheres and their suggestions of motion are found mainly at the vague and less specified end of this continuum of meaningfulness. In semiotic terms their relationship is iconic, because the suggestions of motion stand in relationships of qualitative likeness to the atmospheric forces that provoke such sensation, as well as indexical, because their relationship is also causal. In this case that means that the perception of atmospheres is meaningful but broad and relatively open, while this vague kind of indexical iconicity is also available for uptake into more qualified directions and meanings through enculturated techniques of the body. The fact that atmospheres' operation also involves the kind of bundling mentioned earlier also means that any empirical instance of atmospheric felt-bodily affectedness involves a broad range, if not the entire range of such a continuum of meaningfulness.

Such a continuum of meaningfulness spans much of the range of positions covered in an earlier debate about sensory anthropology between Tim Ingold and David Howes (2011; Howes 2022). Tim Ingold, following Merleau-Ponty's understanding of the body as a synergic system, stresses a relationship of relative interchangeability between the senses, as they are part of holistic perception through human activity and bodily motion: "the eyes and the ears should not be understood as separate keyboards for the registration of sensation but as organs of the body as a whole, in whose movement, within an environment, the activity of perception consists." Ingold's perspective on sensory perception as a "bodily synergy of the senses" is proximate to what we, following Schmitz, describe as atmospheric intermingling with the felt-body that has a holistic character, exceeding any definite sensory impression (2000, 268, 262). In contrast, Howes, accusing Ingold of universalizing a certain European phenomenological analytic of sensory perception, argues for a very extensive cultural constructedness of the senses, including their variable interrelationships. Also, according to him, the range and very subdivisions in the human sensorium are variable cultural sensory regimes (see also the discussion in Pink 2011). This in turn evokes the more socioculturally qualified end of the continuum of sensory perception mentioned earlier. Atmospheres exert suggestions of motion on felt-bodies, causing vague stirrings while at the same time bundling cultural conceptions of sensory perception and related techniques of the body together with discourses and memories through such stirrings so that all these elements coincide with the feeling of being a body.

We want to avoid a universalist take on atmospheric sensation pretending that felt-bodily sensation occurs in a sociocultural vacuum but also find the hyperparticularism of more pronounced kinds of sociocultural constructionism with respect to the senses unhelpful, because the latter sidelines the shared conditions of human being in the world, whose embodied base arguably has more common than diverging aspects. It is true that phenomenologists such as Maurice Merleau-Ponty and Hermann Schmitz were largely if not entirely insensitive to the diversity of sociocultural contexts of sensation, and this might lead one to conclude that "phenomenological accounts . . . tend to ignore how shared meanings shape the most 'natural' of human actions and perceptions in dance and in life, slighting the cultural content inherently implied by physical and cultural experience" (Bull [1997] 2018, 263, cited in Howes 2019, 20). Nevertheless, particular cultural regimes of the senses and connected sensory techniques of the body are not all there is, because these phenomena cover only part of the spectrum of felt-bodily perception. For a comprehensive understanding of sensation it would not be enough, or even odd, to solely emphasize cultural kinds of sharing while ignoring the aspects of sensation and multisensoriality we share as humans more broadly. One such key aspect is atmospheric felt-bodily affectedness, a condition for being in the world that we humans also share with many other animals. To sum up, to come to terms with atmospheric knowledge, a layered and differentiated approach to sensation and multisensoriality such as the one we are arguing for here is needed.

If, as we stated earlier, sonic motion and felt-bodily motion can at times fall together, fusing into one, then this suggests a small but significant shift of focus away from the questions centered around the (a)subjectivity of sound that has guided much of earlier scholarly perusals. It leads us on to the environmental capacities of sound-based practices (including music making and dance). In inquiring into music as an environmental and epistemological force, as we do in this book, then, we are not exploring the ontological so much as we are interested in the ontogenetic. Sound-based practices "are" not; they are only ever becoming, and that becoming interlaces with our own becoming. In this evanescence lies the efficacy characteristic of the sonic. The sonic affects, and interacts with, the felt-body as a continuous, amorphous stream of layered complexity. This complexity straddles the territorial boundaries of the material and the immaterial, of the referential and the essential. To make and to participate in sound-based practices is to navigate this layered complexity, to know how to ride the waves of music's becoming, to find something new on their cusps, and to transform along the process. It is this transformative modality of knowledge that we are interested in: the atmospheric knowledge of sonic practices. In this book we refer to it as *sound knowledge*.

SOUND KNOWLEDGE

The idea of a sound knowledge inherent in sound-based cultural practices is inspired by the notion of the passageway and of music making as a passageway of knowing. Intellectually, it takes us to the Pacific Ocean and to the intellectual work it has inspired: "The passageway" is central in Tongan scholar Epeli Hau'ofa's reimagination from the 1990s of the Pacific Ocean as a highway that links rather than separates the Pacific Islands (1993; cf. Goldie and Sobecki 2016). Hauʻofa, rather than looking at the Pacific Island world as a set of "islands in a far sea" located in the global periphery, chooses a more holistic perspective, one that opts to see things "in the totality of their relationships" and Oceania as a "sea of islands" rather than as a few disparate, resourceless islands separated by a vast and mighty ocean (1993, 7). Pacific epistemologies tend to seek out connection and contact rather than delimitation and borders, and this is the perspective Hauʻofa chooses.

"Hauʻofa's 'sea of islands' defies the barriers established by development 'experts,' aid agencies, colonial governments, scientists, and select scholars," writes political scientist Karin Amimoto Ingersoll (2016, 16). Drawing on traditional Pacific knowledge, the notion of a "sea of islands" articulates a counter worldview and offers an alternative. Drafting what she calls a "seascape epistemology," Ingersoll is, in some ways, embarking on a project similar to ours here: one that searches for alternative epistemologies, for ways of understanding based on the logic of mediums other than text and sensitive to both ancestral wisdom and the felt-body's sensitivity and sensuality. The knowledge of sound-based practices, too, is all this and more, we argue. It is certainly from Pacific Island perspectives, even though there is neither a dominant conceptualization of what this mode of knowledge might be about across Pacific Islander communities nor would all Pacific Islanders, or members of a specific Pacific Island community, subscribe to this idea. What is shared across Oceania, however, is the sense that what we call sound knowledge here is knowledge not about the sonic but about both sound as a medium and sonic practices as "an interconnected system that allows for successful navigation through them. It's an approach to life and knowing through passageways." Discussing alternative epistemologies, and the seascape epistemology in particular, Ingersoll claims that the Kānaka Maoli (native Hawaiian) seascape epistemology "organizes events and thoughts according to how they move and interact while emphasizing the importance of knowing one's roots, one's center, and where one is located inside this constant movement. . . . The power of seascape epistemology lies in its organic nature, its inability to be mapped absolutely, and its required interaction with the intangible sea" (6).

Similarly, sound-based epistemologies make sense by rendering experiential in sound the sound connection and its dynamics. They enable one to feel one's relationality and trajectory socially and historically but also within one's life worlds more generally. As an epistemic configuration, then, sound allows us to think and feel forward, to relish in sonic motion, and to anticipate its future course and past itineraries all at the same time. This movement, not confined by linearity or direction in any way, is what enables the passage: from sonic event and neural impulse to affect, emotion, historical narrative, and memory revisited.

Sound involves energetic movement: sound waves traveling through a medium. As sound waves encounter bodies, they make them vibrate to the same frequency, creating a connection akin to sympathetic vibration (Titon 2017). This capacity to create a tangible connection—not metaphorical but felt-bodily in nature—is distinct to the sonic.[16] Sound knowledge, then, is a practice: a knowledge practice rendering this kind of connection experienceable (Henriques 2011). Its very possibility arises from the experience of sound, which through its material characteristics suggests an ethical attunement to one's surroundings (Abels 2020; cf. Feld 2017). Defying a Cartesian worldview in which the environment is a detached, external object, sound knowledge enables a heightened sensitivity to the interconnectedness of beings and things (cf. Ingold 2011; see also Ismaiel-Wendt 2011). As a detached object, the environment can easily be exploited; when imbricated with one's own being and doing, it cannot (cf. Titon 2017).

Similarly, in sound, there is no individual entirely detached from another. Sound knowledge thus gives rise to an ecological and ethical understanding that everyone and everything is connected, an insight that deeply resonates with Pacific Islander notions (see Yunkaporta 2019; Hauʻofa 1993). This understanding arises across the various registers of human experience: it is felt-bodily; it is emotional; it is affective; it is visceral; it is shared and hence social in nature. Both process philosophically and acoustically speaking, sound knowledge is brought about in sonic movement: movement between bodies, stories, histories, and truths. Musical conventions, seen in this light, are strategies to discipline and steer this movement in its incipiency, and musical genres are strategies to tap into this energy the very moment the movement commences. Such engagement is always profoundly situational, and so sound knowledge is something like the mercury of epistemology. It is restlessly moving, ever-transforming, and always already the incipiency of something new. Our preliminary working definition of sound knowledge takes Lawrence Kramer's understanding of aesthetic knowledge as one point of departure: "Knowledge in its most robust form is never a matter of simply knowing what is true or false. Knowledge of the world, as opposed to knowledge of data, arises only in understandings that can neither be true nor false, that is, in understandings the epistemic form of which is the form of the aesthetic" (2016, xiii–iv).

In this book we link the epistemological qualities distinct to what we call *sonic privilege* with the environmental and temporal possibilities it creates to take Kramer's idea a significant step further (Eisenlohr 2019). Sound knowledge as Kramer's "knowledge of the world" is always-already environmental, a practical, transforming engagement with our environment; it is also a temporal practice. In keeping with Schmitz's dissolution of the object-subject divide, sound knowledge is therefore not knowledge about the world as an object separate from ourselves. Rather, it is a way of reconfiguring the world as we live in it that arises from thinking, feeling, and traveling along with music as knowledge unfolding. Humans follow the routes of sound knowledge by making, studying, and learning—in short, by engaging in music. The knowledge of sound-based practices unfolds through musical structures, textures, and forms, as well as through the meaningfulness that arises from engaging in these practices (cf. Abels 2022). This is how music making, among many other sound-based practices, makes sense: as an enactment and experience of a knowledge-as-discovery (Kramer 2016, xi). If the ineffability inherent in a modality of knowledge that keeps charting new ground makes it notoriously difficult to frame sound knowledge in academic terms, then this is precisely the quality that also accounts for music making's impact and relevance in daily life. Here the shift of focus away from what music might be onto what music might do is helpful. From a conceptual perspective, what is key here is the transductive process going on in the experience of sound; in the logic of sonic experience, the felt and the thought are not necessarily separate categories. As a sound wave becomes an affect, an emotion, or a shared feeling, one may instantaneously become the other. Sound knowledge emerges gradually, along musical forms, layered discursive formations, emotional dispositions, historic memory, and many other configurations (cf. Abels 2018). It therefore is always one step ahead of the reflexive language that seeks to capture it in full—precisely because, as we wrote earlier, a Husserlian melody is an operational frame in which retentions and protentions interact. This quality has often enigmatically been described as the unsayable and ineffable—even as the power of music.

THE STRUCTURE OF THE BOOK

Transoceanic spaces are not sites of movement; they are constituted by it. The intersections between atmospheric knowledge of such movement and the long-distance connections that make up oceanic worlds are the theme of chapter 2. We take a genre of Islamic vocal recitation in Mauritius as an example in which transoceanic movements and relations become perceivable through felt-bodily affectedness. The knowledge this sonic practice generates is also environmental; in this case it involves a sensing of the interconnected worlds of the Indian Ocean region.

Departing from the previous chapter's discussion of sensing Indian Ocean world connections through sonic practices, in chapter 3 we extend this perspective to the Western Pacific Island world. Shifting from atmospheric knowledge of transoceanic connections in religious recitations to popular music as a way of knowing felt Oceanic connections, we explore the consonances and overlaps between the originally phenomenological tradition of thinking about atmospheres and Pacific Island world epistemologies as ways of knowing and being in environments. In particular, Indigenous epistemologies about the Pacific as a "sea of islands" are built on musical practices as ways of knowing the relationalities that constitute this world from Pacific Islanders' perspectives. There sound knowledge is at the same time knowledge of the environment, and musical practices are "passageways of knowing" Oceanic connections and relations.

In chapter 4 we attend to the political dimensions of atmospheric knowledge, showing how atmospheric sensing also shapes citizenship and belonging in far-reaching ways. We discuss the generation of sonic atmospheres in the

Indian megacity Mumbai, India's economic capital and a major hub of the Indian Ocean world. There such atmospheres play an important role in the making of places and neighborhoods associated with particular ethnic, caste, and religious groups. In the example that is the focus of this chapter, they emerge in ritual performances and processions among Twelver Shiʻi Muslims, at the same time articulating this largely marginalized religious minority's right to the city through atmospheric citizenship.

In chapter 5 we explore how an analytic of atmosphere bridges the gap between the phenomenology of the felt-body and the anthropology of the senses and suggest that atmospheric affection is irreducible to particular sensory modi. We do so by way of two ethnographic studies of atmospheres, one taken from Patrick's own research on vocal recitation of devotional poetry among Mauritian Muslims, the other from Mikkel Bille's (2019) research on practices of lighting in Danish homes. In both examples atmospheres emerge as diffusely meaningful holistic sensations that afford further qualification through the particular discourses and sociocultural framings of sensory perception available in these two settings. Atmospheres are irreducibly multisensory phenomena that partially align with but are also upstream from the culturally specific sensory terms that the anthropology of the senses focuses on. Ultimately, we argue that atmospheric multisensoriality and specific cultural regimentations of the senses are part of a larger sensory continuum of meaningfulness. On this continuum atmospheres operate at its more diffuse end, while the sensory frames and formulations studied by the anthropology of the senses can often be found at its more defined end, its sensory modulations being the outcome of sociocultural, religious, and often also discursive kinds of qualification.

Chapter 6 continues with this exploration of atmospheric knowledge as irreducibly multisensory and multimodal. Expanding on the previous chapter's theme of multimodality, we deepen this line of analysis through the medium of dance or, sidestepping the culturally contingent category of *dance*, practices of structured movement. We demonstrate that such bodily practices of movement can generate and actualize atmospheric knowledge. In this chapter we shift our ethnographic focus back to the Western Pacific, especially to Palau. There such established practices of structured movement can also be interpreted as the aesthetic labor of atmospheric knowledge. In this ethnographic context, practices of structured movement provide another occasion for placing a phenomenologically inspired analytic of atmospheric knowledge in dialogue with kindred Pacific traditions that long predate phenomenology and its insights.

Atmospheric theory is now an established field. It has traveled from phenomenological philosophy to a number of other academic traditions and disciplines. But it is striking that there has been little analysis of atmospheres' temporality. This is all the more surprising because a certain temporality is at the heart of atmospheres' ways of operating. In chapter 7, we propose that latency is this kind of temporality.

Latency is another term for describing how atmospheres intermingle with and impact felt-bodies not through motion but through suggestions of motion. The temporal category of latency thereby also becomes central to all those public and political phenomena in which atmospheres revolving around a complex of incipient motion are important. Our investigation of the temporality of atmospheres returns to the ethnographic setting of chapter 4, the predicament of Twelver Shiʿi Muslims in Mumbai and their struggle for a right to the city, especially through Muharram processions and their mediatizations. We point to the prominent role that notions of latency have long played in Twelver Shiʿi historical memory and how these kinds of latency intersect with the latency at work in atmospheric claims to citizenship.

Engaging with the environmental qualities of atmospheric knowledge and thus coming full circle, chapter 8 explores how sonic atmospheres set the terms on which environmentality unfolds. Offering a close reading of a traditional *chesols*, a chant from Palau, we take a close analytical look at a specific musical situation to trace this idea. This chant is regularly used to frame official statements by Palauan advocates for increased climate-protection measures. The lyrics of the chant detail particular rules for the sustainable use of natural resources. However, in keeping with the rationale of this book, rather than emphasizing the message of the lyrics, we focus on the atmospheric intensity of the chant. We examine both the energetic forces specific to the chant's medium, sound, and the nature of its atmospheric force. We identify sonic suggestions of movement to explore the subtleties of the chant performance's rhythmicity, swirls of sonic intensities, and relationship to sustainability and climate protection. If chanting allows for access to a specifically sonic type of environmental knowledge, then it is potentially resourceful vis-à-vis climate-crisis adaptation strategies and possibly a potent cultural strategy for fostering resilience to climate change. This potential, we suggest, is rooted in the intimacy between the distinct atmospheres chants create, the felt-bodily experientiality they enable, and the somatic knowledge of environmental relations that arises from the felt-bodily sensation of being connected in sound. This is how sonic suggestions of motion mark individual distinctiveness and, at the same time, interconnectedness: the environmentality of individuals, their historicity, and the relationality inscribed into their being in the world. As a temporospatial practice, this is how sonic atmospheres create and prefigure the space in which environmental relations unfold.

2

———

Sensing Transoceanic Connections I

The Indian Ocean World

Movement constitutes transoceanic spaces. In this chapter we explore how atmospheric knowledge of such movement plays into long-distance connections that make up oceanic worlds. We investigate how a genre of Islamic vocal recitation generates atmospheres that make such multilayered movements and connections palpable. The knowledge that this sonic practice produces primarily addresses the felt-body; it makes a web of relations perceivable through felt-bodily affectedness. Therefore such knowledge is also environmental. The sonic practice we discuss in this chapter is an example of atmospheres' continuously hailing felt-bodies into being, because atmospheres actualize the feeling of being and having a body. By virtue of addressing the felt-body as a distinct entity, atmospheres also help to provisionally divide it from the world, thereby marking off environments that felt-bodies interact with. At the same time, it is through instances of atmospheres intermingling with felt-bodies that knowledge of environments becomes tangible; in the example we discuss these are the famously interconnected worlds of the Indian Ocean region.

The double character of environmentality that we laid out in chapter 1 is also relevant to the scenario we discuss in this chapter. On one hand, the sonic practice we discuss is environmental in the primary sense of a far-reaching relatedness and interconnectivity because it revolves around atmospheric forces that address felt-bodies. On the other hand, the practice generates atmospheric knowledge that is also environmental in a second, Foucauldian sense, because it also involves the artful staging and manipulation of atmospheres as a form of subtle discipline and

24

control. This is because it is an integral part of the embodied dimensions of a religious tradition. This religious sonic practice is meant to deepen piety and to reproduce and strengthen Mauritian Muslims' allegiances to a particular Islamic tradition, along with the latter's geographically spread places of importance in the Indian Ocean world. In other words, they aim to generate particular feelings of belonging of a religious kind that in turn have important political ramifications within the national and transnational settings in which they are practiced.

As is the case in India and Pakistan, Muslims of Indian background in Mauritius have long engaged in the recitation of Urdu na'␣t, devotional poetry in honor of the Prophet Muhammad. We examine the interplay between this Indian poetic tradition associated with the Ahl-e Sunnat wa Jama'at Islamic reformist tradition with the sonic dynamics of vocal performance. In particular, sonic dynamics of vocal performance are responsible for the powerful effects of pious transformation and long-distance connection that Patrick's interlocutors spoke about during his field research in Mauritius. To this end we draw on the neophenomenological analytic of atmospheres as emotions poured into space that intermingle with sentient bodies to understand how vocal sound can bring about such transformations. The discursive and sonic dimensions of the na'␣t genre are closely interrelated. Nevertheless, by approaching the sonic through the paradigm of atmospheres, we treat the sonic as a modality of knowledge and meaning making that is in principle independent from the discursive aspects of voice. Understanding sonic religious practices such as reciting na'␣t as atmospheres is also useful because it helps one grasp the role of sensory knowledge in the making and sustaining of transoceanic connections.

We stress the significance of atmospheres as nonverbal and somatic knowledge, but this does not imply that discursive knowledge does not matter or that discursively articulated knowledge cannot also play into the generation of atmospheres and be compatible with atmospheric affection. Nevertheless, the obvious importance of discursively constituted meaning in emotion does not diminish the fact that the sonic is a modality of knowledge and meaning making of its own. This is especially evident in contexts where discursively generated meanings and sonic meaningfulness do not always align, as, for example, in the discussion of atmospheric citizenship in Mumbai in chapters 4 and 7.

In July 2010 Patrick attended a ritual gathering known as *mahfil-e mawlud* on the occasion of a wedding in a village in the north of Mauritius; this devotional event featured the recitation of na'␣t. Men and women were in separate rooms, and Patrick was sitting among the men on the densely packed floor of a moderate-size living room in the bride's family's home. Several of the na'␣t recited by the *na'␣t khwan* (an expert reciter of this poetic genre) were widely known among local Muslims from locally produced audio recordings. This was also the case for the following naʿt, of which a recording was released on a CD by a schoolteacher originally trained by an Indian imam residing in Mauritius (Chady [n.d.], CD 1, track 12). They listened to this Urdu naʿt, some of the men gently swaying to the recital. Like many other naʿt, this poetic recital centered on the Medina theme, with an ardently desired pilgrimage to the tomb of the Prophet standing for a personal encounter with him. Not only the lines of the poetry but also the sonic dynamics of the reciter's voice suggest an experience of travel and removal to a faraway, more desirable place, where one can personally encounter the presence of the Prophet himself.

Sabze gunbad kī ziārat kijiye	Embark on the pilgrimage to the green dome [of the Prophet's tomb in Medina]
Sabze gunbad kī ziārat kijiye	Embark on the pilgrimage to the green dome [of the Prophet's tomb in Medina]
Zairo sāmāne rāhat kijiye	Pilgrims, comfort and calm will be your provision
Zairo sāmāne rāhat kijiye	Pilgrims, comfort and calm will be your provision
Gunbad-e khazrā ke jalwe dekh kar	Beholding the splendor of the green dome
Gunbad-e khazrā ke jalwe dekh kar	Beholding the splendor of the green dome
Khub roshan āpni qismat kijiye	Illuminate your destiny with the most excellent light
Khub roshan āpni qismat kijiye	Illuminate your destiny with the most excellent light
Zairo ro ro ke unke sāmne	Pilgrims, shed tears [of repentance] in front of him
Zairo ro ro ke unke sāmne	Pilgrims, shed tears [of repentance] in front of him
Peish āpni āpni hājat kijiye	Present your requests [to the Prophet] humbly
Peish āpni āpni hājat kijiye	Present your wishes [to the Prophet] humbly

In comparison to other naʿt Patrick knew and had listened to, the recitation of this particular naʿt was in a calm, composed style. However, when the naʿt khwan recited the second iteration of the line *Gunbad-e khazrā ke jalwe dekh kar*

AUDIO CLIP 1. "Sabze gunbad kī ziārat kijiye." Chady (n.d.), CD 1, track 12.

To hear this audio clip, scan the QR code with your mobile device or visit DOI: https://doi.org/10.1525/luminos.244.1

(Beholding the splendor of the green dome), Patrick could feel a slight nudge that also seemed to instantly take hold of the other men seated very closely to him on the floor, a distinct sense of motion seizing the men. This second iteration of the line was especially significant as a moment of intensification, where not just the discursive invocation of the splendor of the famous green dome of the tomb of the Prophet Muhammad in Medina featured as a focus of ardent longing, fusing spiritual travel and pilgrimage to a sacred site across the ocean with the reactualization of diasporic links through specifically Indian Urdu-language Islamic devotional traditions. Also, as evident in the audio example, the intensification of the reciter's voice—with increases along the dimensions of volume and pitch and also on the dimension of timbre with a shift of acoustic energy to higher frequency ranges in the complex structure of overtones that vocal sound is composed of—suggests somatically palpable motion. The drawing out of syllables through ornamental modulation at these points of intensification further reinforces such a sense of motion. This felt-bodily sensation was simultaneously discursively qualified as a rapture and removal toward Medina and the longed-for personal encounter with the Prophet in his favorite city. In an analogous fashion, just a few moments later, the second iteration of the line *Zairo ro ro ke unke sāmne* (Pilgrims, shed tears [of repentance] in front of him) combined the discursive stress of emotional intensity that the encounter with the Prophet would provoke with a parallel vocal intensification. The sonic dynamics again feature a marked rise of volume and pitch, along with a shift in timbre in the sense mentioned earlier, also underlined by the ornamental and modulating drawing out of syllables, resulting in a similar sense of being carried away so subtly. A relaxing sonic motion, with decreases on all these dimensions, immediately followed in the recitation of the next line. In other words, the naʿt khwan brought together sonic motion, suggesting removal or travel elsewhere and the spiritual travel as articulated in poetic discursive in an artful way, the sonic and the discursive not just overlapping but mutually reinforcing each other in their effects.

Ever since the 1980s, recordings of naʿt, first from India and Pakistan and since the 1990s also by local naʿt khwan, have circulated in Mauritius. They have provided influential models of vocal performance so that recitation of the genre is nowadays thoroughly integrated with media practices (Eisenlohr 2006, 2009). At the same time, the cultivation of this devotional genre inspired by Sufi traditions has long been a focus of sectarian disputes among Muslims in India and Pakistan as well as Muslims of Indian background throughout the Indian Ocean world. Among Muslims of Indian background, such disputes have become part of larger concerns of Islamic authenticity in locations that are well connected to, yet far removed from, the South Asian homelands of their ancestors. At the same time, the mediatic circulation of na't raises the question of the technical reproducibility of sonic atmospheres and their transformational effects (Eisenlohr 2018).

For followers of the Ahl-e Sunnat wa Jama'at, the artful recitation of na't is one of the chief means of bringing about the presence of the Prophet in his role as a mediator between Muslims and God (Sanyal 1996). This is very much in line with this reformist tradition's openness to Sufism, which distinguishes it from the contemporary stances of other, more purist South Asian reformist traditions, such as the schools of Deoband and the Ahl-e hadith.[1] The discursive dimensions of the poetry are of great significance; however, the vocal and sonic aspects of the performance are at least as important. A successful performance provokes profound bodily sensations among those present that many speak of as the feeling of being moved and carried away to a better place. In the discursive framework of this Islamic tradition, with its special emphasis on devotion to the figure of the Prophet, this more desirable place is often identified with Medina, considered to have been the Prophet Muhammad's favorite city.

The vocal performance of na't is the main part of *mahfil-e mawlud* gatherings that are held on important days of the Islamic ritual calendar, such as the Prophet's birthday, the death anniversaries (*'urs*) of major Sufi saints, or auspicious events in people's lives such as performing weddings, moving into a new house, or the passing of important school exams. The reciting is often collective but is usually led by solo reciters known as na't khwan, who are known for their voices and skill in reciting this devotional poetry and regarded as models to be emulated when performing the poetry. The performance of na't both expresses and stirs feelings of love and attachment for the Prophet among those present, aiming to turn them into better Muslims in the process. Mauritian Muslims who follow the Ahl-e Sunnat tradition are concerned about the perceived authenticity of the poetry. This is first of all related to long-standing sectarian disputes in South Asia and its diasporas about the extent to which the exuberant personal veneration of the Prophet expressed in na't poetry is legitimate. Opponents of the Ahl-e Sunnat, such as followers of the school of Deoband, manifest in Mauritius above all through the strong presence of the transnational missionizing movement Tablighi Jama 'at. Proponents of the Ahl-e hadith tend to consider the profuse personal praise and exaltation of the Prophet in na't poetry as dangerously exaggerated, elevating the Prophet to a God-like position and thereby diluting the unicity of God. Aficionados of na't poetry have in turn defended the practice by citing hadith, according to which the Prophet himself was fond of the poetry and sanctioned its recitation, and have counterattacked their opponents, accusing them of insufficient respect for the Prophet.

As the texts of the poetry are such a delicate issue, Mauritian Muslims who are fond of naʿt often make sure that the poetry is sufficiently authorized, for example, through having been composed by eminent scholar-saints, such as Ahmad Riza Khan Barelwi, the founder of the Barelwi tradition (Eisenlohr 2018). Ahmad Riza Khan Barelwi was known as a prolific composer of naʿt who wrote naʿt poetry in moments of divine inspiration such as when he felt the presence of the Prophet in front of him (Khan Barelwi, n.d.). Another reason for the major concern about the authenticity and legitimacy of the naʿt poetry recited in mahfil-e mawlud stems from the diasporic context of Mauritius, where Muslims are a minority and perceive themselves as being relatively far removed from the center of religious authority in the Muslim world. In contrast to this widespread perception, Mauritian Muslims are in fact closely connected to several centers of Islamic authority, not only in India and Pakistan but also elsewhere. Much of this diasporic anxiety about orthopraxy is related to the dominant multicultural model of Mauritian nation building, which privileges a group's ownership of a major religious tradition pointing to origins beyond Mauritius as a chief means for inclusion into the nation. The question of who then stands for authentic Islam also matters for cultural citizenship, as Muslims are one of the officially recognized "communities" of Mauritius.

These sensibilities about textual authenticity notwithstanding, the perceived appropriateness of the vocal style and voice quality in the recitation of naʿt is important for the effectiveness of the performance. Several of Patrick's interlocutors told him that they considered the sonic dimensions of the voice even more important than its discursive dimensions. They found the sound of the voice of a particular naʿt khwan so moving that they felt carried away by it. The stirring of pious emotions and the palpable sense of the spiritual presence of the Prophet that the performance of naʿt poetry aims to bring about thus hinges on vocal sound and its qualities. Nicholas Harkness has called this intertwining of vocal sound and sociocultural values the "phonosonic nexus" (2014, 12). Pointing at the expected copresence among specific qualities of vocal sound, certain social actors, and particular social and cultural values, this notion emphasizes how the sonic dimensions of the voice can, under certain conditions, stand for sociocultural values and actors' stances to them. For the Mauritian Muslim interlocutors, the recitation of naʿt among Mauritians actively provokes pious emotions and bodily sensations of being carried away to a better place. Even more, vocal sound brings about such sensations and emotions in a way experienced as going beyond one's agency and intentionality.

An analytic of vocal sound as atmospheres not only explains the co-occurrence of vocal tones and particular sociocultural values but also accounts for its transformative somatic effects on those within its range. Understanding sound as atmospheres draws attention to the ways in which its sonic materiality intermingles with felt-bodies. Such processes of transduction then result in suggestions of movement felt by those exposed to the vocal sound of naʿt recitation. These suggestions of motion become a key part of the emotional force behind this devotional vocal practice, providing the bodily felt evidence for the promise of salvation that is central to this form of devotional, Sufi-inspired Islam.

RECITATION AND SONIC ATMOSPHERES

To understand the effects of vocal sound on participants in a mahfil-e mawlud, one has to pay attention to its dynamic movements. Especially, the widely circulated recordings of the naʿt genre in Mauritius demonstrate how an array of obvious sonic parameters is exploited to this effect (Chady 2001, 2003). Naʿt khwans' voices in these recordings feature a great dynamic along the parameters of loudness, pitch, and timbre. On top of this, another feature of the recordings is the application of a reverb effect throughout. This results in the impression of spatial wideness, this echo effect citing listeners' experience of the azan, the Islamic call to prayer reverberating in a built environment. In crucial moments of the recitation, the naʿt khwan's voice displays an intensification along several of these dimensions, not just an increase in loudness and pitch but, as in the example discussed earlier, also a shift of acoustic energy toward the frequency bins of the three thousand to five thousand hertz range, resembling what Johan Sundberg (1974) has called the "singer's formant" with pronounced vibrato. Vocal sound thus enacts a marked sonic movement, a motion that is a sonic icon of a spiritual movement of the devotees present in this religious context toward Medina and a poetic image of the presence of the Prophet himself. The image of traveling to Medina to personally encounter the Prophet is a stock theme discursively elaborated in naʿt poetry. But a movement that several of my Mauritian Muslim interlocutors described as the experience of being lifted up and taken away to a better place is also quite literally enabled and carried out through the dynamics of vocal sound through the ways such a sonic force affects the felt-bodies of those involved in the practice. The question is how vocal sound can actually function as more than a metaphor for discursive themes of a religious tradition such as the particular South Asian tradition of devotional Islam we are writing about here. Where does its peculiar force come from, which some of Patrick's interlocutors in Mauritius spoke about as really overpowering?

An analytic of atmospheres can account for the somatic effects of vocal movement Patrick's interlocutors described for this ritual setting centered on the recitation of naʿt poetry. We hereby draw on recent work on sound and music as atmospheres (Abels 2013, 2017, 2018, 2022; see also Eisenlohr 2018; Riedel 2015). Atmospheres fill a predimensional space, enveloping and intermingling with felt-bodies who sense atmospheres in a holistic manner that is upstream from definite sensory impressions. The phenomenological distinction between the physical body *(Körper)* and the felt-body *(Leib)* is crucial here, as the felt-body often reaches beyond the boundaries of the physical body, into what is felt to pertain to the body but is outside its physical boundaries. According to Hermann Schmitz, atmospheres are akin to feelings occupying the predimensional space of the felt-body: "feelings are atmospheres poured into space and powers that seize the felt-body" (2016, 30). Atmospheres are not objects but fleeting phenomena that come and go, such as pain, the weather, or silence. "Emotions are atmospheres poured out spatially. An atmosphere in the sense intended here is the complete occupation of a surfaceless space in the region of experienced presence. This surfaceless space, apart from emotions, can also be occupied by the weather experienced as enveloping you or by (e.g., festive, pregnant or calm) silence" (Schmitz, Müllan, and Slaby 2011, 255).

Sound and sonic phenomena such as musical figures enacted by a voice are a very tangible example of atmospheres. They are fleeting and nonpermanent but have an eminently material existence. They cannot be sensed only by the hearing apparatus but in a much more comprehensive way, by potentially the entire body. This is why it is justified to speak of sonic instead of acoustic atmospheres because the entire range of traveling energetic and vibratory phenomena they compose very often exceed the limits of the human hearing apparatus. Very importantly, atmospheres contain suggestions of motion (Schmitz 1967, 1969, 2016, 85). According to Gernot Böhme, sound and music as atmosphere is a "manipulation of space as it is experienced by the body" (2000, 16). The sonic dynamics of vocal sound in naʿt performances thus can be understood as atmospheres, effecting suggestions of motion on the felt-bodies of those participating in a mahfil-e mawlud or those listening to recordings of naʿt recitals in other contexts.

SOUNDING THE INDIAN OCEAN
IN RELIGIOUS NETWORKS

The Indian Ocean has a long history of deep and long-term interconnectedness (Alpers 2014; Bose 2006; Chaudhuri 1985). In fact, some have even seen the Indian Ocean as the "cradle of globalization" (Moorthy and Jamal 2010, 9). Running against many North Atlantic intellectual sensibilities connected to the notion of the cosmopolitan, religious traditions and networks have been among the foremost dimensions of such transoceanic connections in this part of the world. Islamic traditions and links have played an especially important role in establishing multilayered routes and connections across the ocean (Eisenlohr 2012; Ho 2006; Ricci 2011; Sheriff 2010; Simpson 2006), comprising not just the spread of religious knowledge and practices but also migration, trade, tourism, and pilgrimage as well as political alliances and musical traditions (Byl and Sykes 2020; Rasmussen 2016), including those that connect and travel across ethnoreligious lines (Sykes 2018).

The sonic practices embedded in particular Islamic ritual contexts can undergird such transoceanic ties by investing them with a particular felt quality. We contend that the production and cultivation of sonic atmospheres like those in naʿt recitals provide a particular kind of somatic evidence for such transoceanic ties that give the links to places of religious authority beyond Mauritius a certain self-evident character beyond words. As is evident from the example of naʿt recitation, such sonic practices build and maintain relationships to several of such places at once. First of all, they are a central component of a larger complex of piety centered on the person of the Prophet Muhammad. The ardent wish to be close to the Prophet that these devotional practices enact from a Sufi-inspired perspective often comes down to the expressed wish to travel to a holy land elsewhere in this Indian Ocean world, in this case Medina. At the same time, the practice of reciting Urdu devotional poetry in Mauritius also points to the predominantly northern Indian origins of most Mauritian Muslims, the part of the Indian Ocean world where the genre emerged and from where its practice reached Mauritius.

It would be wrong, however, to imagine the recitation of naʿt as a straightforward kind of cultural baggage that the ancestors of Mauritian Muslims brought with them when they migrated from India to Mauritius in the nineteenth century, most of them from present-day Bihar and eastern Uttar Pradesh. The large majority of them were impoverished indentured laborers brought to Mauritius to work on the sugar plantations, replacing the slave workforce after the abolition of slavery in the British Empire in 1834 until the end of the indenture system during World War I (Carter 1995). Their ritual practices were more influenced by caste affiliation and the regional and rural background they shared with their fellow indentured laborers, who later identified more as Hindus than by any clear-cut religious boundaries. The waves of religious reformism that brought about the emergence of a Hindu "religion" and new modern forms of reformist Islam from the middle of the nineteenth century onward had not yet touched the rural peripheries from which the ancestors of Mauritians with Indian backgrounds departed for Mauritius. In other words, for the vast majority of Indian migrants to Mauritius, the sociocultural worlds they left behind in northern India were not yet influenced by the modern religious reformist movements that dominate the field today and that caused the emergence of hard religious boundaries between Hindus and Muslims and, in the case of Muslims, strong boundaries between followers of various reformist sectarian traditions. These modern Indian reform movements made their presence felt in Mauritius only after 1910, when Hindu activists of the Arya Samaj started working in Mauritius, soon to be followed by their competitors from the Sanatan Dharm tradition.

Among Muslims the Ahl-e Sunnat wa Jamaʿat movement established itself in Mauritius through Muslim Gujarati trader networks in the 1920s. This reformist tradition, characterized by a synthesis of ʿulema-based Islam and Sufism, then quickly became the dominant form of Sunni Islam in Mauritius. Much of the emphasis in this tradition is on a complex of piety around the figure of the Prophet. The recitation of naʿt is in turn one of the hallmarks of this Sufi-influenced veneration of the Prophet and is what the Ahl-e Sunnat wa Jamaʿat stands for. In fact, the founder of this tradition, Ahmad Riza Khan Barelwi (1856–1921), was known to be a prolific composer of the genre. The recitation of naʿt is a practice that became established only through modern Islamic reformism, after migration from India to Mauritius had already ended. Recitation of naʿt thus enacts a transoceanic connection that is properly diasporic insofar as it emerged long after migration. It is the product of a new orientation to a place of origin and the religious authority connected to it.

A cosmopolitan set of Indian Ocean "mobile societies," in this case Gujarati trader communities, has long played a crucial role in the deep religious transformations that have taken place among Mauritian Muslims since the period of migration from India (Ho 2017). The Islamic networks through which various kinds of reformism reached Mauritius from India were for a long time almost exclusively in the hands of the Gujarati trader communities, who spread around the Indian Ocean region in the nineteenth century in the wake of empire and had entered Mauritius as free immigrants with their own capital, continuously maintaining dense networks of kinship, trade, and religion with India (Markovits 1999). These endogamous and highly mobile groups with their long-distance networks in the Indian Ocean world became the exponents of an Islamic cosmopolitanism that many Mauritian Muslims who are descendants of working-class indentured laborers from northern India have more recently sought to emulate (Eisenlohr 2012).

The reasons for the spread and popularity of performative vocal practices that signal affiliation with a major Indian Islamic reformist tradition cannot be reduced to the impact of religious activism from India channeled to Mauritius by the well-connected and often wealthy Gujarati trader families found not just in Mauritius but throughout the Indian Ocean region. The internal dynamics of a postplantation Creole society also played a crucial role in the process of religious reformism and purification that turned Indo-Mauritians into either Hindus or Muslims in the course of the twentieth century. As a former sugar colony with no precolonial population whose inhabitants all have origins elsewhere, this Creole society has been profoundly shaped by the experience of slavery and indentured labor. As in other Creole worlds in the Caribbean with which Mauritius shares a fair range of historical commonalities, race played a supreme role in the archipelago's social and economic structure. With a Franco-Mauritian community historically in control of most of the land and the sugar industry, slaves, indentured laborers, and other migrants from around the Indian Ocean world became part of Mauritian society through processes of racialization that simultaneously assigned them particular economic and social roles in a plantation colony. In Creole societies such as in Mauritius and the Caribbean, groups tend to be demarcated and set in hierarchical relationships by race. In colonial Mauritius "Indian" was not a neutral designation of origin but referred to a rather inferior racial category. The existence of a small group of well-to-do Indians did not fundamentally change this reality. Members of the economically and at the time also politically dominant white and non-Indian and nonwhite *(gens de couleur)* Christian elite often looked down on Indians as racial others and because of what they considered their questionable non-Christian ritual practices.

The twentieth-century process of "religionization" that both Muslims and Hindus engaged in also has to be understood in this colonial Creole context, where the claiming of a recognized major religious tradition such as Hinduism or Islam offered an escape route from racialization (Eisenlohr 2022b). The modern Indian reformist movements thereby provided sought-after resources for Mauritians of Indian background to elevate their standing from inferior racial others to proponents of the respectable major "world religions": Hinduism and Islam. Transoceanic religious networks, initially almost entirely controlled by Gujarati trader families, provided the impetus for turning Indo-Mauritians with specific caste-based and rural ritual practices into followers of modern Hinduism and Islam. However, the conditions of a Creole society in which race ruled supreme also played its part. Finally, the lasting transformations of Mauritian society through religionization came about through the official recognition and privileging of religious difference as a main mode of demarcating groups in Mauritian society. An important part of this was the institutionalization and teaching of so-called ancestral languages tied to religion, among them Urdu, in schools. This policy started after World War II in the final decades of colonial rule and was completed by the postcolonial Hindu-dominated governments after independence in 1968. Accompanying this shift was the enshrinement of religion as a major category for distinguishing groups in Mauritius in the census, the constitution, and the political system and through the extension of state subsidies and state recognition to non-Christian religions such as Hinduism and Islam.

All in all, this signaled a momentous shift from a plantation society built on racialization to the present model of Mauritian nation-building, religion-based multiculturalism. The shift from racialization to religionization was empowering for Mauritians of Indian origin because it asserted the autonomy and respectability of Hinduism and Islam and the full recognition of their followers as a community. Nineteenth-century indentured migrants were not yet able to assert this claim and had to undergo the inferiorizing regime of racialization instead. In short, modern reformist religious movements from India enabled Mauritians of Indian origin to greatly improve their standing in the Creole society of Mauritius and to leave behind racial stigma. This is the Mauritian background informing Islamic devotional practices such as the recitation of naʿt. Taken at face value, the practice appears to be a cultural import from northern India, falling within what the Mauritian state officially labels as "ancestral culture." However, reciting naʿt and the long-distance connections that can be felt in it is part of the drama of a Creole society, where newcomers from different parts of the Indian Ocean world struggled to establish themselves, seeking to improve the terms of their incorporation in Mauritian society.

SENSING TRANSOCEANIC CONNECTIONS

So far we have introduced the recitation of naʿt among Mauritian Muslims as an atmospheric practice that exerts somatically felt suggestions of motion on those taking part in it. In the context of a devotional tradition centered on the veneration of the Prophet Muhammad, such visceral invitations to movement merge with the discursive call to travel to Medina to personally encounter the Prophet, a leitmotiv of naʿt poetry. In naʿt recitals poetic discourse and sonic motion work together in the generation of atmospheres. On the other hand, we have discussed the recitation of naʿt as part of a much larger process of establishing modern reformist religious networks between Mauritius and India that set in only years after migration from India to Mauritius had finally ended. This process involved the extension to Mauritius of the deep processes of religious transformation in colonial India that produced modern Hinduism and the modern reformist schools of Islam in South Asia, channeled through cosmopolitan and mobile Gujarati trader communities that had spread throughout the Indian Ocean world in the wake of empire. However, the political, economic, and social setup of colonial Mauritius also played a crucial role. Ultimately, the dynamics of Mauritius as a Creole society built on the logics of racialization made alignment with the new, standardized version of major religious traditions from India irresistibly attractive for Mauritians of Indian origin who inhabited an inferior position in the racial hierarchy of a colonial plantation society. It propelled a shift from race to religion as the chief group-making discourse in Mauritius, becoming the single most important criteria of marking communal boundaries in the final decades of colonial rule and culminating in the enshrinement of religious difference in the census, constitution, and the political system after independence, along with state recognition and promotion of presumed "ancestral languages" with chiefly religious significance, among them Urdu. These dynamics of religionization proved highly empowering for Mauritians of Indian origin, and in combination with their numbers their rising dominance in politics and their economic ascent enabled them to leave behind racial stigma.

The Indian Ocean as a cosmopolitan and highly interconnected space that long predates colonial networks has often been considered the distinctive characteristic of this part of the world from a global perspective (Chaudhuri 1985; Alpers 2014). Historians have pointed out how the Indian Ocean has been a zone of movement and interconnections that fly in the face of modern methodological nationalism and the received boundaries of area studies that have conventionally divided the Indian Ocean world into Africa, the Middle East, South Asia, and

Southeast Asia, while Australia as a European settler state always fell out of the frame of the Indian Ocean's established "regions." In a salutary intellectual operation, historians and members of other scholarly disciplines have pointed to the inadequacy of these North Atlantic political and academic demarcations of "areas" in the Indian Ocean world that has always been defied by long-standing histories of movements of people, religious traditions, political forms of authority, goods, and ideas across such boundaries. Mauritius and the Mascarenes present a rather extreme scenario in this regard, because, as an archipelago in the southwest Indian Ocean uninhabited before colonialism, it never belonged to any established land-based area and became the home of Creole societies exclusively composed of people with origins elsewhere. As such, there are few places where the theme of multilayered transoceanic links is more pertinent, as is also evident in Mauritian musical traditions (Servan-Schreiber 2010).

Recent approaches to transregional spaces, including transoceanic spaces like the world of the Indian Ocean, have emphasized the role of movement in creating these spaces. Far from being preexisting grids or containers, such spaces come into existence through human routes, connections, and links that are built, sustained, and transformed through the travel of people, capital, goods and other material objects, and ideas, as well as practices and institutions like religion. Such crisscrossing connections also constitute the Indian Ocean as an "aesthetic space" (Verne and Verne 2017). The recitation of na't is a small example of these much larger and multifaceted ties. It can, however, help us understand a key dimension of such transoceanic links, with its felt and atmospheric qualities that often evade discursive rendering. As discussed earlier, atmospheres exert their power through somatically palpable suggestions of motion. Sonic practices such as the recitation of na't are a particularly evocative example of atmospheres, because the sonic as traveling energetic flows transgresses boundaries, including bodily boundaries, in obvious ways. Those exposed to the power of sound and the sonic feel the passing of sonic energy through them as suggestions of motion, pointing at the processes of transduction that are central to the perception of sound, whether through the hearing apparatus or other parts of the body.

Sonic practices are especially important in this context, because the subtle sensation of movement central to the atmospheric articulates with the larger theme of movement as producing transoceanic worlds. The atmospheric provides a particular register for experiencing movement, in this case movement that makes the Indian Ocean region a lived transoceanic space. It does so by enabling the somatic registration of aspects of such movements as bodily present and therefore as self-evident.[2] It makes possible the feeling of such movements beyond words but also in a diffuse multilayered way that cannot be reduced to single sensory impressions, exceeding them in a holistic way instead. In other words, the recitation of na't, alongside its more obvious character as a practice of spiritual intercession in a Sufi-inspired tradition, is also a means of providing seemingly irrefutable somatic evidence of transoceanic connections. This is not just a matter of parallelism between atmospherically induced suggestions of movement exerted on felt-bodies and the various forms of ties through movement that constitute a transoceanic space. The recitation of this devotional poetry makes the truth of these connections felt in the flesh. As argued in chapter 1 of this book, environmentality is a web of relations, and the recitation of this devotional poetry actualize the visceral knowledge of such relations, including those relations that establish transoceanic connections. The felt-bodily motion induced by such suggestions of motion in naʿt recitals that make such transoceanic connections palpable are therefore also a kind of environmental knowledge.

As we have pointed out, the strengthening of such transoceanic religious connections is also embedded in a Mauritian politics of privileging religious forms of belonging as part of a specific nation building that foregrounds the performance of ancestral origins elsewhere. Thus not only is the kind of atmospheric knowledge that naʿt recitation brings about disciplinary in a religious sense, but it is also located in a particular Mauritian politics of citizenship and nationhood. Naʿt recitation therefore also illustrates atmospheres as staged and crafted for a regulatory aim with political ramifications. In this way the practice generates a kind of atmospheric knowledge that evokes Böhme's approach to atmospheres as artfully produced and designed aesthetic phenomena that are at the same time environmental in a Foucauldian sense. In other words, vocal recitation of naʿt is environmental in the double sense, as outlined earlier in this book. The practice comprises both bodily felt environmentality, which is at the same time somatic knowledge of the environment, and environmentality as a form of discipline and control. While the former kind of environmentality pertains to the more diffuse kind of meaningfulness generated through suggestions of motion, the latter, Foucauldian kind of environmentality aligns with the more qualified end of a continuum of environmental knowledge, where atmospheric affectedness gets fused with religious discourses and ethics, in the example we discuss in this chapter a particular South Asian tradition of devotional Islam. Environmentality as a broader kind of atmospheric knowledge is therefore often available for uptake and at least partial capture by disciplinary techniques and institutional structures, in this case of organized religion.

Provoking suggestions of movement through the sonic in the recitation of Urdu naʿt is no automatic process that yields the same results for everyone and in any setting. The processes of transduction that result in somatically felt suggestions of motion in participants of a mahfil-e mawlud are central to the power of naʿt to generate atmospheres. Such suggestions of movement also intersect with body memories. These are not just aural but properly sonic "archives" of the felt-body, because they comprise the traces of felt movement beyond the acoustically perceivable. It does not need to be pointed out that these archives are not the same for everyone. Such body memories of movement are the outcome of long processes of socialization. In the case of naʿt recitation, the sectarian differences and antagonisms the practice has long become embroiled in play a crucial role in the formation of such sonic archives in the flesh. Many Salafis would appreciate the beauty of a naʿt khwan's voice but would not be atmospherically moved by the performance. This recalls the observation by Hermann Schmitz that atmospheres can also be merely observed and that a spreading atmosphere does not necessarily seize everyone in the same way. From a Salafi perspective the notion of making the Prophet appear in person through sonic practices to gain his intercession with God is blasphemous. For someone committed to that tradition, the sound of naʿt poetry would not be associated with the vivid experience of traveling to Medina to be in the presence of the Prophet, as it would not be part of that person's body memory.

Atmospheric suggestions of movement generated by sonic practices therefore need to intersect with such body memories of movement, including those contained in sonic archives, for their power to unfold. This intersection takes the form of a bundling that suggestions of motion effect, in which religious traditions, acoustemologies, and enculturated bodily dispositions are made momentarily compatible by suffusing them with the same felt qualities. In other words, atmospheres as suggestions of motion that intermingle with felt-bodies are upstream from sociocultural sensibilities and techniques of the body but encompass and bundle them with other lines of experience into a resonating whole.

CONCLUSION

In this chapter we have introduced the recitation of naʿt poetry among Mauritian Muslims as an atmospheric practice that generates sonic and somatic knowledge of transoceanic connections in the Indian Ocean world. Naʿt recital is not a kind of cultural "baggage" that ancestors of present-day Mauritian Muslims brought from India when they migrated to Mauritius. It is a key devotional practice common among followers of a major Islamic reformist movement, the Ahl-e Sunnat wa Jamaʿat that emerged in India at a time when migration to Mauritius was already in full swing and that reached Mauritius only in the 1920s, quickly establishing itself as the locally dominant form of Sunni Islam. The recitation of naʿt is therefore a sonic religious practice that points to links between Mauritius and India that emerged only after migration from India had already ended. The popularity of the practice was due to the expansion and missionary efforts of a modern Islamic piety movement. However, its spread was also driven by the internal dynamics of a Creole society in which people of Indian origin, together almost 70 percent of the population, aimed at empowerment through replacing race with religion as the main principle of making and demarcating communities in a postplantation society.

We have argued that an approach to the sonic as atmosphere is particularly suited to gaining a better understanding of why sonic practices, including music, can be such powerful modes of knowledge of long-distance connections, including transregional and transoceanic ties. In this sense sonic practices such as na't recitation can also be environmental, in the double sense mentioned earlier; their more qualified aspects that align with the discourses and embodied techniques of a particular religious tradition establish environmentality as a mode of discipline and control. The theme of motion is central in this respect, connecting the kinds of movements that constitute a particular space, including the transoceanic world that is the focus of this volume and movement as experienced by the felt-body. The recitation of na't is one way to make the truth and import of such Indian Ocean ties palpable. It therefore constitutes a kind of atmospheric knowledge of its own, irreducible to discourse, providing somatic evidence for the transoceanic connections that play a major role in the lives of Mauritian Muslims.

3

Sensing Transoceanic Connections II

The Western Pacific Island World

Building on the previous chapter's discussion of sensing transoceanic connections through sonic practices in the Indian Ocean world, we now shift this perspective to the Western Pacific Island world. There, too, sonic and musical practices play crucial roles in simultaneously establishing oceanic connections and ways of knowing them. While in the previous chapter atmospheric knowledge of transoceanic connections emerged in devotional recitations that are part of a major religious tradition, we now investigate popular music as a sonic vector of such felt oceanic connections. Moreover, in the Pacific Island world, atmospheric knowledge of oceanic connections and its links to music is contiguous with Indigenous epistemologies about the Pacific as a "sea of islands," where musical practices work as alternative ways of knowing the relationalities that make up this world from Pacific Islanders' perspectives. In this chapter, therefore, we put this Pacific perspective of oceanic relationalities in which musical practices actualize knowledge of such far-flung connections in dialogue with the originally phenomenological tradition of atmospheres as ways of knowing and being in environments. In other words, we explore sound knowledge as knowledge of the environment from these dual and, as we see it, consonant perspectives, taking music and musical practices as "passageways of knowing" oceanic connections and relations in Epeli Hau'ofa's sense.

"The world of Oceania may no longer include the heavens and the underworld," wrote Tongan and Fijian anthropologist, writer, and cultural visionary Epeli Hau'ofa (1939–2009), "but it certainly encompasses the great cities of Australia, New Zealand, the USA and Canada. And it is within this expanded world that the extent of the people's resources must be measured" (2008, 36) Hauʻofa, here referring to the impact labor migration has had on communities and their life-worlds across the Pacific Island world, never ceased to point out how relationality, not difference, is the key theme in oceanic cultures. To be a Pacific Islander, to him, was to view the ocean as a passageway rather than as water masses separating islands and to see migration to other parts of the world as the expansion of one's lifeworld rather than the diasporic separation from loved ones and family. Hauʻofa inspired a whole lineage of postcolonial thinkers, writers, and artists from all over the Pacific Island world who, against the scholarly paradigms of modernity, choose to think with the sea and connection rather than in terms of (land) territory and boundaries (see Wesley-Smith, 2010; for a more critical perspective on Hauʻofa's writings, see Jolly 2001). To him the sea and its primary gift to Pacific Island communities—connection—have always been the defining forces for Pacific Island culture:

> We . . . draw inspiration from the diverse patterns that have emerged from the successes and failures in our adaptation to the influence of the sea. From there we can range beyond the tenth horizon, secure in the knowledge of the home base to which we will always return for replenishment and revision of the purposes and directions of our journeys. . . . Taking a cue from the ocean's ever-flowing and encircling nature, we will travel far and wide to connect with oceanic and maritime peoples elsewhere. . . . We may even together make new sounds, new rhythms, new choreographies, and new songs and verses about how wonderful and terrible the sea is, and how we cannot live without it. We will talk about the good things the oceans have bestowed on us, the damaging things we have done to them, and how we must together try to heal their wounds and protect them forever. (Hauʻofa 2008, 57)

Travel, transformation, and connection, then, are among the key themes throughout Hauʻofa's work. The people of Oceania are of the sea, but the sea in turn is also of the people: "above [the] level of daily experience, the sea is our pathway to each other and to everyone else, the sea is our endless saga, the sea is our most powerful metaphor, the ocean is in us" (2008, 58). Hauʻofa's thinking goes beyond the taken-for-granted ideas that have been formative for scholarly traditions of the Global North: here the subject-object divide, the hylomorphic divide between form and content, and a number of other formative binaries give way to South Pacific lived truths that have grown out of a deep connection with the ocean-as-pathway.

The primacy of connection—in general but also in its relevance to Western Pacific Island cultures and to Palau in particular—is also the underlying theme of this chapter. We explore how music as a cultural practice seeks to render experiential relationality and then work with it. Tracing this process, we will frame music in terms of the procedural knowledge inherent in and specific to it. To this end, we think through popular music making in Palau as a knowledge practice imbricated with connection and connecting. We use "popular music" to describe what Palauans refer to as *beches chelitakl*, literally, "new song." *Beches chelitakl* is the counterpart of *chelitakl rechuodel*, "old song": the traditional performing arts repertoire strongly associated with precolonial Palau. The disjuncture between *old* and *new* is generally taken to coincide with the advent of colonial powers and church music in Palau in the 1890s (Abels 2008, 54). In the second half of the twentieth century, a great part of *beches chelitakl* benefited from the parallel rise of various media of dissemination in Palau, radio in particular; social media (Diettrich 2016) and other transnational networks continue to "play an important role in creating and disseminating local popular music" (Diettrich, Moulin, and Webb 2011, 125). The recordings we discuss later in this chapter attest to this development.

Music, throughout this chapter, always implicitly refers to dance at the same time, as the two are too closely linked across Pacific Island cultures to be considered separately. It is important to note that the kind of knowledge we are interested in here is not knowledge *about* something. Rather, it is a way of knowing *how*: *how* we are interrelated, *how* that relationship transforms, and *how* the aquapelago in the Western Pacific Island world is an ever-transforming assemblage that is so much more, after all, than water and land (Hayward 2012). To know through music, then, is not to relish the musical meaning, an external quality that to a considerable extent is identifiable, objectifiable, and subject to debate. Instead, it is a cultural practice rendering experiential the layered complexity of interrelation- and interrelating-as-process. As in making music, bodies on the islands materially resonate with sound, as do the land and the sea. This sound connection, while it lasts, connects bodies and their natural environment. Taking shape in age-old musical forms such as ritual chants but also more recent ones such as string band songs, it also bridges the mythical past to which these chants harken back with the present and therefore always with the ensounded bodies and natural environment as well. Infusing a musical situation with a chant's or a popular song's historicity (see Abels 2018), the sound ties that emerge from the performance situate those they link historically, emphasizing their lived interconnectedness rather than the discrepancies between memories, narratives of (pre- and postcolonial history, and shared mythologies.

And, finally, in all this, sound ties invariably make felt how these spatial and temporal processes are imbricated with social life on the islands. Experiencing the connection both sonically and metaphorically, island communities can *feel out* for one another, for memories and remnants of the past, and for possible futures. From this the temporal, the spatial, the social, and the felt-body emerge as a relational entity, and music making serves as a means to bundle this relationality atmospherically (see Abels 2020). To know with music is to explore this relational capacity of music making and to follow the sound ties that reveal themselves. If, with Epeli Hau'ofa, Oceania is "humanity rising from the depths of brine," then it is not least the sound ties of knowing in and through music that mold the very humanity of people who are at home with the sea into the aquapelagic assemblages that are, after all, so much more than water and land (1993, 8).

Especially since the 1990s, scholars in Pacific Islander music have carefully explored Indigenous place-making practices in their interlacing with the social frameworks within which they unfold and with the cultural beliefs they embody. Steven Feld's analysis of Kaluli place making as an acoustemology—that is, as "local conditions of acoustic sensation, knowledge, and imagination embodied in the culturally particular sense of place resounding in Bosavi" (1996, 91)—has played an important role in directing attention to the imbrication of place with music making and the epistemological possibilities inherent in its social and cultural surroundings. Edward Casey's work has pointed to motion as occurring both within a place and between places—that is, as an energetic force contained within place. (1996, 23–24; also see Diettrich 2018a, 45). Feld's and Casey's publications have fueled an increasingly nuanced scholarly discussion of local and regional manifestations of such interlacing of music making, notions of place, and knowledge (e.g., Gillespie 2009; Diettrich 2018b, 2018a). Oli Wilson, for instance, has inquired into the cultural beliefs intrinsic to Indigenous notions of place. Discussing the Papua New Guinean notion of *ples* (a word relating to the English "place") as the place of one's origin and primary identification in Port Moresby, Papua New Guinea, he emphasizes that such cultural beliefs may include "ideas about tradition, language, genealogy, marriage and land, as well as rights, such as the right to speak, learn and impart knowledge" (2014, 428). For Micronesia specifically, Brian Diettrich has shown how performances constitute linkages across ocean places and how chanting can be a "participatory means of being with and knowing the ocean environment through performance" (2018a, 47). Micronesian Indigenous epistemologies position relationality as central to such being with the sea and so performance, motion, and belonging emerge as an ontological triangle. Accordingly, Diettrich understands "performance, voyaging, and movement as fundamental links with the sea in Micronesia. Motion is intrinsic to life both within and upon the ocean, and this kinesis is enacted and actualized through practices of music and dance" (54). In the words of Chamoru poet and scholar Craig Santos Perez, "We belong to Oceania. We belong to a diverse sea of moving islands, peoples, cultures, languages and ecologies. . . . We named and recognized the sacredness of waters and lands. We storied our homes with songs, poems, and chants" (2016, 373).

Our exploration of the notion of sound ties builds on these discussions and the avenues they have opened. But it also takes them into a slightly different direction. We use the idea of sound ties to tease out some of the more elusive facets of the Micronesian cultural practice Perez refers to as storying one's home with songs, poems, and chants (2016, 373). Atmospheric in nature, these facets arise from within the ontological triangle of performance, motion, and belonging we mentioned earlier. As such, sound ties point to the overlaps and crossings between

Micronesian sound-based ways of knowing oceanic environments and oceanic connections and the phenomenologically inspired analytic of atmospheres that we have used for framing the question of knowledge that is central to this book. The sonic, more particularly felt-bodily intermingling with the sonic, also plays a special role in this analytic of atmospheres. Moreover, it is also clear that the Micronesian sound and music-based ways of knowing the environment as a sea of islands do not just stand in a relation of overlap and consonance with this phenomenological analytic but also anticipate and predate many of its insights.

In the following we first explore what sound ties are and how they manifest and transform in music making. Grounding these conceptual reflections in music, we turn to "Aloha 'Oe," one of the most popular songs across the Pacific Island world for most of the twentieth century, to trace the sound ties this song and its many versions have created. We then ask how we as researchers can represent sound ties in our work. What ethical implications emerge as critical when we do? The pursuit of answers to these questions will bring us, in closing, to the idea of ecologies of knowledges, which originates from the theory of the South and points to the usefulness of sound ties beyond specific musical instances (Santos 2014). In exploring this set of questions, we also contribute to the important discussion surrounding island(er)ness that has gained momentum in the past decade. Corresponding to a similar argument made by Yaso Nadarajah and Adam Grydehøj (2016), we believe it is absolutely crucial to this debate that we explore alternative epistemological frameworks that may enable new perspectives on how island(er)ness manifests in terms of knowledge production.

Such alternatives have to grow, in one way or another, from lived experience. *Lived*, in this context, refers to the lived experience of those who have often been excluded from the production of knowledge in modernity: here Pacific Island communities. A part of the postcolonial complexity characterizing both local and global conditions, their perspectives are not necessarily identical or even partly commensurable with Indigenous epistemological configurations, even though that may at times be the case (see Teaiwa 2020). But in the spirit of Walter Mignolo's (2009) border thinking, trying to understand music making as a knowledge practice is a strategy to "open . . . up a way of thinking that delinks from the chronologies of new epistemes or new paradigms." The goal is to mediate between the competing epistemic orders characteristic of postcolonial settings: those Indigenous, those dominant in North Atlantic scholarly traditions, and those in between. Enabling an ecology of knowledges, as proponents of the Theory from the South have called it (e.g., Santos 2008), this approach seeks to expand our notion of what all knowledge might legitimately be. To listen out for the sound ties "rising from the depths of brine and regions of fire deeper still," then, is an endeavor to contribute to the decolonial shift in Pacific Island studies—one that addresses urgent epistemological and methodological challenges in current scholarship and allows for the rethinking of Pacific Islander identities, mobilities, and relations through music (see Baldacchino 2008; Grydehøj 2017; Nadarajah and Grydehøj 2016).

SOUND TIES: KNOWING THROUGH MUSIC

At its very core, sound is energy and movement—sound waves traveling through air or another medium. Ethnomusicologist Jeff Todd Titon, whose pioneering work in ecomusicology has helped bring issues of relationality and sustainability to the fore in music studies, describes the unique relational potential of music making as follows:

> When we hear a sound, we're connected through these sound waves with another vibrating body. Sound connects the two of us. We both vibrate to the same frequency. The metaphor for that connection is sympathy—sympathetic vibration. . . . The "sound connection" . . . is a . . . powerful, lasting connection. Sound makes a connection between two beings . . . , and that connection leads to what I call "co-presence." Sound is the most powerful means of co-presence. When we talk about two beings that are co-present, we're talking about community: a sound connection. (2017, 4)

This capacity to create a tangible felt-bodily connection in nature is unique to the sonic. It is this phenomenon that we refer to as *sound ties*. Choosing the concept of sound ties over Titon's "sound connection" here, we wish to emphasize a closely related yet slightly different aspect of the capacity Titon describes. Connection opens up channels; ties bind. Ties also evoke a key dimension of atmospheres, in the way that they are also a name for atmospheres as a bundling mechanism, tying a range of elements of a situation such as discourses, musical traditions, and memories of travel and migration as well as learned techniques of the body together by imbuing them with a shared feel (Abels 2020; Eisenlohr 2022a). That is to say, music making in the Western Pacific Island world not only connects people, land and seascapes, feelings, and ideas; it binds them together, creating an elastic network able to withstand strain and pull people back together. Ties, as we use the word here, are more inevitable but also more reliable than connections. *Sound ties* as a description of what music offers to oceanic communities is reflective of Epeli Hauʻofaʻs sentiment of "how wonderful and terrible the sea is, and how we cannot live without it" (2008, 57). It is something to fall back on, something Pacific Island communities share and hold dear.

Sound ties are distinctly sonic in nature in that they put to work the specificities of the medium sound. Straddling the presumed boundaries between the material and the immaterial, their sonic nature suggests an ethical and sensual attunement to one's surroundings because it makes felt and emphasizes resonance between beings and things (see Titon 2017; cf. Feld 2017). Sound ties alert, both physically and emotionally, to the interconnectedness of beings and things (cf. Ingold 2011;

see also Ismaiel-Wendt 2011). If I consider it detached from myself, I can easily exploit my environment; if I know it is imbricated with my own being and doing, I cannot. Similarly, when I am in a social situation that involves a sonic experience, no one partaking in this situation can entirely detach themselves from me because sound materially ties us together. In this sense sound ties as an analytical concept give rise to an ecological and ethical understanding that everyone and everything is connected (see Titon 2017). It is no coincidence that this is an insight deeply resonating with Pacific Islander notions (e.g., Yunkaporta 2019; Hauʻofa 1993). Sound ties reach, grow, and transform across the various registers of the human experience: the felt-body, the emotional, the affective, and the visceral.

They are also deeply social in nature. Sound ties arise where people make music together or for one another. At their heart sound ties point to motion: to the motion of the sound waves themselves; to their journey between bodies, stories, histories, and truths; and to the resonances emerging from in between the latter. In the spirit of Jonathan Pugh's (2013) suggestion, they seem to confirm that to think with the archipelago is to think with motion and fluidity. Musical conventions, seen in this light, are strategies to discipline and steer motion, and musical genres are strategies to tap into this energy the very moment the motion commences. Such engagement is restlessly moving, ever-transforming, and always already the incipiency of something new. Sound ties are the tissue that holds the parts of an invisible organism in place and gives them a sense of belonging together. This sense of belonging is deeply atmospheric in nature, which means that, as sonic materiality is transduced through the felt-body into a shared feeling, multiple frameworks resonate along the process. This is humanity rising from the depth of brine in music: Oceania atmospherically.

"ALOHA ʻOE" AND "BKUL NGEREMAML"

Inquiring into sound ties and how they emerge in musical practice, we are here exploring how they manifest *experientially*: how, in a musical situation, they infuse a specific experience with a deep sense of belonging rooted in cultural beliefs and historicity. To explore this process, we would like to turn to a song that has been immensely popular throughout the twentieth century across the Pacific Island world: "Aloha ʻOe." Recorded in 1963, "Bkul Ngeremaml" (Point of Ngeremaml Island) is a Palauan version of this well-known tune. The Republic of Palau, Belau in Palauan, is an island nation in the Westernmost corner of the Pacific Island world. Geographically a part of the western Caroline Islands, it belongs to Micronesia. At the time of the recording, Palau was a Trust Territory of the Pacific Islands, the United Nations trusteeship of the region that for Palau meant the next chapter of de facto colonial rule following German (1899–1914) and Japanese (1914–45) rule. The original tune was composed by the last queen of Hawaiʻi, Liliʻuokalani, probably in 1877 (see Elbert and Māhoe 1970, 35; H. Allen

1994, 85; Chow 2018, 110), and it bears resemblances with several European and U.S. American melodies popular at the time (see King 2007). "Aloha 'Oe" is arguably the most iconic Hawaiian tune, carrying global recognizability as an emblem of Polynesian Pacific Islanderness (Elbert and Māhoe 1970, 35; Thomas et al. 1998, 353; Wolfe and Imada 2013; Chow 2018). The song became a popular exoticist trope for Polynesia all around the world when Elvis performed it as a part of the movie *Blue Hawaii* in 1961. This particular Palauan adaptation, performed by the string band Friday Night Club, uses an adjusted melody and a Palauan text (for further information on the band, see Geselbracht, n.d.). The recording was made by music professor Barbara B. Smith of the University of Hawai'i in Koror, Palau's largest town, on October 8, 1963. There is conflicting information on who penned the Palauan lyrics, but it seems to have been either Kebekol N. Alfonso or Bobai Weloi: Barbara B. Smith's field notes identify Kebekol Alfonso as composer of the lyrics, while Junko Konishi includes this song as "Orekii[1]" and identifies Bobai (Weloi) as the author (Konishi 2014, 73). Based on his personal collection of song books as well as historical contextualization, Jim Geselbracht, an expert on Palauan string band music of this era, seconds the attribution to Bobai (pers. comm., June 15, 2020). In any case the performing band's singer was Teich Tiou.

The recording is three minutes and thirteen seconds long and opens with a brief instrumental introduction, followed by five stanzas with a refrain. The refrain is similar to that in "Aloha 'Oe," whereas the stanzas take greater liberty compared to the Lili'uokalani composition. In keeping with genre conventions, a very brief instrumental interlude separates stanzas four and five, and the song concludes with a repetition of the refrain. The song remains popular in Palau, to the extent that it is included in Palauan songbooks. Ethnomusicologist Junko Konishi included it in her songbook of fifty Palauan popular songs (2014, 72n); in Konishi's collection, the song is titled "Orekii." It is also included in Jim Geselbracht's "Adidil er a Klechibelau" (2020). In 1936 Japanese anthropologist Iwakichi Muranushi had already recorded another version of the song in Palau, this one titled "Etud e chochedengei" (recording A-22 of the Muranushi collection, published as Tatar 1985). While "Etud e chochedengei" bears a clear resemblance with "Aloha 'Oe," its tune is equally clearly different from "Bkul Ngeremaml"/"Orekii[1]."

AUDIO CLIP 2. Friday Night Club, "Bkul Ngeremaml." Recorded by Barbara B. Smith in Koror, Palau, October 1963.

To hear this audio clip, scan the QR code with your mobile device or visit DOI: https://doi.org/10.1525/luminos.244.2

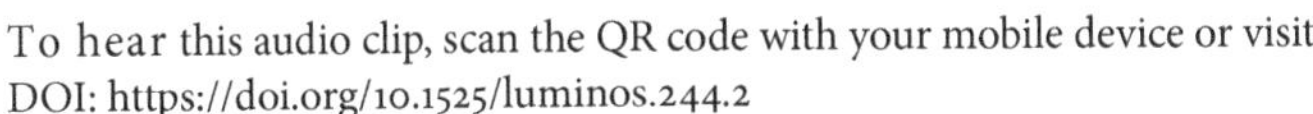

AUDIO CLIP 3. "Etud e chochedengei." Recorded by Iwakichi Muranushi in 1936. For further details, see Tatar (1985).

To hear this audio clip, scan the QR code with your mobile device or visit DOI: https://doi.org/10.1525/luminos.244.3

In Palau we have not been able to find reliable information as to when and how the song may have arrived on the islands. But there are several recordings of local versions of this song from across Micronesia dating from the 1930s (e.g., Tanabe 1978). In her appraisal of Muranushi's work, anthropologist Elizabeth Tatar considers the song's wide distribution and adaptation "perhaps . . . not as surprising as it may seem, since several missionaries to the area came from Hawai'i" (1985, 19). While this was not the case for Palau specifically, missionaries may have played a role in popularizing the song in Micronesia, either by performing it or by spreading recordings elsewhere in the Caroline Islands, from where the song may then have come to Palau. Another possibility is for "Aloha 'Oe" to have arrived in Palau by ship—either with Palauans who sailed with U.S. American sailors or with Hawaiians who were traveling in Micronesia (Carr 2014). In any case by the time Muranushi arrived in Palau in the mid-1930s, "Aloha 'Oe" had already entered the region's song repertoire (Pureyar, in Kaeppler et al. 1998, 159). Regardless of how exactly the tune arrived in Micronesia, its longevity, ongoing journey across the Pacific Ocean, and musical metamorphoses attest to its meaningfulness for the region.

The notion of sound ties can help put a finger on this more specifically, we believe. Tatar, assessing the early recordings and their contextual framework in the 1930s, refers to U.S. American Christian missions and quasi-colonial frameworks as constitutive of the song's general popularity in the larger region. Muranushi, who had collected the recordings Tatar discusses, labeled "Etud e chochedengei" as belonging to the genre of *derebechesiil*, as did Konishi, with reference to "Orekii[l]," another version of the same song still current in the second decade of the twenty-first century. *Derebechesiil* belong to what is called *beches chelitakl* in Palau: new music and dance. Often the term *beches chelitakl* is translated as "popular" music. In any case *beches chelitakl* originated out of the colonial encounter and the music that came with that encounter. *Derebechesiil*, specifically, refers to a group of songs set to Palauan, semi-Palauan or non-Palauan (typically Japanese or English) lyrics and based on a non-Palauan tune of either Japanese origin or in Japanese style. Like "Bkul Ngeremaml"/"Orekii[l]," many *derebechesiil* were based on U.S. tunes with a recognizably Japanese twist, marked, for instance, by a mostly pentatonic melodic framework. Both Muranushi and Konishi worked with local collaborators, and their usage of the term *derebechesiil* reflects the local categorization of the songs they recorded: *derebechesiil* belong to a specific historical context and speak of the historical relationship involving both Japan and the United States. At the same time, like many *derebechesiil* do, the lyrics of "Bkul Ngeremaml"/"Orekii[l]" reference Palauan places. Konishi cites the lyrics and offers translations into English and Japanese (2014, 72), as does Jim Geselbracht. The Palauan places the song refers to are all situated in Chelbached (popularly known as Rock Islands), a group of small limestone and coral islands off the coast of Palau's main islands. This is why *derebechesiil* are standard repertoire until today: because in bringing together these divergent frameworks, they tie together the bits and pieces that will then make up the layered complexity of the genre.

Derebechesiil's genre conventions, including the flexibility inherent in them, are capable of transducing the relationship complex involving their framework into a lived experience and a shared feeling that resonates in contemporary Palau. This is what makes sound ties so much more than musical references: their capacity to bring together the conflicting loyalties that result from colonial history, the contradictory loyalties and aspirations that bind Palauans to their postcolonial islands and globalized networks, and the contradictory, sometimes painful truths contained in collective and generational colonial memory. Coming together in musical experience, none of these conflicts are resolved. Yet in the musical situation itself, they make utter, if vague, sense. They all belong. Here the medium-specific logic of music making aligns with Hauʻofa's dictum of the ocean as a pathway. Like the ocean, sound is not about boundaries but about connection. This is why from a scholarly perspective, the notion of sound ties has merit: with sound ties, a song becomes an analytical gateway to situational relationality and the history of that relationality.

"Bkul Ngeremaml" is a string band recording. String band music everywhere in Oceania is a pan-Pacific yet distinctly local phenomenon, a trait that in itself already speaks to the regional sound ties the music makes resonate (Kaeppler et al. 1998, 137). Like the lyrics of Liliʻuokalani's "Aloha ʻOe," "Bkul Ngeremaml" is a farewell song, describing two lovers parting. It is written from the perspective of the person staying behind at Ngeremaml, from where they must watch the boat carrying their lover move farther and farther away. Geselbracht (2022, 261) renders the lyrics as follows:

1. *Ngar sel mobedul a minami*
   el kmal di kmeed er a Bkul a Chesemiich Ngerechol beluu el kekerei
   e le ng meral blil a klengiterreng
2. *Kmerael el mora hamabe*
   e a sils a di uangera el mochu er ngebard mak mo omdid a ultil ochim er a
   chelechol mobedul a Bkul Ngeremaml

3. *Adidil sel tal bilas el kebesengei e ng kol mochu er keltang*
   e diak be ltab me desterir
   e bai kuk louchais a chisel Belau
4. *Dibe lobuu a daob er a*
   ongesecheliil e ng mo medidelangel a renguk munasiku omoeba
   ng renguk re kau eng me ringelii er a uluk
5. *Me a dilkea rongel a sils*
   e ngak a mo merorael er a tebetab
   el mengerengekl a oiloled
   me a kingelled el ngara orekil

His translation of "Bkul Ngeremaml" is as follows:

1. It is when you go toward the west really close to Bkul a Chesemiich
   Ngerechol is a small island and it is truly the home of sorrow
2. I journey to the beach and just how is the sun as it travels westward and, so,
   I will follow your footprints on the beach toward the point at Ngeremaml
3. Connecting with that one boat in the evening where is it heading?
   Won't it come so we can see them and, instead, they can tell us the news of
   Palau?
4. The crash of the waves on the place we collect white-wedge clams, it makes
   my heart lightly cry recalling with no purpose my feelings for you brings
   me a pain in my stomach
5. The light no longer reflects off the ocean and I go strolling toward the view
   point walking about and looking around at our place to play and our
   special place, where it ended

As the song progresses, the lyrics trace how the pain of separation becomes a viscerally felt movement away from the first-person narrator ("I journey"), on to the open ocean ("connecting with that one boat"), and back to the Palauan coast ("our place")—a lyrical illustration of Casey's idea of motion as an energetic force not only contained within a specific place but also constitutive to it. But "Bkul Ngeremaml" also points to the musical interlacing of Japanese, U.S., and pan-Pacific connections. It does so through the melody's primary derivation from the Hawaiian Islands, its connection with U.S. culture and circulation within the Trust Territory of the Pacific Islands, and its adjustment, compared to Liliʻuokalani's original composition, to *derebechesiil*'s melodic and rhythmic conventions. Both songs are performed in a $\frac{4}{4}$ meter.

The stanzas of "Bkul Ngeremaml" correspond to the first half of the stanzas of "Aloha ʻOe," mostly maintaining the intervallic frame but otherwise adjusting the melody to the Palauan lyrics and rhythmic structure typical of *derebechesiil*: the dotted notes characteristic of the stanzas of "Aloha ʻOe" do not feature in the stanzas of "Bkul Ngeremaml." By leaving out the second part of the stanza of "Aloha ʻOe" entirely, "Bkul Ngeremaml" further avoids the chromatic melodic motif that is characteristic of the "Aloha ʻOe" tune. This same chromatic motif returns in the refrain of "Aloha ʻOe," and here too the tune of "Bkul Ngeremaml" stays within the tonal material of the diatonic scale instead. These two details show by example how "Bkul Ngeremaml" adjusts "Aloha ʻOe" musically to the then contemporary musical characteristics of *derebechesiil* while at the same time maintaining the musical recognizability of "Aloha ʻOe." The result is a song that is distinctly Palauan (marked by the lyrics), Palauan-Japanese (marked by its *derebechesiil* musical features), and Hawaiian (marked by the recognizability of the original tune) at the same time. The song thus combines musical markers that also act as geographic references. But they are temporal markers at the same time: all members of the Friday Night Club had lived through the Japanese period (1914–45), with its exposure to Japanese language, culture, and schooling. Their life histories were imbricated with the Japanese-Palauan colonial encounter; Japanese Palau, in other words, was inscribed in their biographies, analogous to the U.S. American presence on the islands after World War II.

Sound ties such as those "Bkul Ngeremaml" offers make heard those (post)colonial connections in a way that is not a priori positive or negative by nature. Primarily, sound ties are about individual and collective positionality, and they bring together the temporal, spatial, emotional, and social aspects of that positionality in musical experience. There is a transductive process going on in the experience of sound. In the logic of sound experience, the felt and the thought are not necessarily two separate categories; the experienced and the imagined are not mutually exclusive. In music one may instantaneously become the other, just like material sound waves become a spatially extended emotion or an atmosphere (Schmitz, Müllan and Slaby 2011, 255). Music making is a cultural practice transforming sound into meaningful lived experience. Sensations of meaningfulness in turn allow one to know, and confront, one's truths. This is how a song like "Bkul Ngeremaml" acts as a passageway: it enables reconnection, re-creation, and reimagination through a sound-based epistemology. In "Bkul Ngeremaml" the seemingly disparate bits and pieces of (post)colonial life in Palau come together and add up to a meaningful whole.

ETHICAL REPERCUSSIONS:
WRITING ABOUT SOUND TIES

The sound ties "Bkul Ngeremaml" offers for experiential manifestation articulate the potential power that music making has as procedural knowledge: a type of knowledge that emerges in the process of making and engaging with music and that, as it manifests as lived experience, opens a passageway to new ways of knowing one's world. Sound ties, in this sense, are the manifestation of a knowledge inherent in music. Like other alternative epistemologies of the Pacific Island world, such as *hoʻokele*, "Hawaiian navigation," or *heʻe nalu*, "Hawaiian surfing," music as knowledge offers an alternative trajectory of experiencing the world within the realities of a postcolonial world that continues to subject local knowledge systems (Ingersoll 2016). Seeking out connection and encounter, then, the idea of knowing about connectedness through music moves music making into an ontological perspective that speaks to an ethical experience of the world and life through music: where there is connection, there is responsibility (Titon 2017).

Music, in this sense, is a gesture toward those copresent, the knowledge inherent in music, knowledge about the potentials of both that gesture and the connection itself. Here it becomes abundantly evident how music making is an aquapelagic practice: if the aquapelago is constituted centrally by "ways of being, knowing, and doing—ontologies, epistemologies, and methods—that illuminate island spaces as inter-related, mutually constituted and co-constructed," then music is a key practice of rendering the aquapelago and its interconnectedness experienceable (Hayward 2012; Stratford et al. 2011). This experience in turn suggests an ethical attunement to the aquapelago. In sound the aquapelago is connected. From that connectedness, there arises responsibility for one another. Music makes that ethical moment immediately felt emotionally, felt-bodily, and mentally. This is where the region's music making speaks to Hauʻofa's idea of humanity rising from the depth of brine: the sound ties of knowing through music mold the very humanity of people who are at home with the sea into aquapelagic assemblages that reach much farther than the coastlines of their islands (1993, 8). As a passageway, music making also instigates transformation: part of an interconnected aquapelagic system, it allows for new connections or the renewal of connections. Music, then, is where we tarry with the pain of colonial violence, we feel out for the complexity of the present, and we work toward our future selves and collectives. Traveling the passageway moves the focus away from where the islands end and the ocean begins, redirecting all energy to exploring the distinctly musical knowledge it enacts. By virtue of its medium-distinct materiality, it reconnects Pacific Islanders and their ancestors through resonance and resonant movement.

Importantly, sonic movement is not confined to a linear trajectory. Instead, sound allows for flexibility and any direction, extending into the past and possible futures just as to all directions in space. This is music's very own passageway of knowing. In making accessible new pathways and connections to choose from, it privileges, and possibly, in a postcolonial world, reinstates alternative political and ethical relationships with the surrounding physical and spiritual world.

Working with music making as an aquapelagic voyage of the Pacific passageway brings up issues that are similar to yet different from empirical work in the same context, primarily the centrality of Indigenous voices and their representation in Euro-American academic frameworks. As Margaret Kovach puts it,

> Representation and voice in research put the researcher knee-deep in the muddy waters of the objectivity/subjectivity discourse. Too much story, with its inherent subjectivity, can find itself out of favour with those who ascribe to empirical quantification or qualitative generalization. Too much story can be subjected to the label "experimental research" and risk being discredited by conventional academics. Those involved in Indigenous research experience this dynamic in several ways. Their research methodology may be highly congruent with an Indigenous worldview, but not understood by Western knowledge keepers and thus not recognized or diminished. A more common difficulty is that in an effort to serve both Indigenous and Western audiences, without clearly identifying epistemologies the methodology becomes . . . difficult for either audience to assess. While the resolution to this dilemma requires more than a decolonizing lens, incorporating such an analysis brings awareness of this contradiction, thus readying it for transformation. (2009, 82)

Contradiction, a prerequisite and powerhouse for change, necessitates a significant degree of specification. Music making and its meaningfulness, however, follow the logic of the pathway, as we have argued in this chapter. They are not necessarily always specific in their referentiality. The vagueness and sometimes ambivalence of their signification may well be what allows it to speak so well to the pathway rather than the boundary—to the concurrent rather than the contradictory. If, in the case of stories and language-based ethnographic data, "the function of a decolonial objective is to provide Indigenous researchers with a context-specific analytical tool for making visible contradictions and bringing Indigenous approaches out from the margins," then the forte of analyzing music making in the spirit of a decolonial approach may well be that which has historically relegated it to a lesser priority in the ocularcentric traditions of thinking prevalent in the North Atlantic world: its attention to that which opens up rather than defines in exact terms, its emphasis on process rather than state, its attunement to becoming over being, and its medium-specific capacity to connect rather than to demarcate (Kovach 2009, 82). In seeking out resonance, music making as a knowledge practice is akin to Indigenous Pacific notions of knowledge that seek to gather "knowledge based on oral story tradition congruent with an Indigenous paradigm. It involves a dialogic participation that holds a deep purpose of sharing story as a means to assist others. It is relational at its core" (2010, 40).

In 1963 Koror "Bkul Ngeremaml" was not Hawaiian, Palauan, Japanese, or U.S. American. It was all these and more at the same time, exploring interconnectedness and feeling out for the new passages that would open. To represent this journey academically is to travel along for a fraction of the way and to talk about it. This is an academic practice invested in exploring *how* the people engaging with "Bkul Ngeremaml" knew through the song, not of *what* they knew. Music works with resonance—if it resonates, it is connected. To explore the knowledge inherent in music is to learn about interconnectedness.

CONCLUSION

Sound ties, then, manifest as resonance—a resonance pointing to interconnectedness. In the logic of the pathway, to trace sound ties academically is to follow the knowledge unfolding that is unique to music making. Herein lies the academic benefit of understanding music making as a knowledge practice: to explore the routes sound ties have taken is to inquire into distinctly musical knowledge configurations. How are Pacific Islander musical epistemologies specific, and how are musical epistemologies relevant to the study of the Pacific Islands? Proponents of the Theory from the South have argued for "ecologies of knowledges" premised on the idea of epistemological diversity, proposing a theoretical and methodological framework for challenging the dominance of Eurocentric thought that stays clear off "the potential neocolonial trap of 'universalism'" (Santos 2008; Aluli Meyer 2003, 146). Acknowledging knowledge systems born from the experiences of marginalized peoples, Boaventura De Sousa Santos suggests that global justice can come about only through an epistemological shift that facilitates cognitive justice. Such a shift is aimed at creating new, alternative strategies for political mobilization and activism that give oppressed groups the means through which to represent the world as their own and in their own terms (Santos 2018).

To accept Pacific Islander music making as a knowledge practice is to acknowledge the centrality of the connections music knows about. To Palauans attending the Friday Night Club performance of "Bkul Ngeremaml," the song was "capable of transforming temporal sequence into spatial organization, because once established, the points of connection continue to exist as a stable, structural linkage which transcends the particular founding act. . . . Spatiotemporal linkages once established can become the template . . . for future actions and relationships" (Parmentier 1987, 136). This is how the connections sound ties render experienceable are a resource. Especially for societies under threat, such as many Pacific Islander communities, it is therefore essential to explore the alternative knowledge the performing arts hold. In Pacific Island culture, performance "communicate[s] multiple messages about a culture simultaneously. These messages, however, are not overt, and often go unnoticed by academics, who are more adept at reading between the lines on a page than reading the messages implicit in the kinds of costumes being worn, the way space is negotiated, the arrangement of dancers, the hand, feet, and facial movements, and other elements of performance that embody a culture's aesthetics and values," writes Vilsoni Hereniko, calling for academic practices that create a space for Pacific Islander truths rather than Eurogenic epistemologies (2000, 89, 90). In this spirit, to listen out for the sound ties of "Bkul Ngeremaml" is an attempt to "reengage with life and attentively walk along the amazing diversity of forms of knowledge held by those whose experiences can no longer be rendered legible by Eurocentric knowledge in the academic mode, if they ever were" (Escobar 2020, 67).

Pacific Islander musical epistemologies, in their aquapelagic setting, are a central tool to think, feel, and connect beyond the island and into the ocean as a passageway. Sound travels beyond the shore and onto the ocean, and it may resonate farther than the eye can see. At the same time, as a sonic strategy to make sense of one's environment, musical epistemologies are more than a framework for spatial practices. Like other alternative knowledge systems of the region such as paddling, surfing, and navigation, they involve "a knowledge situated in a specific place and space, which is oceanic. These enactments involve a knowledge that reconnects [Pacific Islander communities] to [their] pasts and to [their] ancestors as understood through [their] oral histories. They involve a literacy that empowers [Islander communities] because they offer self-sufficiency, honor [Indigenous] native histories, allow for flexibility and movement, and offer philosophical nourishment for visions of alternative and self-determined future" (Ingersoll 2016, 5).

Literacy, in Karin Ingersoll's sense, is the capacity to explore alternative "political and ethical relationship[s] with the surrounding physical and spiritual world." Writing about what she terms "seascape epistemologies" and specifically Kānaka Maoli (Indigenous Hawaiian) surfing, she takes an approach to knowing presumed on a "knowledge of the sea, which tells one how to move through it, [and] how to approach life and knowing through the movements of the world" (2016, 5). An oceanic literacy of music making is as embodied a literacy as Ingersoll's literacies of the ocean, but it thinks *with* the ocean, not *through* it like surfing (see also Diettrich 2018a, 57). And here we come full circle: to think with the ocean through music is to think with the ocean as a passageway. To return one final time to Epeli Hau'ofa's dictum of Oceania as humanity rising from the depths of brine and regions of fire deeper still, sound ties are the connections that resonate across the land and the sea, choosing the vastness of oceanic space rather than insularity as frameworks for belonging.

4

Atmospheric Citizenship

Atmospheric knowledge can also be deeply political. Knowledge through atmospheric affection shapes citizenship and belonging in the most consequential ways. In this chapter we examine such formation of citizenship and belonging by way of the generation of sonic atmospheres in the Indian megacity Mumbai, which is not only India's most populous metropolis but also perhaps its most globally connected, having expanded on its long-standing role of a hub of the Indian Ocean world.[1] Mumbai is known not only for its great urban diversity but also for its history of intense struggles over urban space and claims to belong to the city.

In Mumbai the sonic dimensions of place making and religious life are strongly connected to the right to the city. For Twelver Shi'i Muslims, who are marginal to both the city and the nation, public religious rituals and processions have long played very important roles in staging claims to the city. Investigating the sonic aspects of urban place making, including its religious dimensions, this chapter analyzes place making through sonic performances as atmospheric knowledge. Through its coupling with the felt-body, the sonic plays a privileged role in giving urban locales a specific feel as belonging to particular groups, investing this feel with an air of facticity that is largely immune to discursive critique. We examine the feeling of belonging to the city through ritual performances and processions among Twelver Shi'i Muslims during the Islamic month of Muharram to foreground nondiscursive and atmospheric forms of citizenship.

Urbanity and urban belonging not only are approachable in terms of architectural and population density, patterns of consumption, or nodes of global capital flows but also often manifest themselves as specific urban atmospheres (Hasse 2012). These are related to visual, sonic, and olfactory impressions that convey the mystique and feeling of being in the city. Being able to understand and contextualize these sensory impressions enables the urban dweller to successfully navigate the city, and mastery to do so across the internal boundaries of a highly segmented and residentially segregated postcolonial city constitutes a prized kind of knowledge, giving those in command of it a specific "urban charisma" (Hansen and Verkaaik 2009). But urban atmospheres, the main topic of this chapter, do not just emerge through sensory impressions and their interplay; they also involve a somatic dimension of bodily encounter and immersion. Such atmospheres are holistic gestalten that cannot be fully reduced to particular sensory perceptions, even if, as in the case discussed here, the auditory plays a central role in the production of urban atmospheres. We take the notion of atmospheres as distinct, material entities that felt-bodies encounter and intermingle with to be useful for examining questions of belonging to the city and the forms of citizenship they entail. Sonic phenomena can be very concrete exemplifications of atmospheres understood in such terms. Atmospheric knowledge of the city is at the same time also an illustration of environmentality as a register of belonging. While the somatic intermingling with urban atmospheres is an extension of the broader, elementary kind of environmentality that Martin Heidegger referred to as *Umweltlichkeit*, in this chapter we take the politically contested aspects of such environmentality as central. As mentioned earlier in this book, environmentality can also feed into forms of discipline and control, as is evident in the atmospheric dimensions of a struggle for belonging and citizenship by members of a beleaguered religious minority.

Our focus is on sonic atmospheres in the Indian megacity Mumbai and their connection to religious practices and forms of belonging. In Mumbai religious festivals have played a long-standing role in the claiming of urban space. Mumbaikars often conceive such struggles over the right to the city in terms of competing religious communities that also have regional identifications. Religious processions have constituted an important part of this often violent mode of claiming of urban space that in Mumbai/Bombay was already notorious and subject to government regulation in the nineteenth century (Masselos 1982; R. Kaur 2003). There religious processions, including their intense sonic dimensions, turn urban space into places associated with a specific community and their moral right to belong to the city, with far-reaching implications regarding housing, employment, and access to public services (Lynch 2019). This making of urban places is not just a matter of contest between religious communities but often also stands in tension with practices of urban planning and governance in Mumbai, not to speak of the intense competition over urban space and housing that the city has become notorious for (Appadurai 2000). Against the background of a history of intercommunal violence, more recently featuring Hindu nationalist and majoritarian targeting of

Muslim minorities in the city and the latter's progressive ghettoization, the ritual and performative marking and place making of particular urban locales as specifically "Shia Muslim" is a powerful way of publicly claiming and reconfirming the right to be recognized as belonging to Mumbai, as it is in other Indian cities (Halder 2019). Hindu nationalist and Maratha regional chauvinists have in recent years violently rejected such claims.

This in turn raises questions of citizenship, more specifically the problem that "formal membership in the nation-state is increasingly neither a necessary nor a sufficient condition for substantive citizenship" (Holston and Appadurai 1996, 190). The notion of cultural citizenship points to the fact that there is no known polity in which legal citizenship is factually decoupled from the performance of ethnic, ethnolinguistic, and religious forms of belonging, or a combination of them all, further reworked through social stratification, even in nation-states that present themselves as highly inclusive, such as India and the United States (Rosaldo 1994). With the rise of Hindu nationalist visions of the Indian nation in recent decades, the range of sociocultural elements that falls within the limits of such cultural citizenship has further narrowed. Indian Muslims' citizenship has become ever more precarious, despite their increasing attempts to justify their citizenship in terms of minority rights (Fazal 2012; Shani 2010; Williams 2012).

In everyday life citizens displaying markers that identify them as Muslims have faced growing difficulty asserting their citizenship, as to many the performance of Muslim identity has placed them outside the boundaries of the nation, to a position of "abject citizenship" (Sherman 2015, 12). Even among those who do not subscribe to Hindutva ideology, the citizenship of those who are recognizably Muslim is frequently considered conditional. For example, non-Hindutva nationalist discourses have long drawn a distinction between Muslims engaged in shrine-based "syncretic" ritual practice influenced by Sufism that they consider as proper to India and Muslims who are followers of movements of self-understood Islamic purification. The latter are more likely to be placed outside the boundaries of the nation, despite the centuries-old presence of such traditions within the boundaries of present-day India (Menon 2015; see also Das 1984; Robinson 1983). The notion of atmospheric citizenship we introduce in this chapter also starts from the premise that the performance of cultural signs and their ratification by others is central for full inclusion in a nation. However, in contrast to previous formulations of the concept of cultural citizenship (but see Trnka, Dureau, and Park 2013), it places greater stress on the felt dimensions of such citizenship in such performances, highlighting its somatic dimensions that often evade discursive rendering.

Returning to questions of citizenship and belonging in urban settings, such as Mumbai, there is a growing body of research asserting that sound and sonic performance can mark spaces, especially urban spaces, as belonging to a particular group and make a case for their inclusion and belonging or can be flashpoints for contestations over cultural citizenship. In this struggle over aural borders and the city as "aural borderland" (Western 2020, 297), the Islamic call to prayer *(azan)* is among the most notorious examples (Lee 1999; Tamimi Arab 2017; Weiner 2014) but so can be other Islamic genres, such as broadcast sermons (Eisenberg 2013; Larkin 2014). What is the specific role of sound in accomplishing such links between people, places, and forms of belonging? There is much more to sound than its affordances as a marker, as an indexical or symbolic sign that stands for something, in this case Muslims. Markers need not be sonic to do their work of representation, and this raises the question of where the specific sonic contribution to such forms of belonging lies. To take sound seriously, one needs to also engage with the proprium of sound—that is, the modalities of knowledge and meaning making that make it special and that are not reducible to discourse, images, or visual signs. What is it about sound and the sonic that makes them a focal issue in this regard?

Our answer is that there is a privileged relationship between the sonic and the emotive that makes it central to urban contests over belonging to a city and, by extension, in our Mumbai example, also belonging to the nation. This is not about resuscitating the tired contrast between supposedly distancing and objectifying visuality—an untenable notion in its own right—and aurality as a domain of intimacy and nonseparation, a contrast traceable to Christian theology about spirit and letter that Jonathan Sterne has aptly called an "audio-visual litany" (2003, 15–17). There is a privileged link between the sonic and the emotive because the sonic engages the felt-body in a most encompassing way, as it is not just perceived by the hearing apparatus but potentially the entire body, its flesh.[2] In this the phenomenological distinction between the felt-body *(Leib)* and the physical body *(Körper)* is important.[3] Sonic phenomena are processes of wavelike, vibrational passing of energy through a medium, and these processes often ignore the boundaries between objects, humans, and their nonhuman environments. Several scholars have therefore likened sonic phenomena to affect (Goodman 2010; Shouse 2005).[4] The workings of sound often appear ineffable to those exposed to them; this is also related to the often-remarked power of particular forms of organized sound like music to profoundly move people in ways they often struggle to describe in words. Here we take atmospheres as an analytic that does justice to this proprium of sound. At the same time, atmospheres also allow a new perspective on urban space as something that is felt and provokes particular sensations, sensations that in turn impinge on the crucial urban question to whom that kind of space belongs.

AN ATMOSPHERIC RIGHT TO THE CITY

Much Twelver Shi'i activism in Mumbai bases its claims for the inclusion of Twelver Shi'is in the city and by extension also the Indian nation on discourse, including religious narrative.[5] But the "live" Muharram processions also contribute to the Shi'i claim to a right to the city in a different way, even though they certainly also involve discourse and images. The processions commemorate the Battle of Karbala. In this battle in the Christian year 680, Hussain, a grandson of the Prophet Muhammad, along with other members of the family of the Prophet (the *ahl-ul bayt*), were killed by an Umayyad army in a struggle over the leadership of the community of Muslims. Ever since, the Battle of Karbala has featured as a traumatic *ur*-event and moral-political paradigm for Shi'is. The commemorative processions' sonic aspects and their quality of dynamic movement are crucial in this respect. The drumming, the rhythmic breast-beating, the amplified chanting of *nauha* (a genre of poetic lament for the martyrs of the Battle of Karbala), along with the dynamic movement of bodies and ritual objects through the streets, combine to emit a palpable atmosphere that give the neighborhoods through which the procession passes a certain Shi'i quality in nondiscursive ways.

This spreading of the quality of being "Shia" is not just an arbitrary, symbolic marker.[6] It is about a collective experience of suggestions of motion exerted by sounds and the actual movement of people and objects through a neighborhood. While this evokes the work of Henri Lefebvre (1968, 2004), both his notion of the right to the city as well as his work on rhythmanalysis, we suggest that neophenomenological approaches to atmospheres are more useful to understand bodily felt qualities of city neighborhoods that go beyond what can be discursively specified. Drawing on an understanding of atmospheres as energetic forces that fill spaces and act on felt-bodies, as formulated by Hermann Schmitz and Gernot Böhme, we investigate how atmospheres blur the boundaries between subjects, as well as the boundaries between subjects and their nonhuman environments.

One reason why atmospheres are important is their emotive qualities; they are environmental in lending a diffuse and holistic "feel" to situations and surroundings. According to Schmitz, emotions are not a matter of subjective interiority, but atmospheres are themselves emotions as they spread and fill spaces and touch and become entangled with feeling bodies. They move the feeling body, and their perception through somatic mingling with them is similar to feelings of warmth, cold, being under the weather, and pain or being immersed in sound. As mentioned earlier, atmospheres are palpable through the subtle suggestions of motion they exert on those intermingling with them. We suggest that sonic events and the flow of bodies, as in the Muharram processions, are very tangible exemplifications of such suggestions of motion that those exposed to them feel. They are modifications of the felt space of the body that provoke emotions.

When such atmospheres fill urban space, as in the unfolding of the Muharram processions, with its sounds of mournful poetry and rhythmic self-flagellation with blades fastened to chains and breast-beating, drumming, and the dynamic flow of masses of black-clad participants pressing through the streets, carrying large and elaborately decorated ritual objects linked to the events at Karbala such as *alam* (ornate battle standards with signs of the family of the Prophet) and tazia (decorated replicas of the tomb of Hussain and other martyred imams), they exude a feel that lingers on and pertains to a city neighborhood. Such an atmospheric feel of a neighborhood is akin to what Schmitz has called "internally diffuse meaningfulness," an excess and plurality of meanings that are holistic and inexhaustible and blend into one another to such a degree that they are hard to specify (2016, 53). Therein lies the palpable and environmental "feel" of a neighborhood as "Shia" that can never be verbally described in an exhaustive way. Its diffuse holism conveys the feel of a neighborhood as something difficult to render into language but as an undeniable presence. Video and audio recordings of the Muharram processions and the events linked to them, such as *majalis* (assemblies where devotional and mourning poetry are recited and chanted) on the days preceding the processions, circulate very widely in Mumbai and are nowadays posted on online video portals. Part of the appeal of such recordings is their affordance and invitation to relive the ritual events or to witness them in a multisensorial way, even though one did not participate in them at the time and place of recording. This also includes their atmospheric qualities that can be conveyed to some extent, especially in their sonic dimensions.

The undeniable presence of an urban atmosphere like the one created by the Muharram processions cannot be argued away, because it operates on the non-discursive level of somatic evidence. It therefore constitutes a powerful register for making claims to the city, alongside the affirmation of Shiʿi belonging to the city through discourse and imagery, aided also by the character of South Asian Muharram as a moment of "moral exception" that crosses common communal boundaries, highlighting values broadly accepted across such multiple communal and religious demarcations (Cooper 2024, 129). Such emotional and felt aspects of belonging are often highly consequential, even as they are difficult to describe in a precise way. Despite the fact that such atmospheres can be created, recreated, manufactured, and even reproduced though media practices, there is an air of facticity and givenness about them. They constitute a kind of evidence for belonging that is felt in the flesh and that is largely immune to discursive critique.

THE ATMOSPHERE OF MUHARRAM PROCESSIONS

Muharram ritual in Mumbai, as elsewhere, is geared to the production of pious emotions. Its spectacular and sometimes also bloody dimensions have long been the focus of controversy, with Twelver Shiʿi Muslims disagreeing about the ways and extent to which the mourning for and the memory of the tragic events at Karbala should find expression in ritual practice. Patrick's interlocutors in Mumbai often spoke about a contrast between "rational" and "emotional" ways to commemorate the tragedy of Karbala. This is related to changes in the interpretation of Karbala since the Iranian Revolution, when an earlier quietist emphasis of traditional mourning practices was complemented and sometimes replaced by an activist commitment to political and social improvement in the here and now (cf. Deeb 2009). Among Mumbai Twelver Shiʿi Muslims, both tendencies persist; however, many among the younger generation are often attracted to bringing about reform in the field of education and social reform that they view as modern and progressive. As Abbas, a young man in his twenties, told Patrick, "To be a Shia does no longer mean to cry and be a victim. We can make life in the community better, such as through efforts in education and health care." This newer sense of agency and mastery over one's own fate so typical of the postrevolutionary and activist interpretation of the message of Karbala was also central to local Twelver Shiʿi media activism (Eisenlohr 2015a, 696–97). In fact, several interlocutors linked the emergence of activist engagement with the memory of Karbala to the influence of the Iranian Revolution. In particular, a local media center known as World Islamic Network seeks to balance the prevalence of established forms of ritual commemoration in its programming with "modern, rational" television programs geared to a younger audience. These include news programs in a sleek studio setting, commenting on world news from an Islamic perspective, or talk show and call-in programs such as *Masael-e zindagi*, where a maulana answers from a Shiʿi perspective a broad range of questions posed by viewers calling in or sending messages by online chat and email. As the director stressed, "Young people are more educated and they want to be given reasons. They will ask [a maulana], 'Why are you saying this? Where is your reference?'"

Others continued to defend the established ritual practices, such as the Muharram processions and the dramatic displays of mourning that play on the emotions of everyone present. When Patrick debated differences among Twelver Shiʿi customs during Muharram across the world with Parvez, a middle-aged businessman, Patrick mentioned that the government of the Islamic Republic of Iran as well as Hezbollah in Lebanon had banned bloodletting during Muharram processions, urging people to donate blood instead. Parvez said that he thought that Indian Shiʿis were very emotional. "They will become angry if you tell them not to do this. They will say, you have no right. You are a Wahhabi. You do not know if Imam Hussain will accept it or not, so why do you interfere?" He mentioned that his own son had engaged in self-flagellation with blades in a procession in the suburb of Bandra, which has a small middle-class Twelver Shiʿi population. "He had to have fifty stitches on his head," Parvez said, and from the way he spoke about his son's participation in these controversial ritual activities, his disapproval was evident. For others, however, there was no doubt about their beneficial and pious nature; it was an important way to show empathy and emotional intensity in the face of injustice, according to a logic of witnessing (see also Eisenlohr 2015c, 293). The "message" of Karbala was to be reenacted through ritual practice, bringing about a purifying effect through experiencing and provoking overwhelming emotions. To most of Patrick's interlocutors, however, the way in which this provoking of emotions unfolds was difficult to put in words. Talking about the broadcast devotional poetry such as dirges for the martyrs of Karbala, Afsar, who worked in a bakery business, told Patrick that "not only the words of the poetry, but the sound of it makes you cry. The sound of it causes crying." But, like others, he found the precise ways in which such sonic events cause strong emotions that make one cry hard to render into discourse. The seeming ineffability of the nexus of sound and emotions and their pious and purifying effects from a Shi'i perspective was also evident in conversations with ritual specialists.

At the fringes of the main afternoon procession on Muharram 10, which that year fell in December 2010, Patrick joined Baqer, a young aspiring maulana whose parents had migrated from Azamgarh in North India to Mumbai before he was born. He had spent two years studying at a Twelver Shi'i seminary in the Iranian holy city of Qom and spoke to me about how much he missed Iran, where two of his children were born, and especially his visits to the shrine of Imam Reza in Mashhad. From Iran he was also able to go on pilgrimages to Karbala and Najaf. The sound of the devotional poetry, he said, reminded him of his pilgrimages. With these sounds recreating an atmosphere of both the pilgrimage and the events at Karbala, he said that he could not find words to describe the feelings they provoked. With eyes wide open and emotion in his voice, he told Patrick how he had always wanted to travel to these Iraqi holy cities and was barely able to believe it when he finally reached them. Also for Baqer, the felt aspects of these experiences in which sounds, memory of the pilgrimage, the tragic events of Karbala, and their commemoration and partial reenactment that we were witnessing blended into one another, giving the situation an overarching feel and seeming to evade discourse.

The main procession on the afternoon of Muharram 10 moves through Dongri, the historic heart of Twelver Shi'i Bombay/Mumbai and also from Dongri to the Rahmatabad cemetery in Mazagaon. Dongri is not an exclusively Shi'i neighborhood; the neighborhood and its adjacent areas are home to a great diversity of other people such as Sunni Muslims and Hindus of different backgrounds. The tense sharing of streets and other urban space that characterizes the procession is iconic of the situation of Twelver Shi'i Muslims in the city at large, where they face an array of contesting claims of belonging (Gupta 2015). As far as the procession is concerned, some Sunni Muslims have strong anti-Shi'i tendencies and reject the massive public ritual spectacles in commemoration of the events at Karbala in the month of Muharram. Added to this, there is the internal fragmentation of Shi'i Muslims in the city, with distinctions of sect, ethnicity, and class separating smaller Bohra and Khoja Ismaeli communities of Gujarati trader background from the Twelver Shi'i, who are in their majority of North Indian origin and overwhelmingly poor. However, there is also marked diversity and stratification among Twelver Shi'i Muslims, as two trader communities among them, the Ithna Ashari Khojas of Gujarati origin and the "Mughals," whose ancestors migrated to Bombay from Qajar Persia in the nineteenth and early twentieth centuries, play the role of social and economic elites who also control most Twelver Shi'i institutions in the city. This contested and fragmented quality of the urban terrain only heightens the stakes for performing claims to belong to the city through the Muharram processions, including their sensory and atmospheric dimensions. In fact, the sidelining of such ordinary social boundaries and the downplaying of conventional discourses of citizenship that the sensory and atmospheric aspects of the ritual spectacle bring about crucially enables the staging of such claims to the city.

Among the participants many express their mourning by wearing black clothes. The processions are an exercise in sensory intensity, for which acoustemologies, ways of knowing and engaging with human and environmental worlds through sound and sounding, are central (Feld 1996). On the morning of the procession, the harsh sounds of pedal-powered grindstones sharpening the long razor blades fastened to chains to be used for ritual and rhythmic self-flagellation can be heard in the street in front of the Mughal Masjid, a main Twelver Shi'i mosque originally built by Iranian traders in the heart of Dongri. Together with the smell of metal dust in the air, they emit a visceral feel of expected events and actions in the afternoon. Groups of devout Shi'is, often organized in associations named for the places of origin from where their families migrated to Mumbai, carry highly decorated tazia, along with tall, ornate *alam*. Often blood-smeared shrouds are fastened to the standards as a dramatic sign of the mourning, suffering, and martyrdom at Karbala. Groups of men with bare upper bodies engage in bloody and spectacular acts of self-flagellation known as *zanjiri matam*, with knifes or sharp razor blades fastened to chains with which they keep hitting their backs. In some locations participants restage the events at Karbala, literally reliving and positioning themselves as witnesses of the tragic events. The rhythmic, amplified chanting of devotional poetry can be heard throughout, expressing grief and pain and sometimes narrating the traumatic events at Karbala and the suffering of the family of the Prophet in heartrending detail (Fa 2022).[7] The sounds of large groups of men beating their breasts in unison while chanting dirges in a show of bereavement mingle with the sounds of drummers that move through the streets (cf. Wolf 2000), heightening the emotional intensity of the spectacle. As a whole, the processions are a highly dynamic event; they are an expression of rhythm and bodily movement.

Consider the sequences and layering of sounds in a recording Patrick made of the main procession on the afternoon of Muharram 10 from Dongri to Mazagaon in December 2010. The recording starts with rhythmic chants of "ya Hussain" by men carrying decorated *alam* with shrouds fastened to them, walking through a side street en route to the main procession. This is followed by a scene of a group of young men and adolescents with bare upper bodies engaging in *zanjiri matam*. The metallic sounds of chains and blades merge with the thumping sounds of the metal implements hitting the bleeding backs of the devotees in unison, as they are egged on by calls from the bystanders surrounding them on the street. Another

FIGURE 1. The Mughal Masjid in Dongri. Photo by Patrick Eisenlohr.

signature sound of the procession by bodily acts of mourning is the clapping sound of men rhythmically beating their breasts with their hands or fists in a show of bereavement, driven on by calls of "Ali, Ali" (Hussain's father and the son-in-law of the Prophet). A cart with a sound system passes by, blaring out the refrain of a dirge in a lamenting voice: "sham ho gayi, sham ho gayi" (evening

FIGURE 2. Still from a video of the Shiʻi Muslim afternoon procession on Ashura, beginning in Dongri. Photo by Patrick Eisenlohr.

has come). The lament evokes the mood of the evening of the day of the Battle of Karbala *(sham-e ghariban)*, when the martyrs had been slain and darkness and despair descended on the survivors among the family of the Prophet. This poetically and sonically evoked scene is a long-established and frequently recurring focus of emotions in Shiʻi commemorations of the tragic events at Karbala. Interlayered with the recited lament are the sounds of ambulances' horns and the loud whistles blown by paramedics as they try to clear a way for the emergency vehicles through the crowd. Not all, but many of the patients in the ambulances are injured mourners who, having fainted, are on the way to the hospital, adding to the feel of drama and tragic urgency that the spectacular acts of the bereavement and their vocal poetic renderings literally spread through the streets. The scene then shifts again to a collective act of self-flagellation, with their telltale metallic sounds of the chains' and blades' impacting each other, mingled with the audible hitting of sharp metal instruments on flesh.

Periodically recurring religious processions like the Muharram processions in Mumbai achieve the production of urban places and forms of belonging connected to them, not just because of the movement of bodies through streets and other public locations but also through the creation of particular sonic atmospheres that convey impressions of one neighborhood having the "feel" of belonging to a certain community rather than others. The Muharram procession is central to a "process of acoustic *territorialization*," making a Mumbai neighborhood Shiʻi (Labelle 2010, xxiii). The rhythmic beating of breasts and the chanting of various slogans and genres of poetry lamenting the martyrdom of Hussain; the broadcasting, mediatic recirculation and public amplification of sermons, intermingled with the sound of ambulances catering to fainted mourners engaging in bloody forms of self-flagellation; the sound of hundreds of razor blades being ground and sharpened beforehand; and the metallic sound of the chains they are fastened to during flagellation compose some of the key sonic components marking the south central neighborhood of Dongri and surrounding areas as specifically "Shia." This shows how urban places such as neighborhoods are both produced and known through experiences that bring about urbanity as a felt quality, here in particular the creation of sonic atmospheres as feelings.

Sonically induced suggestions of motion are the somatic end of a continuum of motion that generate territoriality and belonging through repeated movement. At the other end are the observable movements of bodies and ritual objects through the streets of South Central Mumbai, tracing an established route from Dongri to the Rahmatabad cemetery in Mazagaon, marking and reconstituting this part of the city as a focus of Shi'i Muslim belonging (Masoudi Nejad 2015). Such belonging is reinforced and most powerfully emerges in the interplay between different modes of motion and mobility, such as recurring travel and pilgrimages of persons, the movement of people and sacred objects through the streets, and finally the subtle suggestions of motion that sonic atmospheres exude. The Muharram processions in Mumbai show us how this entire spectrum from transnational travel and pilgrimage down to palpable sonic suggestions of motion is involved in making territories, places, and sites of belonging. These acts of motion in turn vitally contribute to the nondiscursive constitution of citizenship. Their atmospheric dimensions give such belonging an air of somatic facticity.

URBAN ATMOSPHERES

Atmospheres as "ecstasies of the thing" have become a theme in scholarship on cities. Those interested in the aesthetic and affective dimensions of urban places have been spurred by the suggestion that "urbanity has an atmospheric core" (Hasse 2014, 185). Atmospheres as feelings extended in space profoundly affect persons, just as being in warmth or darkness does, shaping a sense of being in the city. In cities a plurality of atmospheres coexist and overlap, in often contradictory and complex ways. Urbanity is palpable through immersion in atmospheres, and the very literal felt-bodily encounter with them. Architecture (Böhme 2006, 2017), sets of illumination (Edensor 2012), smells, the movement of people and vehicles, and urban sounds can all exude feelings of urbanity as atmospheres. According to Schmitz, atmospheres are "half-things," phenomena that are fleeting and immersive, such as sounds and rainstorms that disappear and return (2016, 74–75). Frequently, those affected by an atmosphere resort to synesthetic descriptors to report their experience, such as when describing a city as "lively." Furthermore, residents can identify and locate particular neighborhoods of a city through their atmosphere, while contemporary urban planners also deploy the atmospheric character

FIGURE 3. The afternoon procession on Ashura, beginning in Dongri. The red stains on the white shrouds are meant to resemble blood, as a reminder of the tragic Battle of Karbala and the martyrdom of members of the family of the Prophet Muhammad. Photo by Patrick Eisenlohr.

of a neighborhood in marketing strategies and even aim at manufacturing atmospheres in the construction of new neighborhoods, as in Hamburg's "Hafen-City," a new part of the city built on the site of former port warehouses dating from the nineteenth century (Hasse 2014, 257–58). This line of work on urban

FIGURE 4. The afternoon procession on Ashura, moving from Dongri to Mazagaon. Photo by Patrick Eisenlohr.

atmospheres in philosophy and geography is highly relevant for our discussion of the atmospheric dimensions of the Shi'i character of Dongri as a distinct Mumbai neighborhood. In contrast to most previous studies of urban atmospheres, our investigation focuses on the sonic rather than architecture and illumination as generators of atmospheres. The sonic creation of a specific character of Dongri tied to its Shi'i history mainly becomes palpable in two ways, or steps, the first more general, the second more specific.

First, the sounds that emerge from the procession, whether the repetition of slogans, the sound of rhythmic breast-beating, the devotional genres of recited poetry commemorating the events of Karbala, or the sounds of metal chains and blades used during flagellation have one quality in common: they are sounds of rhythmic movement, they comprise an alternation between strong and weak elements on multiple dimensions. This is plainly obvious in the case of breast-beating, the repetition of slogans, and the flagellation with metal implements. But also the musical rendering of commemorative and mournful poetry of the nauha genre shares this quality of rhythmic, here musical, vocal movement. These sonic manifestations are ecstasies of the procession, which itself is a movement of bodies and ritual objects through the city. The sounds of collective movement emanating from the procession have a capacity to seize and affect those exposed to them. Returning to the theme of sonically generated atmospheres, in this context it is useful to draw a link to Hermann Schmitz's suggestion that atmospheres are not just feelings poured into a predimensional space but also suggestions of motion (1967, 1969, 2016, 85), an insight that resonates with Böhme's point that sound as atmosphere acts through modifying space as it is experienced by the body (2000, 16). In other words, those affected by sounds like those emerging from the procession do not just hear movement, but their felt-bodies are also touched and immersed in a way suggesting or driving toward analogous motion. Through sound, suggestions of motion work on the felt-bodies of those witnessing the performance. These sonic movements are a chief means of making the specific urban atmosphere of Dongri as a Shi'i neighborhood perceivable as a socially shared experience, as a mode of intercorporeality (Csordas 2008). Atmospheres become shared and social through processes of encorporation, which is how we translate Hermann Schmitz's term *Einleibung* (1965, 343; 2016, 59). Especially in the case of sonic atmospheres acting out the same suggestions of movement on a multitude of felt-bodies, the felt-bodies that encounter such an atmosphere can temporarily become part of a larger collective entity in which the boundaries between them become permeable, so that they constitute a supra-felt-body or we-*Leib*. Atmospheres therefore are able to create a collective feeling of being in and being part of a shared emotionally charged space.

But the sonic atmospheres generated in the procession also produce the shared experiential Shi'i character of Dongri in a second, more specific way. The sounds of breast-beating, flagellation, and the slogans invoking members of the family of the Prophet, along with the amplified recitation of devotional poetry, bring together those familiar with the narrative of Karbala as a community of witnesses. In other words, the shared emotional space that the process of atmospheric encorporation just mentioned creates and that is atmospheric in its diffuse meaningfulness is in this second step further qualified as specifically Shi'i.[8] Witnessing, in both Islamic as well as Christian traditions, is intimately linked to martyrdom. This entanglement of witnessing and martyrdom is to a large extent based on assumed inner connections between pain, death, and truth that also provide the background to the history of judicial uses of torture in Europe, while in Islamic traditions, *shahid* refers to both martyr and witness (Peters 2001, 711–15). The restaging of events that happened at Karbala during the procession, where sonic and visual reminders of Karbala are thickly present, summons those receptive to the Karbala paradigm as witnesses of the events, thus collectively tying them to the unfolding spectacle. As John Durham Peters has put it in his discussion of media and witnessing, "to witness an event is to be responsible in some way to it" (2001, 708). Witnessing and reliving the mournful events of Karbala is the common theme of many ritual practices of Shi'ism, and it features prominently among Patrick's interlocutors as signs of what they referred to as a "good Shia." Witnessing is an inherently social act and, elaborated as a religious performance, can be constitutive of community. Sonic atmospheres proceeding from the procession help to achieve a rapprochement of a collective of listeners—that is, those affected by the sonic events in the knowledge that the sounds of the events also affect others at the same time—with a Shi'i community of pious witnesses of Karbala. It is through the body and sensations felt through it, such as sorrow and pain, that witnessing occurs: "The body is authenticity's last refuge in situations of structural doubt" (717).

As sonic atmospheres affect the body through its suggestions of motion, they play a powerful role in positioning listeners in the role of witnesses. They thus reinforce the memory and narrative of Karbala by giving the impression of first-hand experience through their affection of bodies. They thereby affirm the moral truths the events have come to stand for among Shi'is, and sometimes even non-Shi'is, including also some non-Muslims. To a large extent this involves sounds coming from painful and mournful events and acts such as breast-beating, flagellation with sharp metal implements, and amplified, sorrowful poetry. In a very literal way, these sounds constitute an atmosphere and therefore a feel of the events and the narrative of Karbala. As periodically recurring urban atmospheres, they contribute to giving the urban setting a specifically Shi'i feel that is as diffuse as it is powerful. The hailing and summoning of listeners as witnesses through the sounds of the performance establishes a connection between the atmosphere of the urban locale and specifically Shi'i narratives and moral stances.

TERRITORIALIZATION,
TRAVEL, AND SONIC MOVEMENT

As much as the sonic movements discussed here contribute to Shi'i belonging in the urban setting of Mumbai, they also have important translocal aspects that interact with other, more visual reminders of the Battle of Karbala, around whose memory the procession revolves. The commemorative processions contain elements of reenacting the events at Karbala, in a sense transporting the devotees to this sacred site in present-day Iraq. It is well known that the events of the Battle of Karbala in 680 CE play a pivotal role in Shi'i self-understanding and religious orientation. Scholars have referred to the "Karbala paradigm," centered on a narrative and images of resistance, just struggle, and sacrifice against overwhelming odds, as a template of Shi'ism (M. Fischer 1980; Korom 2002). Karbala in present-day Iraq, where the pivotal events took place and which is also the site of Hussain's magnificent tomb, has long been a site of pilgrimage, as is Najaf, a city of Shi'ite learning and the site of the tomb of Ali, Hussain's father and son-in-law of the Prophet. Karbala is literally holy ground for Shi'i Muslims. Karbala and other places of pilgrimage and associated centers of Islamic learning such as Damascus in Syria and Qom and Mashhad in Iran, have long featured as places of longing and favored destinations of pilgrimage in Shi'i imaginations; material objects from these sites and the experience of being present there evoke deep emotions and feelings of attachment.

But Shi'i Muslims do not just link themselves to Middle Eastern sacred sites in memory of the family of the Prophet; they also perpetuate a tradition of attachment to India as a holy land. For example, among Shi'i Muslims in Mumbai there are discourses of aligning Imam Hussain's example at Karbala with Gandhi's freedom struggle in India, suggesting that the latter was directly inspired by the former (see Hyder 2006). In 2007 a religious advertising campaign by the Mumbai Twelver Shi'i media center World Islamic Network, announced under the name of Muharram Awareness Campaign in the sacred month of Muharram, prominently showcased an alleged quote by Gandhi: "If India ever desires to be a great nation, it should follow the example of Imam Hussain." Long-standing discourses circulate among Shi'i Muslims according to which Hussain intended to go and settle in India, emphasizing the great respect accorded to India as a site of learning and wisdom in Islamic traditions and sayings of members of the family of the Prophet (Eisenlohr 2015a, 699–701).

In the specific Shi'i ritual context discussed here, sonically enacted movements affect listeners in such a way that both the making of an urban neighborhood as distinctly Shi'i and forms of transoceanic belonging are strengthened in deeply emotional ways. The surrogate character of the procession as a pilgrimage is also important. The ability to recognize and locate such sounds, an acoustemology in Steven Feld's (1996) sense, are not only an important means of navigating the city in its great diversity, because such sounds also contain specific pointers to locations beyond its boundaries. In the ritual setting, the sounds evoking the tragedy of Karbala are not just profound sorrow and grieving, reinforcing a Shi'i claim on a part of Mumbai; they also momentarily transport attuned listeners to a witness position in a distant location in nondiscursive ways, going beyond the narrative construction of Shi'i tradition. The performative establishment of links to places in other parts of the world, far beyond the city's boundaries, does not contradict the efforts of acoustic territorialization that support a Shi'i belonging in Mumbai. On the contrary, the evocation of Karbala and other places in present-day Iraq, Iran, and Syria reinforces such a project, as "acoustic territories should not be exclusively read as places or sites but more as *itineraries*, as points of departure as well as arrival" (Labelle 2010, xxv). The notion of territorialization as travel, including its sonic dimensions, plays a crucial role in positioning those present at the procession as witnesses of the events at Karbala, thereby supporting a specifically Shi'i historical memory. It also speaks to the position of Twelver Shi'i Muslims as people whose lives are organized around intersections of various forms of mobility, as a prime example of the social processes and organizations that have been discussed in the recent literature on a "mobilities paradigm" (Adey 2010; Sheller and Urry 2006; Urry 2007). Our point is that these mobilities do not just comprise actual migration within India, as the great majority of Twelver Shi'i Muslims in Mumbai are migrants or the descendants of migrants from North India who continue to maintain close links to their places of ancestral origin they often refer to as *vatan* (homeland) (Eisenlohr 2015b).

Associations *(anjuman)* of those sharing a *vatan* elsewhere in India play a major role in organizing Muharram ritual in Mumbai, including the commemorative processions. Nor are these mobilities limited to circuits of labor migration to countries of the Persian Gulf that Shi'is are engaged in along with other Muslims in Mumbai (T. Hansen 2001). They also go beyond actual pilgrimages to the sacred sites of Twelver Shi'ism in Iraq and Iran. Muharram processions in Mumbai do not just build on and point to all these forms of mobility and fold them together with movement of bodies and ritual objects through urban streets; they also interweave them with the somatically felt motion of the procession's sounds. They enact a large complex of interlaced motion on a cline stretching from transnational migration and pilgrimage, migration, and travel within India, via recurring forms of travel through an urban setting, to the atmospheric suggestions of motion that the sonic aspects of ritual processions enact on felt-bodies.[9] These atmospheric suggestions of motion provide somatic evidence for both far-flung connections and the making of urban places as "Shia," thereby undergirding claims of belonging to the city. In this sense such atmospheric suggestions of motion are also environmental in a political sense, as a mode of struggle and control, because they are part of a larger project that seeks to imbue the perception of the environment through atmospheres with a felt quality of "Shia-ness," which is in turn linked to struggles over claims of belonging and citizenship in an urban setting.

In this way religious networks and traditions play a key role in sustaining a sense of attachment across the Indian Ocean, with both India and particular religions and sites in the Middle East as foci of belonging and emotionally charged affiliation, highlighting the sensory and material dimensions of belonging that constitute "emotional geographies" (Anderson and Smith 2001). Certainly, long traditions of narration provide a key foundation for translocal Shi'i attachments to holy lands and places in India and beyond, resulting in transoceanic forms of belonging. However, especially in pilgrimage and commemorative rituals, such attachments also emerge as the result of exposure to material sites and environments that affect pious Shi'i Muslims in bodily ways that involve, but cannot be reduced to, the workings of discourse. Sonic atmospheres can be a chief mode for the creation of such attachments.

CONCLUSION

In this chapter we have tried to make a case for the centrality of sonic atmospheres in the constitution of cultural citizenship. Trying to show how sonic practices and performances help to produce the feel of a Mumbai neighborhood as belonging to Twelver Shi'is, we have highlighted the somatic dimensions of belonging to certain places. If cultural citizenship "refers to the right to be different . . . with respect to the dominant national community, without compromising one's right to belong," the articulation of such claims does not merely involve atmospheric and felt aspects (Rosaldo 1994, 57). Atmospheres, including sonic atmospheres, can be of critical importance in contexts where the conventional boundaries of citizenship discourse and powerful counterclaims over contested urban space make the successful articulation of such rights for inclusion and belonging highly challenging. The role that performatively staged and crafted atmospheres can play in constituting and claiming citizenship highlights their character as a form of environmentality that also constitutes a mode of discipline and control and that is at the same time a mode of governmentality as outlined in the first chapter of this book. At the same time, Mumbai Twelver Shi'i place-bound belonging is intertwined and produced by an array of mobilities including migration, pilgrimage, and ritual processions that also include sonic movement. The sonic is a privileged avenue for investigating such nondiscursive and bodily felt aspects of citizenship and belonging because of its intimate relationship with felt-bodies. In exerting collectively felt suggestions of motion, sonic events and performances produce feelings, thereby bringing about an atmospheric, prediscursive sense of place. The sonic dimensions of a regularly recurring religious procession are a vital component of such making of place, interacting with other kinds of mobility. Their bodily felt character invests such place-bound belonging with an air of facticity, foregrounding nondiscursive, somatic evidence for claims of citizenship with far-reaching consequences.

5

Multisensoriality

An analytic of atmosphere bridges the gap between the phenomenology of the felt-body and the anthropology of the senses, offering advantages for understanding sensory cultural practices such as, for example, sounding and lighting. The felt dimensions of these practices often escape full qualification by cultural discourses but are nevertheless deeply meaningful. As holistic gestalten, or figural moments whose multiple dimensions appear as an integrated whole, atmospheres cannot be reduced to single sensory impressions. Even if, for example, sounding or lighting plays a central role in a given atmosphere, the latter will take hold of those exposed to it in a diffuse way that exceeds any single sensory modality. In this chapter we begin by distinguishing the phenomenological tradition of thinking about atmospheres from affect, stressing what we see as the advantages of an analytic of atmospheres over affect. Against the background of this distinction, we explore the potential of the notion of atmosphere for a better understanding of the cultural framing of sensation, suggesting that atmospheric meaningfulness is irreducible to particular single sensory modi. Instead, it rests on diffuse and synesthetic kinds of felt-bodily incitement with a holistic character. Atmospheres are not only spatial phenomena but also impact bodies' felt spatial economy. Much of our discussion of atmospheres is grounded in the sonic as a multimodal phenomenon that comprises, at a minimum, hearing, touch, and kinesthetics. However, the multisensoriality of atmospheres obviously goes beyond these fields.

To support our broader argument, we draw on two recent examples of ethnographic engagement with atmospheres, one taken from Patrick's own research on vocal recitation of devotional poetry among Mauritian Muslims, the other from Mikkel Bille's (2019) research on practices of lighting in Danish homes.

75

The examples suggest that atmospheres generate diffusely meaningful sensations that are available for further specification and qualification through sensory regimes and discourses that circulate in given contexts and settings. In this sense atmospheres as multisensory phenomena comprise, but are at the same time not reducible to, the culturally specific sensory terms that have been analyzed in the anthropology of the senses. In other words, we propose an analytic of atmospheres as multisensoriality that partially aligns with but also differs from other anthropological approaches to multisensoriality or the anthropology of the senses. In this chapter's concluding analysis, we address the question of whether the two kinds of practices in the two contexts we discuss—sonic practices, as different from the merely acoustic, and practices of lighting—entertain different relationships to atmosphere as holistic sensation.

The meaningfulness of atmospheres and their potential for signification can be distinguished from affect. Compared to those notions of affect as intensity, as a nonsignifying, precultural and "autonomous" force, that have become so influential in the humanities and social sciences and that derive from the Spinozist philosophy of Gilles Deleuze and in which the translations and interpretations of Brian Massumi play a major role, an analytic of atmospheres offers advantages for understanding the felt dimensions of cultural practices of sounding and lighting (2002, 27, 35). The felt dimensions of these practices often escape full qualification by cultural discourses but are nevertheless deeply meaningful. In the case for atmospheres as an analytic that bridges the gap between affect and culture and history, it is important to distinguish between anglophone adoptions of the notion of atmospheres and its uses in German neophenomenology. In the former the notion is used flexibly, often as a metaphor interchangeable with mood and affect (Stewart 2011).[1]

Other scholars collapse atmospheres with affect, such as in geographer Ben Anderson's (2009) frequently cited "affective atmospheres." German neophenomenology, in contrast, has since the 1960s developed theories of atmospheres as phenomena in their own right (Schmitz 1969, 98–106; 1978; 2016), building on precursors such as Ludwig Binswanger's "tuned space" ([1932] 1953). Hermann Schmitz, and since the 1990s also Gernot Böhme ([1995] 2013, 2017), the main theorists of atmospheres in this tradition, offer distinct approaches. Böhme has formulated an aesthetic theory of atmospheres that focuses more on the planned and artful manufacturing of atmospheres in fields such as design and architecture, while Schmitz theorizes atmospheres as part of a larger investigation into the felt-body, or *Leib*. Both concur that an atmosphere is not an interior mood, but an entity in the world "that proceeds from and is created by things, persons, or their constellations" (Böhme 1993, 122). Atmospheres as quasi-objective phenomena encounter and intermingle with felt-bodies. According to Schmitz, they are "the occupying of a dimension-less space or area within the sphere of experienced presence" (2016, 30). Emphasizing the production of atmospheres by things, people, and their combinations, Böhme has coined the phrase that atmospheres are "ecstasies of the thing" (1993, 121). Schmitz, however, identifies atmospheres with what he calls "half-things" *(Halbdinge)*, phenomena that are fleeting and can be interrupted such as wind, heat and cold, the weather, pain, and a voice or musical figures (Schmitz 2016, 75; Griffero, 2017). In distinction from bounded things, half-things have no steady locations. These qualities of fleeting half-things also make it possible for them to intermingle with felt-bodies in ways that would not be possible for bounded, relatively permanent things with stable locations, as in the examples of wind, heat, cold, the weather, pain, voices or musical figures as half-things. In his radical attack on interiorist subjectivity, including its felt dimensions, Schmitz has also argued that feelings are atmospheres poured into space, seizing the felt-body (2016, 30).

Human sensations and emotions come about through the felt-body's intermingling with atmospheres as distinct entities in the world. This implies that atmospheres are thoroughly spatial phenomena and that, in the process of seizing someone, they also act on the body's spatial economy. Atmospheres, according to Schmitz, affect the body's felt location in space through suggestions of motion. These suggestions of motion are a kind of kinetic energy that feeds into the body's vital drive that alternates between states of contraction and relaxation (Schmitz 1966, 77; Schmitz, Müllan, and Slaby 2011, 245). This spatial manipulation of the felt-body is the ground not just for the holistic affection that atmospheres bring about but also for the diffuse meaningfulness of atmospheres.[2] Such meaningfulness "manifests atmospherically and as a corporeal impression" (Abels 2018, 2) and distinguishes atmospheres from notions of affect as interpreted by Massumi (2002), which the latter conceives as autonomous from signification and therefore prehistorical and precultural.

Böhme's and Schmitz's approaches to atmospheres are rather different. Unlike Schmitz in his thoroughgoing decentering of subjectivity that goes as far as locating feelings outside the material body, Böhme is more committed to a subject-object divide. In Böhme's focus on the production of atmospheres, he tends to view atmospheres as ecstasies generated by objects and perceived by subjects. Schmitz, in contrast, describes atmospheres as properties of situations, or larger contexts and constellations that are at the same time feelings and emotions, phenomena traditionally considered as locatable in subjects. However, Schmitz and Böhme concur that atmospheres are closely tied to suggestions of motion. For Schmitz this is a generic property of atmospheres, while for Böhme this is at least characteristic of atmospheres related to sound. For him, as for Schmitz, the perception of atmospheres generated in such performances unfolds through motions sensed by the felt-body: "To be present in a space means to reach out into this space through the sensing of the felt-body *[durch das leibliche Spüren]*. This occurs through feeling oneself contracted or expanded, pushed down or lifted up and much more. . . . The extraordinary effect of voices on our present emotional state is due to them immediately modifying our presence in space as sensed by the felt-body" (2009, 30–31).

Schmitz ties such modification of the felt-body's sense of being in space to the broader theme of the felt-body's continuous vital dynamics. While drawing a link between felt-bodily suggestions of movement and atmospheres in general, he also writes of a close relationship between sonic phenomena and such movements: "The dynamic volume of sound is the same as the volume of the vital drive pertaining to the felt-body consisting in tension and swelling, as in breathing in, including the privative dilation that releases itself from the swelling, as in the state of fatigue. These kinds of volume come about through suggestions of movement. Such suggestions of movement correspond in the cases of felt-body and sound, and far beyond that, as they make communication through the felt-body *[leibliche Kommunikation]* possible" (Schmitz 2016, 85).

From an anthropological and historical perspective, however, this phenomenology of atmospheres poses a number of problems. If we take the sonic as atmosphere, for example, it evokes a split in the study of sound in the social sciences and humanities between those who claim that sound itself has the power to affect bodies, nowadays often argued through theories of affect (Goodman 2010; Cox 2018), and those, typically anthropologists, musicologists, and historians, for whom human actors ascribe power to sound through cultural practices (Bull and Back 2003; Feld et al. 2004; Kane 2015). In particular the diversity of auditory cultures makes the question whether sound itself is powerful or whether people invest it with power an urgent one.

According to neophenomenological approaches to atmospheres, there is a causal connection between the materiality of sonic movements and the perceived stirrings of the felt-body *(leibliche Regungen)*. This is what Hermann Schmitz describes as suggestions of movement whose role is to make "the perceived and the felt-body's palpable condition comparable *[das Wahrgenommene und das spürbare leibliche Befinden vergleichbar]*" (1978, 54, cited in Hasse 2013, 49). Taken at face value, this would imply that, much like in the European baroque *Affektenlehre*, the shapes and movements of sound directly and invariably generate particular feelings and passions in listeners in a universal way (Großmann 2014). In Islamic traditions, too, the notion that emotions and particular kinds of music, or modal components within them, are intrinsically connected is evident in, for example, Al-Farabi's *Great Book of Music* (Shaw 2019, 44). Al-Ghazali's consequentialist theorizing of the value of music from an Islamic perspective in terms of whether it leads Muslims to God or distracts them from that path relies on the idea, inherited from ancient Greek traditions, of inner connections between types of music and particular emotional states (Shehabi 1995, 119–31). The latter idea also informs Indian raga music, where the performance of a raga and listeners' emotional states are often assumed to be directly connected

(Jairazbhoy 1971; Kaufmann 1965). From an anthropological perspective, however, the relationship between particular types of music and certain emotions is less self-evident, against the background of research on auditory cultures and other culturally and historically shaped engagements with sound and sound as knowledge. One way to bring together this anthropological sensibility for auditory cultures and the phenomenology of atmospheres is to take the holistic character of atmospheres seriously.

THE SEMIOTICS AND MEANINGFULNESS
OF SENSORY HOLISM: SOUND AND SOUNDINGS

The holistic character of atmospheres can never be tied down to single, particular sensory impressions but emerges prior to the singling out of such impressions. Atmospheres as holistic gestalten are diffuse and encompassing because the felt-body absorbs sensory impressions in the worldly context of situations and not by putting together separate sensory impressions. This holistic and pluriform character of atmospheres is precisely what accounts for their peculiar power and their frequent appearance of ineffability. Applied to auditory phenomena, such as vocal performance, this suggests that atmospheres cannot be simply acoustic and centered on listening only. Atmospheres also do not emerge from a combination of several of such definite and separate sensory impressions, such as a combination of sound and light, on the basis of a "substitutability of sensory qualities" as Böhme (2013) has argued. In comparison with Schmitz, Böhme's understanding of synesthesia is more focused on the exchangeability of separate sensory modalities and less concerned with the felt-body as a holistic entity. His notion of the substitutability of sensory qualities is therefore also less suitable to the analysis of atmospheres as "synesthetic characters" (Schmitz 1968, 51–68), where initial holistic perception in the context of a situation arises through the modulating interplay and the "integral simultaneity" of multiple senses (Hasse 2013, 48). Atmospheres as half-things thereby intermingle with felt-bodies, provoking meaningful stirrings that stand in a relation of qualitative similarity to the integral gestalten though which such half-things present themselves.

To return to the topic of sound, music, and voice, an emerging focus in work on atmospheres (Abels 2013, 2022; Eisenlohr 2018; Riedel and Torvinen 2020), there can only be sonic instead of merely acoustic atmospheres. The sonic as traveling vibratory and energetic phenomena not only exceeds the realm of the audible but also provides an overall paradigm for the stirrings and suggestions of movement that atmospheres provoke. There is an intimate relationship between the sonic and the suggestions of motion that play such a pivotal role in the phenomenology of atmospheres. While the acoustic pertains to the sense of hearing only, the sonic as the broader energetic phenomena from which the acoustic derives is a compelling example for the suggestions of movement around which the perception of atmospheres revolves.

Where does this leave the anthropological question of auditory cultures? After all, we are talking about causal and analogue couplings between the integral gestalten or half-things and the felt-bodily stirrings that their perception provokes. The base for the suggestions of movement that atmospheres contain is to be found in the material properties of energetic flows of which the sonic is a chief mode. If there is a rather direct connection between such properties and the stirrings of the felt-body, where does undeniable auditory cultural difference come in? The question of auditory culture points to the meaningfulness of atmospheres. Contrary to ontological claims about the sonic as an "asignifying material flux" (Cox 2011, 157) that correspond to Massumi's (2002, 23–25) "autonomy of affect," a material flux that is prior to culture, history, and signification, sonic movements such as those that make up atmospheres are deeply meaningful. From a Peircean semiotic perspective, they are shot through with iconicity (relations of qualitative likeness) and indexicality (relations of contiguity, co-occurrence, or causality). For example, the correspondence or likeness between the stirrings of a felt-body seized by an atmosphere, and the sonic gestalt of the atmosphere, is a relationship of qualitative similarity and therefore a relationship of iconicity in semiotic terms. The causal coupling between the sonic as atmospheric and kinetic force and the bodily stirrings and suggestions of motion is simultaneously a relationship of indexicality.

The meaningfulness of atmospheres inheres in the materiality of its semiotic forms (Peirce 1932, 170) and is not the result of a superposition of conventional meanings through a socially shaped mind following a "half second delay" (Massumi 2002, 28–30). The diffuse complex of signification that revolves around the indexical-iconic links between sonic half-things and bodily sensation is less qualified than the meanings often found in sociocultural and religious discourses. This, however, does not make it a less important dimension of sociocultural practices such as sounding and lighting that are recognized to have an atmospheric force. If anything, their diffuse meaningfulness provides somatic evidence undergirding these atmospheric practices. More broadly, this points to how atmosphere as a concept not only addresses many of the same intellectual concerns as the Deleuzian genealogy of affect through Massumi but can do so without sidelining signification, thereby making it a more useful notion for the humanities and social sciences.[3]

While there are other understandings of affect compatible with signification, an analytic of atmospheres brings in the diffuse meaningfulness of felt-bodily stirrings from the outset, which in semiotic terms amount to indexical iconicity. In ritual studies and anthropology, the latter sign relationship is especially known from contexts in which social processes and rituals are framed as "natural" or as part of a cosmic order, because contiguity and copresence (indexicality) can be represented as grounded in inherent likeness (iconicity) (Parmentier 1994). In the ethnographic examples that follow, I show that this semiotically induced naturalization effect is not unlike the ways in which atmospheric sensations provide seemingly irrefutable somatic evidence for the tenets of a particular Islamic sectarian tradition or for a social aesthetics of home design that draws hierarchical distinctions between different groups of people.

If the intermingling of sonic atmospheres with felt-bodies is deeply meaningful, how does this meaningfulness relate to the differences in meaning that auditory cultures and situationally shifting personal stances produce? Our answer is that, in the case of atmospheres, we have to distinguish between different levels of signification. The meaningfulness that inheres in atmospheres' materiality such as in the sonic movements that we have discussed is of an internally diffuse kind.[4] Taking one of the two examples discussed later, culturally situated practices such as Mauritian Muslims' artful recitation of devotional poetry in honor of the Prophet Muhammad known as naʿt revolve around and also generate much more clearly delineated kinds of signification. In this practice the more diffuse significations of sonic suggestions of movement become further qualified through the discourses and histories of a particular religious tradition, thus acquiring more specific meanings in the process. The atmospheric component of a vocal performance's meaningfulness is the ground on which more specific meanings such as narratives and discourses about spiritual travel to personally encounter the Prophet arise. Auditory cultures and other kinds of social and historical difference is the more defined and qualified end in a continuum of meaningfulness. This suggests that the analysis of sonic atmospheres in empirical sociocultural settings needs a layered account of signification and meaningfulness.

In this sense the analytic of atmospheres as multisensoriality we propose relates to, but also diverges from, other anthropological approaches to multisensoriality or the anthropology of the senses.[5] The latter tradition assumes that the senses are socioculturally constructed to a very large extent and that they "are made, not given," while stressing "the imperative to approach each culture on its own sensory terms" (Howes 2019, 17, 18; Classen 1993; Stoller 1989). This emphasis on the sociocultural modulation of the senses, including relative subdivisions in the sensorium and their variable interrelations is important. In the example of Mauritian Muslim devotional vocal recitation just mentioned, religious discourse, acoustemologies (Feld 1996), and techniques of the body qualify diffuse atmospheric felt-bodily stirrings as the felt aspects of a particular Islamic tradition and practice. In other words, these sociocultural modulations of felt-bodily sensation correspond to the more qualified end of the continuum of meaningfulness mentioned earlier. However, the diffuse meaningfulness that the intermingling of atmospheres as spatially extended emotions with felt-bodies engenders is upstream from such socioculturally framed sensory regimes.[6]

There is nothing inherently religious, still less Islamic, in sonic atmospheres with their suggestions of motion; these require further specification to manifest as dimensions of Islam. Nevertheless, atmospheres also comprise such religious or sociocultural sensory regimes because they bundle them along with techniques of the body, discourses, and memory, making them resonate with one another by imbuing them with the same overarching feel. The "bridging qualities" at work in atmospheric suggestions of motion bring together different lines of experience into a resonant whole (Schmitz 2009, 33). With respect to sonic atmospheres, "when musical movement acts on bodily movement in this way, music and dance create resonances between the divergent registers from which lived experience emerges. Among these resonating registers are affect, emotion, discourse and memory. . . . The resonances themselves are atmospheric" (Abels 2020, 166). In other words, atmospheres make such disparate strands of life such as acoustemologies (Feld 1996) and other techniques of the body, discourses, and memories commensurable with one another by fusing them with the feeling of having a body (Eisenlohr 2022a, 625). In such a way, atmospheres are inseparable from sociocultural modulations of sensation but also irreducible to such more qualified cultural renderings of the sensory.

For a better understanding of the continuum of meaningfulness along which atmospheric sensation operates, an earlier debate on sensory anthropology between Tim Ingold and David Howes (2011) is instructive (Howes 2022). Drawing on the work of Maurice Merleau-Ponty, Ingold argues for a "bodily synergy of the senses," a relative interchangeability of the senses and the primacy of holistic perception out of bodily motion and activity (2000, 262, 268).[7] This is close to what from a phenomenological perspective can be described as atmospheric felt-bodily sensation revolving around suggestions of motion, which cannot be reduced to particular sensory impressions. Howes, in contrast, critiques Ingold for allegedly universalizing a European phenomenological model of perception, arguing for the thorough sociocultural variability and shaping of the senses instead. The latter position, in turn, points to what we have called the more qualified end of a continuum of meaningfulness in sensory perception. In our view the upshot of this is that both positions are correct; they point only to different poles on such a continuum of meaningfulness along which the multisensoriality of atmospheres unfolds.

ATMOSPHERIC DIMENSIONS OF VOCAL RECITATION

Let us draw on an example from Patrick's research on the recitation of naʿt among Muslims in Mauritius, who are of Indian background, that demonstrates this progression from the diffuse meaningfulness of sonic movements to more specific enculturated signification. As mentioned earlier, the naʿt genre of devotional Urdu poetry is most commonly recited in religious gatherings known as mahfil-e mawlud, held on prominent dates of the Islamic ritual calendar such as the Prophet's birthday or the death anniversary (ʿurs) of a Sufi saint or auspicious occasions in peoples' lives such as having weddings, passing important school exams, or moving into a new home. The performance of naʿt is especially associated with the Ahl-e Sunnat wa Jamaʿat, or Barelwi Islamic reformist movement, which historically had the greatest following among all modern Islamic reformist movements in South Asia, as well as in Mauritius. A particular complex of piety focused on the figure of the Prophet Muhammad is a hallmark of this movement. The recitation of naʿt is not just showering praise on the Prophet and an expression of deep affection for him but is also a performative practice in the sense that it aims at transformative results. For Patrick's Mauritian Muslim interlocutors, this practice, if performed in the appropriate manner, can bring about the spiritual presence of the Prophet among his devotees even long after his death, affording the possibility of a personal encounter with him. The practice is thus part of a Sufi-inspired quest for a spiritual journey to meet the Prophet in person, a possibility and wish that is denied and rejected by followers of other Islamic traditions. Therefore, the recitation of naʿt in such devotional gatherings is subject to sectarian contestation and critique in South Asia as well as in Mauritius. Both the popularity of the genre and the salience of the sectarian contestation around it have been amplified by the circulation of audio recordings of this genre, first on audiocassettes in the late twentieth century, followed by a shift to audio CDs and mp3 disks in the late 1990s, and then eventually audio files through internet-based mobile devices and social media.

Consider the sonic suggestions of motion in the following spectrogram and waveform of a naʿt recording from Mauritius that features an alternation of contraction and expansion or relaxation (Chady [n.d.], CD 1, track 11). These can be traced through the alternation of increases and decreases on several acoustic parameters.[8] The excerpt features the recitation of three poetic phrases or lines, separated by brief pauses visible on the spectrogram and the waveform, of which the second line is a repetition of the first and is approximately forty-five seconds long.

Voh tujhe bacāeinge pār bhī lagāeinge	He will save you and guide you to a safe haven
Voh tujhe bacāeinge pār bhī lagāeinge, pār bhī lagāeinge	He will save you and take you to a safe haven, take you to a safe haven

The first line and its repetition on the second line do not just feature a striking increase of loudness and pitch or fundamental frequency (traceable through the bottom layer representing the buildup of the frequency bands across a broad

AUDIO CLIP 4. "Voh tujhe bacāeinge." Chady (n.d.), CD 1, track 11.

To hear this audio clip, scan the QR code with your mobile device or visit DOI: https://doi.org/10.1525/luminos.244.4

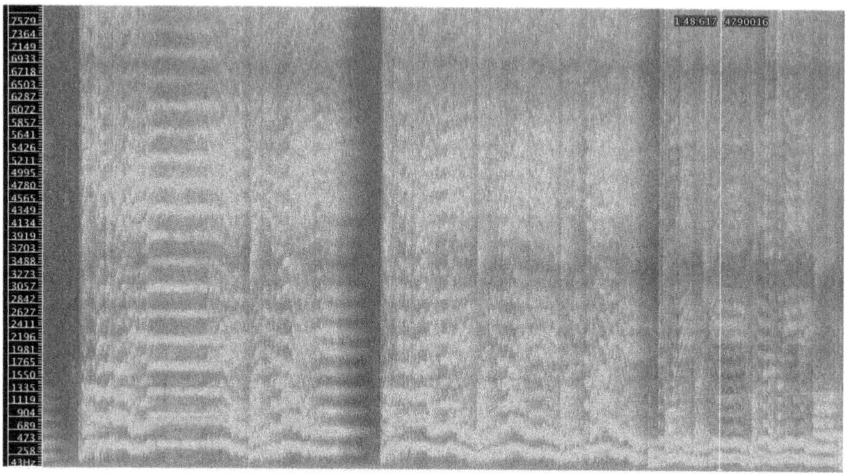

FIGURE 5. Spectrogram of a recording of the devotional Islamic vocal recitation "Voh tujhe bacāeinge."

range in complex sounds like a voice). An examination of the timbre of the voice also shows that much of the acoustic energy is concentrated in higher-frequency bands, reminiscent of the "singer's formant" (Sundberg 1974). On the spectrogram the intensity of acoustic energy is indicated by coloring, from low (green) to intermediate (yellow) to high (orange-red). Particularly striking is the markedly long drawing out and modulation of the syllable *–ge* of *bacaenge* for approximately 5.5 seconds in the first phrase, where the voice peaks in terms of loudness, pitch, and the concentration of energy in higher-frequency ranges. This contrasts with the third line, which shows a marked decrease in acoustic energy in these ranges.

> *Un pe choṛ de kashtī, gham na kar*   Leave the vessel's course to him and do
> *safine kā*   not worry

A look at the spectrogram tells us that most of the sonic energy is now concentrated in lower ranges up to approximately seven hundred hertz, coinciding with a drop in loudness and pitch. The waveform diagram, which tracks volume (the wave amplitude between hypothetical 1 and –1 values, the 0-axis representing the given atmospheric air pressure) also provides a striking illustration of these alternations in sonic movement.

The recitation of this na't revolves around such alternations of contracting and relaxing movements. The na't khwan's voice carries out these movements between high energy and decreases in acoustic energy, which are at the same time

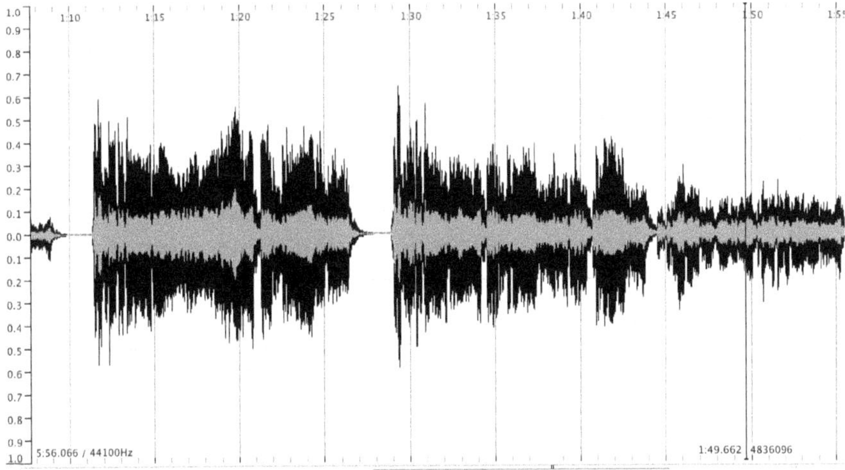

FIGURE 6. Waveform of a recording of the devotional Islamic vocal recitation "Voh tujhe bacāeinge."

alternations between bodily contraction and relaxation. Because listening to naʿt is typically a socially shared, collective experience, listeners perceive these suggestions of motion together, synchronically, as a form of intercorporeality (Csordas 2008). Patrick's Mauritian Muslim interlocutors described the experience of feeling such sonic suggestions of motion as something that "grips you powerfully" and "makes you vibrate," something that "directly enters your soul." They also used metaphors of movement when talking about the power of naʿt recitals, such as "getting onto a bus" or the feeling of being carried away to another place (Eisenlohr 2018, 79–108). From the perspective of an analytic of atmospheres with its decentered understanding of subjecthood, in which felt-bodies intermingle with atmospheric forces such as the sonic, this synchronous perception can also bring about a blurring of boundaries between participants' felt-bodies. It can bring about a temporary merger into a shared we-*Leib*. The we-*Leib* emerges through rhythm, the synchrony and bringing together of sonically enacted contraction and dilation. As a result, the participants in a naʿt recital are subject to a process of solidary encorporation (Schmitz 2016, 59). The sonic creation of such a shared whole then establishes a somatic base for a community of Muslims yearning to personally encounter the Prophet, in a shared, bodily event and for repeated movement toward him and his favorite city, Medina. Listeners feel and realize that they have joined in the same movements, oriented toward their common pious destination.

As mentioned, such sonic suggestions of motion are meaningful in a diffuse way. They stand in an iconic relationship with alternating movements of other kinds. At the same time, the bodily felt sensations of motion that participants in naʿt recitation perceive also stand in an indexical relationship with the sonic movement enacted by the naʿt khwan's voice, because of their habitual co-occurrence and the causal link between the latter and the former. Thus suggested body movements could be taken to be immanent in sonic motion (cf. Downey 2002, 503). The bodily felt movements provoked by the intermingling with sonic movements as atmospheres are therefore indexical icons, akin to diagrams, of sonic movements, which means that they in themselves are awash with semiosis. To qualify such seemingly immediately felt movement as part of Islamic traditions and cosmologies, further qualification is necessary. This is where the discursive and iconographic dimensions of a religious tradition come in. Throughout this book we stress the significance of atmospheres as nonverbal and somatic knowledge, but this does not imply that discursive knowledge does not matter or that discursively articulated knowledge cannot also play into the generation of atmospheres and be compatible with atmospheric affection. In the example mentioned here, the discursive aspects of the poetry, too, underline the sonic suggestions of movement as atmosphere. The latter align with and fit into particular sociocultural and historical narratives and images, such as devotion to the Prophet as someone who is capable of intercession and who can be personally encountered even long after his death and the desire to spiritually travel to Medina, his favorite city, to be in his presence. In such a way, the diffuse meaningfulness of sonic movements acquires more specific layers of meaning, layers that are not only Islamic but Islamic in a particular sectarian sense. At the same time, such a specific sectarian Islamic tradition then benefits from being undergirded by the seemingly irrefutable verification through somatic experience, with the result that it appears as self-evident. The interplay of sonic movements and the discursive and poetic dimensions of the naʿt genre result in a powerful Islamic summon to encounter the prophet that is felt in the flesh. The recitation of naʿt shows how the atmospheres that this religious practice generates bridges across a divide of affect versus history and culture.

ATMOSPHERES OF LIGHT AND LIGHTING

The embeddedness of one sensory modality in synesthetic and holistic felt-bodily perception is also characteristic of light and lighting as atmospheres. Mikkel Bille's (2019) rich ethnography of creating homely atmospheres through lighting in Denmark also draws on phenomenological approaches to analyze how his interlocutors in Denmark produce and carefully attune atmospheres through lighting. Like Patrick's analysis of the recitation of devotional poetry among Mauritian Muslims, Bille shows how the diffuse meaningfulness of atmospheres that emerges in sensory practices merges with cultural discourses, such as those on the proper mood of a middle-class Danish home. The now internationally famous and increasingly imitated Danish preoccupation with making homes feel *hygge* (cozy) is a salient example of this. Atmospheres may therefore also have a strong normative bent, such as in a voice that sounds right in a given religious setting or in the right kind of lighting that enables a desired from of homeliness.

On the other hand, atmospheres also exceed full qualification by cultural discourses and can be difficult to pinpoint, let alone exhaustively rendered into language. Nevertheless, as Bille's ethnography demonstrates, his interlocutors often had a keen sense for the kind of lighting that felt right, even if they could not exactly say why, and tried to practically adjust their homes' lighting accordingly (2019, 46–47). Just as sound in Patrick's ethnography of devotional vocal performance among Mauritian Muslims, for Bille's Danish interlocutors, lighting is diffusely meaningful rather than affective in Massumi's sense. Bille's analysis of atmospheres is conceptually most indebted to Gernot Böhme, who, reversing Hermann Schmitz's earlier analytical move, reintroduces a subject-object divide into his phenomenology of atmospheres (2017, 12, 26; cf. Bille 2019, 68). This is probably why the felt-body as the zone where the sensing of atmospheres unfolds in a manner sidelining any subject-object distinction, and where the feeler and the feeling momentarily become one and the same, features less prominently in Bille's ethnography.[9] In it Bille draws a direct connection between the atmospheric quality of light and cultural discourses as well as normative practices of lighting. However, just like in an investigation of sounding as atmosphere, there are intermediary steps between the realization that lighting has an atmospheric force and the qualification of such atmospheres through cultural discourses. It is therefore also important to pay attention to the mechanisms that generate atmospheric meaningfulness in lighting, a meaningfulness that then becomes available for developing further discursive qualification or embedding in sociocultural practices and values.

It is not that Gernot Böhme pays no attention to the body when writing on light as atmosphere. He points out that light facilitates a body's location in space, a location that in turn comes with felt qualities attached to it (2017, 199–200).[10] Schmitz, however, provides a richer account of felt-bodily affection through light that is based on his understanding of light as a fleeting half-thing that primarily generates atmospheres through synesthetic characters (1969, 373; 1978, 64; see also Hasse 2014, 283).[11] The case for synesthetic characters is based on the idea, in European intellectual traditions already articulated by Johann Gottfried Herder, that prereflective bodily perception has a holistic quality, while its separation into distinct sensory modalities unfolds through abstractions after the fact (1772, 96; cited in Hasse 2014, 57). In Bille's ethnography of lighting in Denmark, an example of such synesthetic characters is the pervasive contrast between "warm" and "cold" light (2019, 52–53). There warmth and coldness are unrelated to the actual sensation of temperature. In fact, the distinction is deployed in opposition to the temperature of light color measured in kelvin established in physics, where the kind of light that appears warm to Bille's Danish interlocutors, such as candlelight, is actually assigned a lower temperature and where, conversely, the light spectrum emitted by strip lighting with its felt quality of relative coldness is in a higher temperature range. Instead, the felt warmth and coldness of light are synesthetic characters that point to bodily states of felt relaxation and contraction that cut across the distinctions between thermic, optical, acoustic, and kinesthetic sensory modalities. In such a way, the warmth of candlelight and the variety of settings and activities described as *hygge* go together, the latter term, as a descriptor of atmospheres, "is about expressing personality in a relaxed manner"; it is "a classification of a variety of atmospheres where informality and relaxation is in focus" (Bille 2019, 50, 51).

Relaxation, in an atmospheric sense, is more than a metaphor for security, recuperation, and well-being; it is above all a holistically palpable bodily sensation. When light as atmosphere intervenes in bodily economies of relaxation and contraction, it exerts suggestions of movement on felt-bodies. According to Schmitz, such suggestions of motion are alongside synesthetic characters the main mechanism through which atmospheres intermingle with and affect humans through acting on their felt-bodies. In Patrick's example of sonic atmospheres, there is a rather direct connection between the sonic as traveling kinetic energy and such suggestions of motion, while the atmospheric sensation of parts of the spectrum of electromagnetic waves that humans perceive as warm or cold light potentially brings about such suggestions of motion through warmth and coldness as synesthetic characters that in turn provoke such bodily felt suggestions of motion. The diffuse meaningfulness of suggestions of motion as interventions into the body's subtle spatial economies and synesthetic characters becomes in a further step fully culturally qualified in Danish discourses of *hygge* and even turned into a socially shared aesthetics. The latter then is available for the drawing of hierarchical distinctions between the homes of middle-class native Danes and the homes of working-class Danes of migrant origins located in less desirable parts of Copenhagen (Bille 2019, 103–18), the comparatively cold and bright strip lighting associated with the latter kind of homes makes them, and by implication its inhabitants, less respectable. In such a way, like in the atmospheric sonic practices we discussed earlier, lighting as atmosphere displays an entire continuum of signification, from the meaningfulness of diffusely felt-bodily stirrings to fully qualified sociocultural discourses and distinctions, the former acting as somatic evidence for the latter.

CONCLUSION

In this chapter we have argued for an analytic of atmosphere as a way to bridge the gap between the phenomenology of the felt-body and the anthropology of the senses. By way of conclusion, let us return to a question raised earlier, whether the sonic, as different from the merely acoustic, provides a privileged paradigm for the workings of atmospheres. What can the two ethnographic examples, dealing with sounding and lighting as atmospheres, respectively, tell us about this question? Patrick's example of the vocal performance of na't suggests that, while acoustic dynamics are obviously important in the generation of atmospheres, the suggestions of motion and the stirrings of the felt-body they provoke are traceable to something more encompassing and are not reducible to particular sensory impressions, acoustic or otherwise. The suggestions of motion the felt-body perceives point to the holistic character of atmospheres that is prior to specific acoustic or other single sensory impressions.

This holistic character of atmospheres corresponds to the sonic, traveling vibratory phenomena that exceed the realm of hearing and that impress themselves on and in the felt-body in a comprehensive way, going beyond particular modalities of the sensorium. Certainly, sound can also be fed into synesthetic characters, such as in voices felt to sound "warm" or "cold" in a manner unrelated to thermic sensation, as Schmitz discusses at length (1968, 56–67). But the coupling of the felt-body and the sonic as traveling kinetic energy through suggestions of motion does not necessarily depend on synesthetic characters, although the latter can of course contribute to sonic atmospheres. The visual representations of acoustic and by extension sonic movements that we have used to illustrate the example of vocal recitation of Islamic devotional poetry in Mauritius depict such movements as occurring in a dimensional space. But this dimensional space is not the same as the diffuse nondimensional spatial economy of the felt-body and cannot be reduced to the former. In the same way, the sonic as the source of holistic suggestions of movement cannot be reduced to definite sensory impressions or even a particular dimension of the sensorium. The intimate and relatively direct relationship between the sonic as traveling kinetic energy and the suggestions of movement that are central to the workings of atmospheres and in which sonic motion and felt-bodily motion may at times simply fall together indicates that sonic motion plays a pivotal role in the constitution of atmospheres.

Can a similar claim be made about lighting as atmosphere as examined in Mikkel Bille's ethnography of lighting in Danish homes? As with sound in our discussion, it is apparent that light as a single sensory modality becomes inextricably embedded in the kind of primary felt-bodily and holistic perception that is a hallmark of the atmospheric. However, in contrast to Patrick's study of Islamic devotional vocal performances in Mauritius, in Bille's ethnography of lighting as atmospheres in Danish homes, suggestions of motion as the central working mechanism of atmospheres from a Schmitzean perspective stand in a less direct relationship with lighting. Instead, lighting's intervention into vital corporeal dynamics of relaxation and contraction unfolds through synesthetic characters, such as warmth and coldness, not understood as thermic sensations but as cross-modal sensations that in turn translate into suggestions of motion. This implies that lighting, at least in this case, has a more oblique relationship with such interventions into felt-bodily economies of space compared to the sonic as kinetic energy propagating though space in Patrick's example, where its coupling with felt motion of the body is of a more obvious kind.

Accordingly, in this example lighting as atmosphere depends largely on synesthetic characters for its effects, while in Patrick's example of sonic atmospheres sonic motion and felt-bodily motion can simply fall together, even though synesthetic characters can also contribute to felt-bodily affectedness in sonic atmospheres. It might be too far-fetched to take this more immediate relationship of the sonic to felt-bodily stirrings of atmospheric sensation as a reason to elevate the sonic as the central paradigm of the atmospheric as such. But it is notable that, at least in the two examples discussed, the sonic already comprises cross-modal sensory characteristics that correspond to the holistic taking hold of felt-bodies through atmospheres in a more straightforward and extensive manner than lighting appears to do. As such, the sonic's intimate relationship with felt-bodily suggestions of movement as the central mechanism of atmospheric world making gives it a particular place in the study of atmospheres.

6

Structured Movement
as Aisthetic Labor

Atmospheric knowledge, as we have explored it in this book, is irreducibly multi-sensory and multimodal. In this chapter we continue this line of analysis through the medium of dance or, more broadly speaking, practices of structured movement. It is our contention that such bodily practices of movement can make and actualize atmospheric knowledge. We shift our ethnographic focus back to the Western Pacific, especially to Palau, where traditional "dance"—Palauans mostly use no overall generic category of dance, only of particular named genres considered to be inherited from the gods or the ancestors—plays precisely such roles. Therefore, in this chapter, we again position a phenomenological analytic of atmospheres in dialogue with Indigenous Western Pacific epistemologies. Striking similarities and overlaps between a phenomenologically inspired analytic of atmospheric knowledge and of these Pacific traditions that long predate phenomenology and its insights emerge in the process. Pacific traditions of structured body movement, we argue, can be understood as the aisthetic labor of atmospheric knowledge.

For the neophenomenologist Hermann Schmitz, any creative process is by nature a dancing movement: drawing on the felt-body's sensing its motion-laden environment, a motional motive grows into a gestalt. This gestalt in turn literally takes form as it transitions from abstract inspiration into a visible, audible, or palpable medium. The process in which a creative impetus becomes manifest—as a gesture, a music performance, or a piece of art—therefore is at heart a motor practice. This is why any piece of fine art, for Schmitz, is "dance solidified into fixed form" (1966, 77). With this Schmitz suggests that dancing is a motional phenomenon located in primary proximity to any aisthetic comprehension of the world we live in; it is felt-bodily communion with the tempo-spaciousness surrounding us.

In this chapter we critically reflect on this conceptualization of dance, because it has far-reaching implications vis-à-vis human being-in-the-world. Specifically, it invites inquiry into the relationship between felt-bodily sensing and cultural qualification. Expanding on Gernot Böhme's notion of aisthetic labor and Hermann Schmitz's suggestions of motion, we understand structured movement as a practice of dwelling on the threshold: it sounds out the interfaces of felt-bodily sensing with specific performance conventions and of diffuse meaningfulness with cultural qualification. On a conceptual level, dance allows us to think of atmospheres together with the cultural frameworks within which they unfold their efficacy. Our argument springs from a consideration of traditional dance practices in the Western Pacific Island world, which we suggest invites thinking phenomenology through dance rather than dance through phenomenology.

Owing to the nature of what he terms "suggestions of motion" *(Bewegungssuggestionen)*, Hermann Schmitz casts any and all creative processes as dancing movements by nature: "The felt-body, not the artist's mind, receives the inspiration: In the felt-body's perception, a mentally or emotionally conceived motif grows from suggestions of motion to the *gestalt* in which it can then, as it transitions into a visible, audible or tactile medium, literally or metaphorically see the light of the day. *Thus, an artwork is an objectified gesture inspired by felt-bodily sensing, a dance coagulated into fixed form*" (1966, 77; italics in original).[1] Where artistic creativity transforms from inspirational spark into manifestation, the felt-body draws on its ability to sense its motion-laden environment, he argues. The felt-body, which, recalling Maurice Merleau-Ponty's reflections of the chiastic quality of the body as simultaneously perceiving and perceptible, is also the feeling body, sounds out the complex stream of parareflective sensory information it finds itself thrown into, and a motional motive grows into a gestalt ([1964] 1968, 148, 248; see also Schmitz, Müllan, and Slaby 2011). This gestalt, then, literally takes form as it transitions from abstract inspiration into a visible, audible, or palpable medium. The process in which a creative impetus becomes manifest—as a gesture, a music performance, or a piece of art—therefore is at heart a motor practice. As such, it is intimately tied to the felt-body. This is why for Schmitz, a piece of art is in essence suggestions of motion that, sensed by the felt-body, have manifested into an objectified gestalt. In the course of this process, human felt-bodily experience translates into an unfolding of gestalten *(Gestaltverlauf)*. Specific gestalten tend to merge with specific kinds of suggestions of motion; otherwise, a *Gestaltverlauf* would be arbitrary (Schmitz 1966, 77).[2]

Schmitz hereby suggests that dancing is a motional phenomenon located in primary proximity to any aisthetic comprehension of the world we live in. It is felt-bodily interaction with the tempo-spaciousness surrounding us and with the holistic meaningfulness present in our felt-bodily surroundings. Schmitz's suggestions of motion are a type of kinetic atmospheric energy that feeds into the rhythm of individuals' vital drive, thus impacting them in their entire being. As Schmitz positions suggestions of motion as the heartbeat of vitality in a general sense, his philosophy should be intuitive to choreomusicologists, and it already has been to dance therapists in particular (Schwarz 2015; Willke 2020). It resonates well with key ideas in the philosophy of dance, ranging from Friedrich Nietzsche (e.g., 1883, 54) to Rudolf von Laban (e.g., 1920, 14). Yet, as felt-bodily holisms, Schmitz's suggestions of motion fail to address an analytical category that is fundamental to any structured movement activity: the cultural distinctiveness of performance conventions without which, paradoxically, a specific dance movement's meaningfulness will forever remain out of reach. The Schmitzian notion of suggestions of motion therefore invites inquiry into the continuum between felt-bodily sensing and cultural qualification.

In this chapter we follow this invitation by making a foray into dance as a threshold practice in the sense of the continuum that strategically links felt-bodily sensing with specific structured movement conventions and diffuse meaningfulness with cultural qualification. We are, then, not interested primarily in a choreomusical analysis of structured movement activity that seeks to analyze choreographic structure alongside connotative semantic content (Jordan 2007, 29; see also Stepputat and Seye 2020). Rather, following up on Schmitz's notion of the motor quality of all creative movement, we inquire into configurations of structured movement as a distinctly kinaesthetic type of aisthetic labor in Gernot Böhme's sense.

To scholars in the study of Pacific Island performing arts, the insight that the movement dimension of activities or activity systems often referred to as "dance" in a northern Atlantic context systematically works across several distinct layers, thus bringing divergent levels of meaningfulness in conversation with one another, is not new at all (Kaeppler 1995, 41). In her work on Hawaiian hula, Adrienne Kaeppler has emphasized the importance of the processuality behind the emergence of such complex meaningfulness in performance, underlining how "often, the process of performing is as important as the cultural form produced" (1995, 32). Scholars working in other areas of Oceania second this appraisal (e.g., Nero 1992). In keeping with Oceanic notions of deep meaning versus surface meaning, also relevant across the entire region (e.g., Diaz 2011), she describes how movement motifs may depict specific animate beings (such as flowers or animals) or inanimate things (such as objects) but at the same time also refer to "veiled or hidden meanings, making reference to genealogical lines, chiefs, and their deeds and thus enhancing the texts" (Kaeppler 1995, 33). This leads her to distinguish between the "visible," or the actual performance, and the "invisible," or the "aesthetic system" by which specific movements are engendered with meaningfulness: "Only if one knows the social and cultural background will the visible and the invisible emerge in all their dimensions to reveal the political acumen of the creator or . . . the reinterpreter. The resulting products were passed from generation to generation to become chronicles of history and social relationships objectified in verbal and visual forms" (39).

A key to understanding hula is *kaona*, a Kānaka Maoli (native Hawaiian) concept embracing the idea of the "hidden meaning" and significatory stratification inherent in both language and cultural practices. Only with a deep understanding of *kaona*, Kaeppler argues, a performance's meaningfulness "becomes visible as a product of human action and interaction in the context of a socially constructed movement system. The system itself is invisible, existing in the minds of people as movement motifs, specific choreographies, and meaningful imagery" (1995, 42). Kaeppler's interpretation is reminiscent of Schmitz's distinction between suggestions of motion as an invisible kinetic impetus and motional sensory energy bursting with meaningfulness on the one hand and their manifestation as physical movement or a piece of art as "dance having taken shape" on the other. In several ways, however, Kaeppler and Schmitz are coming from opposite directions. Kaeppler's interest is on the culturally specific manifestations in structured movement of the "invisible system," and Schmitz is interested primarily in the holistic experientiality through which felt-bodily sensing affects human being-in-the-world.

Our own interest in this contribution is piqued by what one could refer to as the missing link between the two perspectives. By taking a step back and looking at the upstream qualities (Eisenlohr 2018, 97) of aisthetic labor, we extend the well-established viewpoint that the human body is a "moving agent in a spatially organized world of meanings" (Farnell 1995, 7), suggesting that to engage in structured movement activity is to go beyond dimensionally anchored meaning. We argue that to partake in structured movement is to take a plunge into the chaotic and messy intensity of what Schmitz calls "surfaceless space" (2016, 83) and to navigate its complexity to then dwell on the threshold between the surfaceless space from which creative energy emerges, the directional space in which felt-bodies incorporate creative energy along culturally qualified conventions, and the directional space in which the now-transduced energetic flow takes shape as kinetic movement. This is what we mean when we refer to structured movement activity as a threshold practice. Framing structured movement activity as a threshold practice, in the following we explore structured movement activity as a specific type of aisthetic labor. The actual "labor" is to manifest meaningfulness into visible structured movement. Regardless of its (in)visibility, however, the holistic meaningfulness energized by the flux of suggestions of motion intervenes into felt-bodily tempo-spatial economies and, as such, is engendered with cultural qualification. Cultural qualification enters the energetic flow of suggestions of motion in directional space, strategically oscillating in the directions of both surfaceless and dimensional space at all times. Cultural qualification, then, is no less a phenomenon of dimensional space than of surfaceless space but also goes beyond both. To take a closer look at structured movement activity at the interfaces of surfaceless and dimensional space, we briefly turn to the *ruk*, the traditional men's dance in Palau, in western Micronesia, exploring the oral history of its origin. In closing we reflect on the conceptual implications for this chapter's central question: What is the aisthetic labor distinct to structured movement?

LABORING AESTHETICALLY
IN STRUCTURED MOVEMENT

Gernot Böhme, the second pivotal figure in neophenomenology next to Schmitz and one generation the latter's junior in terms of his work on atmospheres, contends that aisthetic labor is implicitly or explicitly central to any post-Benjaminian aesthetics. It is "generally conceived of as the production of atmospheres, and as such, ranges from cosmetics to advertisement, from interior and stage design to art in a more specific sense. Autonomous art, in this context, is simply one specific form of aisthetic labor, and even where it is autonomous does it have a social function: to impart, in situations that relieve their participants of their agentivity (such as in museums and exhibitions), familiarity with and exposure to atmospheres" ([1995] 2013, 25).[3]

To labor aesthetically, then, is to invest skill, time, and energy in the emergence of atmosphere as collective feelings poured out in space. Böhme strategically distinguishes between the production and the reception side of aisthetic labor, identifying aisthetic theory as a general theory of the production of atmospheres on the one hand and, from the recipient's perspective, as a theory of perception in an encompassing sense on the other. In context of the latter, "perception is understood as the experience of the presence of people, things, and surroundings" ([1995] 2013, 25).[4] In application-oriented contexts such as architectural design, Böhme's categorical distinction between the dynamics governing the production and reception of atmospheres, respectively, has been useful; in connection with structured movement, however, it is of little analytical value because the "producing" movement artist is always already the "receiving" participant as well. Movement artists do not create an objectifiable atmosphere; they are throughout the process enveloped by the atmosphere their aisthetic labor creates. The atmospheres created by structured movement, through their performative processuality, are characterized by a heightened immediacy of Böhme's "presence of people, things, and surroundings."

This is where we locate structured movement's ability to intensify—Kaeppler (1995, 39), in connection with hula, uses the word "enhance"—the meaningfulness inherent to the complex and ongoing stream suggestions of motion by transducing them into, and manifesting them as, culturally qualified bodily, structured movement. This intensification occurs through a bundling of diverging spatial and temporal modalities of experience (Abels 2020). Any type of bodily movement can experientially bundle such divergent experientialities and, by doing so, produce atmospheric energy. Through structural self-referentiality—Kaeppler's "invisible system"—however, the culturally qualified nature of structured movement can open dance situations up toward their own historicity, thus dynamically positioning a structured movement performance vis-à-vis the situation's tempo-spatial positionality. For the brief duration of the performance or just a moment thereof, this positionality emerges from the aisthetic stream of meaningfulness atmospherically through the aisthetic labor of structured movement. Through this process a performance movement becomes meaningful. It takes cultural conventions of structured movement for Kaeppler's (1995) "deep meaning" to manifest, and it takes deep meaning for cultural conventions of structured movement to self-referentially bundle divergent experiential frames into atmospheric intensity.

In Böhme's aisthetic labor with Schmitz, a key moment of the transductive work that occurs as a gestalt unfolds and manifests as musical motif, structured object, or physical object is the transition of felt-bodily sensed suggestion of motion in surfaceless space to, in one way or another, physical motion in dimensional space. For Schmitz space "is not originally encountered as the measurable, locational space assumed in physics and geography, but rather as a predimensional surfaceless realm manifest to each of us in undistorted corporeal experience, for example in hearing voluminous sounds or sensing atmospheres." Schmitz gives the examples of the resounding of big church bells, the sonic immediacy of which envelop those within hearing range. Another example would be the weather, which "presents surfaceless spaces that are felt immediately in our bodily responsiveness to the atmosphere surrounding us. Crucially, the felt-body itself is a surfaceless space, or more precisely an assemblage of many such spaces: corporeal 'islands' such as the stomach region or the soles of feet are felt as diffuse but still separately identifiable spatial realms" (Schmitz, Müllan, and Slaby 2011, 245). In Schmitz's neophenomenology, surfaceless space is primary; dimensional space, to him, is an abstract construction and a secondary spatial experience. Structured movement activity impacts on surfaceless space in a way that introduces directionality to surfacelessness. In the now-directional space of structured movement activity, suggestions of motion, for instance as exuded by chants and music, can be incorporated felt-bodily and fed into one's own movement practice (Schmitz 1967, 179, 71).

As in structured movement activities, a suggestion of motion enters directional-spatial experience; its motional energy transduces from energetic flow into palpable structured movement. Such transduction intensifies the synesthetic quality of structured movement: that which we know in directional space and that which we felt-bodily sense in surfaceless space enters into correspondence. "Body-spaces of sound and sound-spaces of the body enter into conversation with one another to give rise to new body-sound-spaces," writes Stephanie Schroedter (2012b, 48).[5] Such new body-sound-spaces are always transitory and ephemeral, and we suggest we conceive of them as the threshold of surfaceless, directional, and dimensional space. To dance, then, is to experientially explore and savor a spatial threshold experience and to actively engage with the spatial properties of one's environment. This accounts for the experiential intensity of structured movement.

WEAVING TOGETHER TEMPO-SPATIAL COMPLEXITY BEYOND TIME AND SPACE: PALAUAN *RUK*

If all creative processes are, at heart, motional in nature, then against this backdrop it makes sense for Pacific Indigenous communities to not traditionally have used a category that compares to the notion of dance. *Dance*, in its academic usage, is a distinctly North Atlantic category that sets apart (from daily life activities but also from other types of cultural practices) a specific type of kinaesthetic repertoire, assigning a bounded category to it. In most of Oceania, kinaesthesia is deeply entangled with daily practices, and to think in terms of dance as a distinct category would conflict with lived experience. Kaeppler has suggested the term "structured movement systems" instead (1985, 1995). Structured movement systems, by her definition, include some that are integrally related to music. They are "systems of knowledge, the products of action and interaction, and processes through which action and interaction occur" (1998, 311).

> [They] denote specially marked or elaborated systems of movement . . . that result from creative processes that manipulate human bodies in time and space in such a way that movement is formalized and intensified in much the same manner as poetry intensifies and formalizes language. . . . These specially marked movement systems may be considered art, work, ritual, ceremony, entertainment, or any combination of these. . . . A person may perform the same or a similar sequence of movements (consisting of grammatically structured motifs) as a ritual supplicant, as a political act, as an entertainer, or as a marker of identity. Thus, the same movement sequence may be meant to be decoded differently if performed for gods, . . . for a human audience, or . . . as a participant for fun; and it may be decoded differently depending on an individual's background and understanding of a particular performance and the individual's mental and emotional state at the time. (312)

The Austronesian language spoken in Palau, a small island nation in the westernmost part of Micronesia, has the neologism *dangs*, adopted from the English word *dance*. Generally, however, Palauans discuss specific dance forms by the name of their dance genre (e.g., *ngloik*, *ruk*) rather than a generic category. The actual movements and motion-based gestures are inherited from either the gods or the ancestors. Like elsewhere in Oceania, they therefore "may be perpetuated as cultural artifacts and aesthetic performances, even if their meanings have been changed or forgotten." Importantly, such underlying systems of structured movement themselves are invisible, "existing in the minds of people as movement motifs, specific choreographies, and meaningful imagery" (Kaeppler 1998, 312). But, as the performers move their bodies through time-space, the dance takes shape as visible form. This is, in a tangible manner, reminiscent of Schmitz's archetypical creative process, which transduces motional energy into a visible medium and impacts on the performers' spatial surroundings.

Schmitz's notion of space(s) radically complicates notions of space as established in the North Atlantic philosophical traditions. At the same time, however, it remains indebted to European conceptualizations of space, which make a basic distinction between the spatial and the temporal. Many Oceanic languages, by contrast, know the word *space-time* in one form or another (Salesa 2014, 41), which reflects a conceptualization based on the sense that time, place, and space cannot categorically be distinguished from one another: "The *va* [i.e., space-time in Samoan and Tongan, see Staley 2017] is necessarily relational, implying not a static point of observation but a movement, or possible movement between" (Salesa 2014, 43). More specifically, *vā* perceives of space as points and their inter-relationships rather than a bounded area (see Staley 2017, 52; van der Ryn 2007, 3). Tēvita O. Ka'ili conceives of the Tongan practice of *tauhi vā*, the nurturing of sociospatial relationships, as a cultural practice of establishing and strengthening beautiful relationships. He emphasizes how it is impossible to think of *vā* (space) without *tā* (time), both in Tonga and Hawai'i. In Hawaiian culture "the past is the time in front and the future is the time that comes behind" (2008, quoted in Staley 2017, 53; see also Kame'leihiwa 2009). Ka'ili's thinking is closely related to Tongan historical anthropologist 'Ōkusitino Māhina's *tā-vā* theory of art (see Lear 2018; Māhina 2010). Māhina sees *tā* and *vā* as the common medium of all things natural, mental, and social that exist.

Accordingly, all things unfold in time and space, with nothing whatsoever existing above or beyond this realm. All things in nature, mind, and society have four dimensions: three spatial dimensions (height/depth, width/breadth, length) and one temporal dimension, which is form (see also Staley 2017, 54). Ka'ili explains how *tā-vā* is "collective and communal but . . . also arranged in a circular fashion": "The purpose of ontologically organizing these concepts in a cyclical fashion is to bring multiple entities into harmonious relations with one another. This is made visible in the practice of *tauhi vā*, especially among closely related people in a 'aiga or kin group" (2008, 41; Staley 2017, 55). At the same time, *tauhi vā* underlines the social importance of *tā* and *vā*, which literally mean "beating space": as a cultural practice, *tauhi vā* regulates and maintains social relations between groups by performing reciprocity. The symmetry or asymmetry of such exchange-based relationships leads to either a harmonious relationship or conflict (see Ka'ili 2008, 42). This illustrates the deep entanglement of notions of time-space and sociality.

Oceanic temporalities thus tend to place emphasis on the interlacing of the cultural, the relational, and the spatial with the temporal. While this differs significantly from Schmitz's understanding of space, it does resonate with his acknowledgment that music making and structured movement are spatial practices of the felt-body but at the same time engrained with a fundamental historicity: "[In sound], sound's history often lives on," contends Schmitz (2016, 88).

This is certainly the case for *chelitakl rechuodel*, the traditional repertoire of the performing arts in Palau, Micronesia. In traditional Palauan thinking, space-time is engrained with motion to begin with: "[traditional Palauan] culture unites [the two categories of space and time] through the notion of a journey (*omerael*, from the verb *merael*, 'to walk, to travel,' itself derived from the noun *rael*, 'path, road, way' [PAN **dalan*]). The journey of a god, person, group, or mythological creature provides a basic space-time continuum for conceptualization and discourse" (Parmentier 1987, 134).

Chelitakl rechuodl are not the result of the specifics of Palauan tempo-spatiality; in fact, they are a set of cultural conventions to practice Indigenous time-space that render them experiential in their deep sense. *Deep* here refers to what Kaeppler has called the "invisible system," the complex entanglement of cultural, social, and aesthetic values interlacing with Oceanic spatio-temporality (note here that while surfaceless space is primary to Schmitz, he also refers to it as the "deeper layers" of spatiality [2016, 83]). Importantly, the spiritual world is a fundamental component of Palauan deep time, and Palauan structured movement activities were originally created by *chelids*, the Palauan gods. During the Hamburg South Seas Expedition of 1908–10, Augustin Krämer recorded the following oral history describing the invention of the Palauan *ruk* (men's dance):

[Uchelchelid] is considered the inventor of the *ruk*. It is said that once when he sat on the shore of a Ugél pelú, he saw a *gorovídĕl* [caranx] jumping after a *tebér* sardine. The jumps inspired him so much that he decided to adopt the caranx as a symbol of the dance. In *a* Iraĩ, especially, this is observed, because their god Medegeĩ is a descendent of Ugél'lĕgalíd [Uchelchelid]. In *a* Iraĩ, during the period of seclusion, the dancers have in the bai [men's house], in addition to their *tet* hand baskets, another little basket called *gomsangĕl*. This basket contains the betel quid for the god and is hung on the bai wall behind the back of its owner. In *a* Iraĩ, where several other unusual things occur, the *klemeaĩ* ["locked in," i.e., secluded for the purpose of the *ruk* preparation] people engage in something special. Everyone from [a specific house] makes thread *(ker'rĕl)* and weaves a net with a particular mesh size; even the *uriúl* members [i.e., the ones of lower rank in the social hierarchy] take part. All of the nets are then tied together, resulting in a long net, which is spread out over the water on the Megórei stone wharf . . . , as a soul-catching net for the protective deities, the 7 Galid [Gods], the Tekíĕl maláp [man-eating devils]. . . . These special practices apply only to *a* Iraĩ and Ngátpang, however, which are the villages of Medegeĩ pélau [a specific *chelid*]. . . . After all of these activities, the day of coming out begins in earnest.

In the morning, the village women go to the village bai and rub turmeric on the *klemeaĩ*. Each of them puts on a women's skirt. In this state, the men now advance in a festive procession toward the ocean, holding the wooden *gorovídĕl* in their raised right hands. At the edge of the path, at some distance, lies a tridacna clam shell filled with water. The leader dips the head of his dance rod figure into this, an act known as *omárĕg ra gorovídĕl* "the dipping of the caranx." After this, the group returns to the bai in silence, where the women perform their dances on the stage. Now has come the time for the dancers to show what they have learned while being sequestered. First, they do *klemeaî* a little dance and then return to their bai. it is not until the afternoon that the great dance *gorovídĕl* is performed; it is followed by the *kotebádĕl*, the other clubs. (KETC 2017, 295; for the German original see Krämer 1926, 315)

The *ruk*'s choreography is predetermined by the ancestors (Palau Society of Historians 2002, 8); the actual dance, of divine origin, and the actual performance of a *ruk* calls on the deities and ancestor spirits to an extent that determines the structure of the months-long seclusion period prior to the performance of a grand *ruk*. Ritual objects manifest and further consolidate this link into the spiritual realm, rendering the presence of spirits felt. To perform the *ruk* following the ritual observance of the traditional *klemeaî*, then, is not only to dwell on the threshold of surfaceless, directional, and dimensional space. It is also to commune with spiritual beings in the here and now and to dissolve the boundary between what is past and what is present while performing in the present, along linear time structures. The *ruk* makes this possible by creating a performance space in which the performers can kinaesthetically listen (Schroedter 2012b, 2018; Brandstetter 2012, 114, 123) and, in Schmitzian terms, act on suggestions of motion. Through its genre conventions, it also provides a set of cultural strategies for both the performers and the audience to navigate the wealth of suggestions of motion it creates space for. These strategies are based on structured movement's ability to guide the felt-body in bundling suggestions of motion and transduce them into an encompassing sensation of meaningfulness.

CONCLUSION

The dancing felt-body's aisthetic labor is based on its kinaesthetic awareness (Brandstetter 2012). As in our discussion of the multisensorial character of atmospheric knowledge in chapter 5, kinaesthetic listening emerges as a participatory, multimodal practice of attunement to motional energy. In this way attuned to motional energy, structured movement activity in Palau can be cast as a cultural strategy to intensify, through the felt-body's sensibilities, the sensation of human interconnectedness with everything and everyone around—in an ontological and epistemological but also a social, cultural, historical, and tempo-spatial sense. As the dancing felt-body bundles and condenses atmospheric suggestions of motion through bodily movement, these suggestions of motion connect the *ruk* performers both with the aisthetic stream of sensory perception and with those beings and things that share the same space.

Expanding on Schmitz, we see that cultural techniques of the felt-body such as structured movement are strategies to interact with and intensify the holistic meaningfulness present in our felt-bodily surroundings. In doing so they significantly alter surrounding spatial economies, giving rise to the emergence of new suggestions of motion and changing extant ones. It is of central importance to note here that structured movement activities do not change space as a dimension external to the felt-body; the space of structured movement is by nature space-as-felt-bodily-connection. Against this background, then, it is no coincidence that Schmitz's conception of dance reflects almost literally in the reflections of one of the seminal figures of expressionist dance, Mary Wigman (1886–1973), who in 1922 described the ballet dancer's sensation as she does a *piqué tour* as one of becoming one with "all the oscillating celestial bodies" and of "communion with space" (1922, 864–65) or in Japanese *butoh* performer Min Tanaka's statement that "when I dance, I don't dance in the place, but I am the place" (qtd. in Grant 2013, 14).[6]

Böhme, in recourse to Baumgarten, seeks to emphasize the ultimately epistemological nature of sensory perception and, as such, aisthetic labor (Fahl 2016, 14). According to Schmitz, such knowing emerges as the unfolding of *Gestalten*, which manifests in one palpable form after another. Wigman's "communion with space," for Schmitz, would be a natural effect of dance ecstasy: "ecstatic dance completes itself as an intoxication [Rausch] in which the present and the self . . . are surrendered to an unmeasurable expanse" (1967, 173).[7] In her very own words, Wigman describes quite vividly the unfolding of *Gestalten* in this process: "A [sense of] knowing flashes up in her. The wide, invisible, transparent space extends in formless waves, a lifting of the arm will change it. Ornaments emerge, massive, big, disappear again; delicate arabesques dance past, subside; a jump, right in; forms burst, with an evil fizzle; a fast spin; the walls give way. She drops her arms, standing still again, looks into the empty room: the dancer's realm" (1922).[8]

Structured movement activity, then, is intense aisthetic labor. The multimodal dynamics of structured movement allow for the "sensation of dropping through space" (Brandstetter 2012, 118); space in turn is filled with suggestions of motion and shared feelings. To drop through space with structured movement, then, is to surrender to the tempo-spaciousness surrounding oneself; to feel out for the otherwise ineffable holisms of lived experience is the aisthetic labor of kinaesthesia.

Latency as the Temporality of Atmospheres

Atmospheric theory in the tradition of phenomenology dates back to the 1960s, and atmosphere as a concept has long spread from philosophy to a broad range of other academic fields. Nevertheless, there has been a curious lack of sustained analysis of atmospheres' temporality, even though a certain temporality is central to the way they function. In this chapter we propose that latency is this kind of temporality. Latency is proper to the mechanism through which atmospheres seize bodies and make themselves felt, which is suggestions of motion. However, far more than remaining just an internal property of atmospheres, latency is also foundational for the different kinds of atmospheric knowledge we explore in this book. For example, the temporal category of latency thereby becomes highly consequential for all those public and political phenomena in which atmospheres play central roles. Namely, there has long been interest in the links between regimes of time and inclusion or participation in a body politic. Well-known examples are Walter Benjamin's (1968) connection between "messianic time" and political revolution and redemption, and the link Benedict Anderson (1991), building on Benjamin, draws between modern nationhood and a linear, "empty, homogenous" time. Scholars have also sought to connect particular dominant forms of temporality to late capitalism (Jameson 2003; Guyer 2007). If, since Benjamin, there has been a rich tradition of writing on the links between temporality and political community and belonging and if it has long been clear that a full understanding of contemporary politics needs to have the latter's felt aspects at its center, the temporalities of atmospheres appear to be highly significant.

It is not coincidental that our exploration of the temporality of atmospheres unfolds through returning to our discussion in chapter 4, taking up again Twelver

Shi'i Muslims' struggle for a right to the city in Mumbai, most notably through Muharram processions and their mediatizations. We in particular focus on the role of videos of these processions, including the atmospheric dimensions of this instance of digital religion. As we lay out, Twelver Shi'i cosmology, historical memory, and ritual practice have long revolved around notions of latency. At the same time, the articulation of such claims to the city through Twelver Shi'i public ritual and processions foregrounds aesthetic, performative, and felt dimensions of political belonging, which, as we have argued in chapter 4, may be taken as a form of atmospheric citizenship. Furthermore, interconnections between temporalities and modes of inclusion or belonging can be characterized by the occult, the hidden, and the unknown. These often reappear in surprising ways, defying and exceeding the kind of agentive juggling of multiple temporalities that has emerged as an important theme in, for example, recent anthropological writings on time (Bear 2014; Ringel 2016). In Twelver Shi'i Muslims' struggles for inclusion and belonging in the Indian megacity Mumbai, these frequently obscured connections articulate in particular atmospheres as vaguely qualified but intense feelings of belonging, as well as in the technical functioning of media that simultaneously circulate acts of ritual devotion as well as claims to the city. The temporal figure of latency is useful to make sense of the spectral temporality of Twelver Shi'i ritual and media practices that articulate such claims through public performance and aisthesis. Latency points at the hidden and obscure dimensions of the link between forms of time and political belonging.

On the morning of the tenth of Muharram, Patrick was walking with Jafar and his son-in-law along the stalls set up in the Mumbai neighborhood of Dongri by numerous *matami anjuman*, smaller Twelver Shi'i associations for organizing ritual commemorative activities in the month of Muharram, pushing through crowds overwhelmingly dressed in black as a sign of mourning.[1] The names of these associations often referred to localities in Uttar Pradesh and Bihar as the original home *(vatan)* of Twelver Shi'i migrant families who have settled in Mumbai since independence. Jafar is a middle-aged Twelver Shi'i businessman from a suburb of the city, while Baqer, his son-in-law, is an aspiring maulana who had returned from studies in a *hauwza* (seminar for training Shi'i 'ulema) in Qom, Iran. We were passing several *sabil*, water dispensers that are a reminder of the terrible thirst that the pious victims of the Battle of Karbala had to suffer, having been cut off by their enemies from access to the Euphrates River. We also passed a particularly richly decorated tazia, next to which a large amount of incense was burning, with passersby fanning the smoke to their faces while touching their foreheads. They also touched the banners as well as shrouds draped on the tall battle standards *(alam)* with signs of the family of the Prophet on them that are, along with tazia, among the main ritual objects to be carried in the processions later in the day as reminders of the Battle of Karbala and as indices of the lingering presence of the members of the family of the Prophet who lost their lives in this battle long ago (Ruffle 2017). We could see and hear long razor blades held to grindstones, anticipating their uses in bloody acts of self-flagellation later in the afternoon.

A team with a TV camera from Haq Channel, a Shia television and video producer broadcasting nationwide, was also on the scene, as *niyaz* (food items and dishes distributed in the month of Muharram), from cookies to *khichra* (a stew of goat meat and lentils) with roti, was served from the stalls or directly from vans and small trucks. Some stalls also kept blue containers and bottles of rose water (*gulab pani*) ready for the procession, to be sprayed on the wounds of the flagellants. Several stalls had screens on display with sermons by Shi'i 'ulema, as well as *azadari* videos of the performance of mourning rituals, while some of the younger men would start filming the surroundings with their cellphones as the procession got into motion and a certain mood, a particular mixture of excitement and mournfulness, wrapped the streets.

Baqer and Patrick were talking about the ever-growing number of Shi'i websites and video channels, and Baqer said, "They are so important. The enemies of the Shia make use of them, and we have to be there too. We have to explain what we do and why," pointing at the procession as an example. Abbas, an elderly relative walking with us, agreed, saying, "Yes, there are two Islams in the world; one is truth, the other *duplicate*" (using the English term). Baqer was palpably embarrassed at this crass sectarian judgment of his relative, likening Sunni Islam to a cheap, inauthentic copy of the real thing.[2] The figure of the duplicate is good when thinking about Shi'i media. It points at Indian mediascapes and urban infrastructures in which informality and piracy play such large roles, also undergirding religious media such as azadari videos showing mournful Shi'i ritual commemoration of the events of the Battle of Karbala (Sundaram 2009). *Azadari* is a cover term for the highly expressive, often dramatic practices of Twelver Shi'i ritual mourning in honor of the victims of the Battle of Karbala (Hyder 2006, 9). At the same time, the figure of the duplicate points at struggles in a contested religious tradition, in which religious media such as azadari videos feature prominently in the shaping of ethical selves. In its Mumbai context, such shaping of ethical selves is also intertwined with questions of citizenship and the right to the city and perhaps no more so than in its mediatic aspects (Lefebvre 1968).

Conventional citizenship discourse in India has a built-in tendency to marginalize Muslims. At the same time, intra-Islamic sectarianism has been on the rise in recent decades, posing a special challenge for groups like Twelver Shi'i Muslims, who inhabit the disadvantageous position of a minority within a marginalized minority. In the highly diverse urban context of Mumbai, a city long notorious for contests over housing and conflictual sharing of urban space that often has

FIGURE 7. Muharram in Dongri. The Mughal Masjid is in the background on the right. Photo by Patrick Eisenlohr.

FIGURE 8. Preparing an *alam* in the courtyard of the Mughal Masjid on Ashura. Photo by Patrick Eisenlohr.

communal connotations, Twelver Shiʿis have long participated in the locally established tradition of staging religious processions as a way to claim a right to the city. Like other public ritual performances, the Twelver Shiʿi processions in the month of Muharram articulate such a right not through deliberative discourse and argument but through aisthesis, sensorially investing neighborhoods or particular locales with a certain Shiʿi feel. My Shiʿi interlocutors in Mumbai often used the term *mahaul*, which in Urdu translates as "mood" or "atmosphere," when speaking about such felt qualities of neighborhoods. The undeniable facticity of such a somatically felt atmosphere in its phenomenological sense of a spatially extended emotion transgresses the boundaries of conventional citizenship discourse. It is therefore especially relevant for the marginalized when they claim particular places as belonging to them.

Atmospheres can be understood as energetic forces that fill spaces and intermingle with felt-bodies, in the process blurring the boundaries between subjects, and subjects and their nonhuman environments. Through suggestions of motion they exert on felt-bodies, they generate an intermingling between bodies and their environments that invest situations with a diffuse and holistic feel. The manifestations of public religion with their performative and ritual dimensions and their powerful sensorial presence discussed here are rather salient generators of atmospheres in the phenomenological sense. Atmospheres thus understood are not unconscious phenomena but often linger in an oblique state of ambient half-awareness, underlying a situation in ways that are hard to pinpoint through language. They can invest spaces with a diffuse and powerful feel that in turn has implications for who that kind of space belongs to. In a dense and conflictual urban setting such as Mumbai, atmospheres as "emotions that are poured out spatially" have obvious implications for questions of belonging in ways that bypass and undercut established discourses of citizenship (Schmitz, Müllan, and Slaby 2011, 255).

Such felt aspects of belonging with their related claims on the city through aisthestis and performance also hinge on a distinctive time of their own. The temporal figure of latency is one of the chief features of such atmospheric forms of citizenship and their power. At the same time, the temporal mode of latency is also helpful to think about the mediatizations of the processions or other ritual performances that Twelver Shiʿi religious life and Shiʿi claims to the city are thoroughly enmeshed with. One useful way to define latency is "acutely given non-presence," a hidden force or phenomenon that is neither present nor absent (Khurana 2007, 143).[3] As in the encounter with the preparations and start of the Ashura procession together with Jafar and Baqer, a particular mood and atmosphere was already obliquely present in the locality before we became fully aware of it, that is, it was in a latent state before becoming fully actual.

This particular kind of latency of atmospheres as underlying phenomena already there in occultation before appearing to us is a more general condition of atmosphere and central to its operation in several ways. Nevertheless, latency as the modus operandi of atmospheres, along with the kinds of claims and forms of belonging the spreading of atmospheres enables, resonates with the Muharram processions and their mediatizations in a particular way. This is because of its interaction with the kinds of latency built into Twelver Shi'i cosmology and ritual life. Moreover, the atmospheric right to the city through ritual performance and aisthesis is also intertwined with its media-related aspects. In the process the atmospheres generated by the Muharram processions in Mumbai combine with latency as a hardwired mode of temporality in the technical functioning of audiovisual media. Thus the ethnographic setting features a combination of mutually reinforcing latencies, inhabiting the atmospheric, the religious, and the mediatic. We therefore take the temporal figure of latency as the key to understanding how the production of felt aspects of belonging to the city as articulated by Mumbai Twelver Shi'i Muslims unfolds. Latency is the common thread bringing together the power of atmospheres, Twelver Shi'i ritual life, and related media practices in their urban setting.

MUHARRAM PROCESSIONS AND THEIR MEDIATIZATIONS

In the late nineteenth century, the Muharram processions were the largest public religious event in Bombay/Mumbai, before they were eclipsed by the Ganapati processions at the turn to the twentieth century in the context of rising Hindu nationalist mobilization (R. Kaur 2003). The city has a long history of claims to it through huge public religious performances, along ethnoreligious lines.[4] For Twelver Shi'is as a subgroup within the largely marginalized Muslim minority of Mumbai, the processions and other public azadari rituals are a central part of their ethical life, and the sponsorship and organization of the ritual events are also central to Mumbai Twelver Shi'i social life and provide occasions for contests over prestige and leadership. Moreover, as a largely marginalized group who inhabits a tensely shared urban landscape together with Sunni Muslims and Hindus even in those few areas where they have a dominant presence, there is also a lot at stake in claiming a right to the city through public performance. In a context where citizenship discourse and normal social boundaries put Twelver Shi'is at a severe disadvantage, these processions articulate such a right to the city in primarily nondiscursive and sensory ways that, operating at a level of somatic facticity, are often immune to discursive critique.[5] Forms of public religion such as the processions in memory of the martyrs of Karbala in the Islamic month of Muharram address the felt aspects of belonging by emitting atmospheres that intermingle with felt-bodies, stirring them through suggestions of motion. The result are vague but powerful emotions filling urban neighborhoods such as Dongri that seize bodies and invest them with somatic senses of place and belonging that in turn can be further discursively qualified as "Shia."

In recent years videos of such performances have been recorded and shared to the point that the recording and circulating of azadari videos has become commonplace among many Mumbai Twelver Shi'is. Their recording and sharing are an integral, if not banal, part of such religious activities, where participants can be seen recording on their mobile devices and often share them instantly. As mentioned, these videos of ritual mourning practices often make reference to the events of the Battle of Karbala. The tragic event is annually commemorated in public processions, even sometimes involving restaging of the battle, the performance of ritual oratory and poetic genres of lamentation, and dramatic acts of expressing grief and pain, such as in bloody self-flagellation with sharp implements (Halder 2022; Korom 2002; Schubel 1993). Azadari videos certainly testify to the much-discussed mutual imbrication of religion and media, as well as to the centrality of religion to public spheres (Meyer and Moors 2006; Stolow 2005). Until a few years ago they were still primarily distributed on VCDs, or less commonly on DVDs, sold mainly in Shi'i-owned electronic and media stores or stalls. The circulation of this genre of audiovisual media also vividly illustrate the themes of informality and piracy that have become a salient theme in South Asian media studies. Twelver Shi'is who make, circulate, and watch these videos for the most part do not treat informality and piracy as issues that need to be problematized. This is because informal distribution and unofficial copying of azadari videos are considered to have religious merit and be consonant with these videos' main uses, which revolve around shaping ethical selves through witnessing the tragedy of Karbala (Cooper 2022; Fa 2024). Seen against the light of a burgeoning literature on media, religion, and ethical self-cultivation, especially in Islamic contexts, this role of azadari videos in ethical self-fashioning is relatively unsurprising (Hirschkind 2006; Schulz 2012).

In this chapter, however, we are concerned with the role of such videos in an atmospheric right to the city. Extending the analysis of atmospheric citizenship to azadari videos, we ask how the felt and primarily nondiscursive aspects of place making and belonging that are so much in evidence in the Mumbai Muharram processions also owe their force to the circulation of these videos. The temporal mode of latency is in turn central to such mediatized performances and their felt aspects. Latency is a particularly useful notion for the analysis of Twelver Shi'i media and their attendant practices, because it underlies much of Twelver Shi'i cosmology and ritual life. At the same time, latency is also a feature of their mediatic reproductions. Latency features on multiple levels of the kind of performative generation of place and belonging beyond law and discourse that such public religious events and their interlocking media practices revolve around. In what follows we discuss three kinds of latency that cut across atmospheres, Shi'i ritual life, and media practices and that impinge on the felt aspects of belonging and place making among Twelver Shi'is in Mumbai that are so crucially important for them as a marginalized group in the city.

FIGURE 9. Still from an azadari video, showing a crowd of Muslim devotees engaged in a Shiʿi ritual reenacting the tragic events of the Battle of Karbala. From "Year 2017 Ashura in Mumbai," YouTube.

FIGURE 10. Hoisting an *alam*. Photo by Patrick Eisenlohr.

The first kind of latency relates to the question of why and how atmospheric citizenship and its spreading of a felt quality of Shia-ness endure after the performances' atmospheres with their energetic, spatial, and sensory dimensions are gone. The mediatic circulation and reproduction of images and sounds that the azadari videos enable supports this latent state of the performances' atmospheres. They do so by operationalizing a kind of latency that is part of the technical functioning of media reproduction of sounds and images and that in turn bears close resemblance to Benjamin's messianic time. Second, and building on the theme of the messianic, latency as a messianic figure is not a part of Twelver Shiʻi religious and political life just because of the expectation of the hidden twelfth Shiʻi Imam's redemptive reappearance from occultation at the end of times. Latency is also central to Twelver Shiʻi religious and political life because of what scholars of Shiʻism have long called the "Karbala paradigm," a flexible frame to come to terms with conflict and struggle potentially anytime and anyplace, a frame that generally highlights the trauma and tragedy of Karbala but that can also accommodate utopian elements. Latency and utopia are intimately linked because utopia points to premonitions, to feelings of what is not yet there but about to manifest: "The utopia is the place where the not-yet-conscious makes its appearance" (Bloch 1968, 281).[6]

This aspect of potentially limitless transposability of Karbala as a partially utopian paradigm is in turn further amplified through mediatic circulation. Third, latency is a key quality of the kind of atmospheres that produce the somatic forms of belonging and the felt notions of place at play in these Twelver Shiʻi public performances and their mediatizations. This is because atmospheres can be perceived as manifest events and holistic sensory impressions by felt-bodies but also operate through latent, incipient phenomena such as, according to phenomenologist of atmospheres Hermann Schmitz, suggestions of motion in distinction from manifestly carried-out bodily motion. The former is actually responsible for the vague but powerful diffuse meaningfulness of atmospheres that stops short of discursively qualified notions such as "Shia" or "full Indian citizenship." Let us take up these three kinds of latency in the order in which we have mentioned them.

THE LATENCY OF RITUAL PRESENCE
AND ITS MEDIATIC REINFORCEMENT

First, latency underlies the periodic recurrence of the commemorative events and performances in the month of Muharram. These follow a ritual calendar, culminating on the tenth of that month *(ashura)*, the anniversary of the tragic battle. Even though ostensibly absent most of the year, the specter of the events in Shiʻi neighborhoods of Mumbai obliquely lingers on, ready to be reactivated in the future. The cyclicity of the time of this festive commemoration is also reinforced by the fact that, for some Twelver Shiʻis, the processions feature as a surrogate pilgrimage, thereby pointing to the ritual calendar that also shapes pilgrimages of not only South Asian Twelver Shiʿi but also of Shiʿi from all over the world to sacred shrines in Iraq, including in Karbala, and in Iran and Syria. The memory and future expectation of the public rituals' sounds, movements, and spectacular sights is readily available to those who have been exposed to them and to those living in the area in a way that results in a continued presence in absence. Seen from this perspective, latency is a built-in feature of cyclical ritual time and has the effect of permanently establishing a sense of presence of the ritual events and the people performing them even when the events are not actually occurring.

Media practices are integral to Shiʿi ritual events in the month of Muharram, and these add another layer of latency to the ritual events, a kind of latency embedded in technologies of reproducing sound and images. As a salient example of the nexus between religion and media, Shiʿi participants make video recordings of the spectacular commemorative performances, especially the processions that also comprise a restaging of the tragic events of the Battle of Karbala. As already mentioned in chapter 4, there is even an activist-oriented Shiʿi media center in the neighborhood of Dongri, World Islamic Network, which operates a cable and satellite television channel with Shiʿi themes, producing news programs, quiz shows, and question-and-answer shows with religious authorities answering questions posed by viewers live on air or sent by email or social media (Eisenlohr 2015a, 2017; Mirza 2014). It also produces, broadcasts, and its website circulates recordings of devotional events such as the large Muharram processions in Mumbai. These recordings are also shared on social media, where they are frequently commented on. The processes of storing and reproducing images and sounds that audiovisual media technologies revolve around can be understood as a hardwired form of latency or acutely given nonpresence (Volmar and Stine 2021). Recorded images and sounds are not simply past; they can be reactivated through technical reproduction at any time, directly undercutting their classification as *past* on the sensory level. While there is often an enduring difference in kind between representative images and the embodied events they represent, such a difference does not apply to reproduced sound. There is no difference in kind between original sounds that are recorded and their technical reproductions; both are the same kind of acoustic events or occurrences of traveling kinetic energy of not strictly identical but similar characteristics. Reproduced sounds can thus be understood as *gleichursprünglich*, or "equally original" (Ernst 2012). On the level of sensory perception, these ostensibly past sounds are quite simply and undeniably present, a presence that can irrupt into linear time understood as an irreversible succession of events. The specifically mediatic latency proper to reproduced images and sounds of the ritual events then further contributes to and reinforces the centrality of latency as the temporality of the Karbala complex and its rituals.

We find it useful to think about these overlapping modes of latency through the lens of Walter Benjamin's "messianic time." With this Benjamin meant a suspension of linear time with its distinctions of past, present, and future to "make the continuum of history explode," overturning established politics and opening the possibility for revolutionary transformation. This radically expanded, nonchronological "now" irrupts into "empty, homogenous time" (1968, 261). Like the expected return of the Messiah at any moment, this time stands for a radical form of latency "for every second of time was the strait gate through which the Messiah might enter" (264). Such collapsing of linear time yields a "conception of the present as the 'time of the now' *(Jetztzeit)* shot through with chips of messianic time" (263). Benjamin's messianic time is useful to think about the multiple layers of latency that the ritual commemoration of Karbala and its mediatizations build on. The regularly recurring dramatic ritual commemorations of the long-past tragedy make it irrupt into presence again, even involving restagings and reenactments of the particular events and actions of the battle.

The notion of messianic time also describes the functioning of media technology as a technical operationalization of latency and, by extension, messianic time. Like Benjamin's *Jetztzeit*, stored and reproduced sounds and images from the past are in occlusion but can emerge into full presence at any time, sensorially undercutting the linear flow of time. Finally, because of the strong messianic element in Shiʻi eschatology and cosmology, this notion of time as messianic resonates with the commemoration of Karbala and Shiʻi traditions in a particular way. As mentioned, this is because Twelver Shiʻism is also based on the expectation of the return as a savior of the twelfth, last imam at the end of times (hence the name of the tradition), who entered occultation in the ninth Christian century. More broadly, these aspects of Twelver Shiʻism, which differ from both Christian and Jewish notions of the messianic insofar as the hidden imam remains copresent with humanity, along with the proximity of Benjamin's messianic time to the Karbala rituals, highlight that these ritual forms are not just cyclical repetitions. They also produce a generative remainder, pointing to the irruption of the new and unforeseen that is bound up with latency as a temporal category. This latter aspect of latency is also central to the following kind of latency we discuss, which is proper to Karbala as a paradigm.

THE LATENCY OF THE KARBALA PARADIGM

Second, in Twelver Shiʻi history and everyday life, the tragic events of Karbala have long functioned as a highly emotionally charged template for interpreting political events, oppression, deprivation, and suffering of many kinds. As mentioned before, this transposable frame is also known as the "Karbala paradigm," a way of approaching and reacting to different political and social conditions and perceived injustices (M. Fischer 1980). For example, many supporters of the Iranian Revolution of 1978–79 drew on the memory of Karbala: they saw themselves in the footsteps of Hussain, confronting a powerful oppressor, the shah of Iran, whom they identified with Yazid I (646 to 683 CE), the Umayyad caliph whose army had won the Battle of Karbala, killing Hussain and other members of the house of the Prophet. Like Hussain, they were weaker than the mighty tyrant, but many supporters of the revolution were willing to die for their cause, in the end toppling a dictator who commanded a strong military and security apparatus. Immediately after the Iranian Revolution, the Islamic Republic of Iran mobilized the Karbala paradigm in a massive way in its fight against Saddam Hussain's invading army in the bloody 1980–88 Iran-Iraq War. Hezbollah in Lebanon drew on the memory of Karbala in its guerilla war against the Israeli army, while the Iranian supporters of the failed 2009 "green revolution" against the government of the Islamic Republic of Iran again drew on the memory of Karbala in their protests (M. Fischer 2010).

In India some strands of the anticolonial movement also drew on Karbala for inspiration, the Karbala event and narrative being widely known across religious lines among the Indian public (Hyder 2006). Several of Patrick's Shi'i interlocutors in Mumbai were convinced that Gandhi's satyagraha campaigns as well as his anticolonial resistance in general were inspired by Hussain's example at Karbala; in fact, this is a recurring theme in World Islamic Network's annual public Muharram Awareness Campaign (Eisenlohr 2015a). At the Ashura procession Patrick witnessed with Jafar and Baqer, some men wore black T-shirts, with an alleged quote of Mahatma Gandhi in English: "I learnt from Muharram how to win despite being oppressed." While Karbala has also often served to justify a quietist stance vis-à-vis oppression and injustice, in resignation to the fact that the latter are inherent to this world, since the Iranian Revolution a more activist interpretation of the Karbala paradigm has become increasingly popular throughout the Shi'i world. Accordingly, to live as a Shi'i in the wake of Karbala should not mean to be a mournful victim but should motivate to work for the improvement of politics and society such as through political reform, better health care, and education. Among Twelver Shi'is in Mumbai, this take on Karbala frequently appears to be a motivational force behind recent activist initiatives for citizenship and community uplift. These multiple de- and recontextualizations of the tragic memory of Karbala that make up the Kabala paradigm have the effect of constantly revitalizing the ostensibly long-passed event and to cause it to reappear in a myriad of guises.

For Shi'i activists, Karbala is more than a rich instructional narrative. As the Iranian Islamic Marxist thinker Ali Shariati put it, "Every month of the year is Moharram, every day of the month Ashura and every piece of land Karbala" (Rahnema 1998, 315). In its potential omnipresence across space and linear time, the Karbala paradigm is also driven by the traumatic character of the Karbala. This is not only because its outcome was shocking and devastating for the party of Hussain, with whom Shi'i's have always identified. Like in psychological trauma, the disruptive and violent event also repeatedly returns and becomes troublingly present in multiple guises even long after the original event has passed. The Karbala paradigm has latency as its main temporal structure, and, more particularly relating to the tragic and violent loss that Karbala stands for in the Shiʿi world, it inhabits the latency specific to trauma and traumatic events (see Simon 2020).

The kind of hardwired latency built into the functioning of the technical reproduction of images and sounds also feeds into and amplifies this kind of latency proper to the Karbala paradigm. If linear time can be suspended by the mediatic represencing of images and sounds any time and any place, undercutting their classification as *past* on a sensorial level, azadari videos can be regarded as a technical operationalization of the maxim "every place is Karbala, every day is ashura." They afford a suspension of the established spatial and temporal boundaries of Karbala, helping to universalize its message by enabling travel of the Karbala paradigm to new contexts and settings. Circulating these videos adds new layers of pious and sensory contact to the Karbala complex, thereby fueling its constant reanimation.

In such a way, the built-in technical affordances of audiovisual media support the traumatic reappearances of Karbala as a place and event potentially anywhere, both reproducing and aggrandizing its acutely given nonpresence. Several of Patrick's interlocutors referred to using media and watching azadari videos when talking about the long-standing debates about the permissibility of certain forms of azadari involving bloodletting. Some, but by no means all, middle-class interlocutors were in fact critical of *zanjiri matam* (a form of self-flagellation with long sharp razor blades attached to chains for hitting one's bare back), couching their critique in careful, measured terms because of their awareness of widespread passionate support for the practice, especially among the mass of working-class Twelver Shiʿis. Others in turn defended the practice in terms of a logic of witnessing, assuming inner connections between pain, death, and truth that the notion of *shahid* already points at, simultaneously denoting witness and martyr. As Sabir, a young aspiring businessman in his twenties, put it, "A video of *zanjiri matam* shows everyone what injustice and suffering is. People will feel it; they will not be able to look away and forget." According to Sabir, azadari videos can be an extension and amplification of Karbala as a drama to be viscerally witnessed, with its "emotional style" bringing about morally purifying effects (Binder 2021). The body and painful bodily sensation then feature as guarantors of truth and ethical value (Peters 2001, 717).

LATENCY, MOTION, AND THE ATMOSPHERIC DIMENSIONS OF DIGITAL RELIGION

The media-supported Twelver Shiʿi claims to the right to the city do not rest only on manifest performances and discursive articulations. One of their most significant dimensions is the atmospheric—that is, the production of vague, holistic feelings of Shia-ness that operate on the level of the felt-body. The movements of people and ritual objects through the streets and their sonic ecstasies are good examples of such atmospheric energetic forces that envelop and literally move felt-bodies in synesthetic ways, giving the setting an overarching feel. With suggestions of motion as the key mechanism of atmospheric seizure, it is clear that atmospheres owe much of their power to a specific kind of latency.[7] On the somatic level on which they are active, their modus operandi is not manifestly executed and observable bodily movements but *suggestions* of motion—that is, what is felt right before a movement becomes present in being carried out. This is akin to the interplay of what Erin Manning has called "two co-composed streams of movement, one of the virtual but contradictory, one of the actualized," while virtual movement is at the same time a "vibrational force" (2014, 164, 171).[8] In a related manner, atmospheric suggestions of motion operate at a threshold on which the latent makes itself felt right before it emerges or reemerges into manifest presence (Abels 2022, 112–15). Atmospheres are threshold phenomena in a primarily temporal sense, the threshold being the zone stretching from latency and suggestion to manifest phenomena.[9]

This threshold of latency also recalls what Laura Marks (2010) in her study of Islamic media art has analyzed as the movement from the virtual in the sense of a Deleuze- and Spinoza-inspired process philosophy, which she also calls latency, to the actual in manifest objects and artistic practices. The virtuality of atmospheres is a reminder that even though, as Gernot Böhme (2017) has pointed out, particular atmospheres can be performatively generated and sometimes even deliberately designed, atmospheres are also always already there, not necessarily in manifest but in latent ways. They are in this sense incipient, in the sense of being anterior to a threshold of manifest presence. They surround us before we become aware of them, potentially emerging or reemerging from acutely given nonpresence any time.

It might be argued that audiovisual recordings of azadari practices, such as the ritualized commemorations and procession in the month of Muharram, typically involve the reduction of a holistic felt-bodily sense of place to mere visual and aural sensory impressions. Accordingly, these recordings would therefore pose particular limits on such encompassing perceptibility in exchange for potentially endless circulability and the recontextualizations such mediatic reproduction affords. This is what the classical, established Benjaminian perspective on the loss of aura in the process of the technical reproduction of whatever it is that emanates the aura would suggest (1986, 217–51). Aura and atmosphere are related but nevertheless distinct phenomena; the former has a visual bias, while the latter is about holistic felt-bodily perception through intermingling without privileging a particular sensory mode.[10] Atmospheres are also typically grounded in spatial, energetic processes that are less in evidence in the notion of aura. Nevertheless, the question of the technical affordances of the mediatic reproduction of aesthetic phenomena that Benjamin originally raised is also relevant for the question of reproducing atmospheres through azadari videos.

In the atmospheric affordances of azadari videos—affordances in the sense of the kind of holistically diffuse bodily sensations they enable and invite but do not necessarily cause—we suggest a differentiated approach to the mediatic production and reproduction of atmospheres.[11] Embodiment in the sense of an atmospheric affection of felt-bodies remains central also to making, watching, and circulating azadari videos. Rhys Sparey has suggested something similar when he distinguishes "spatial intercorporeality," which relies on spatial proximity of bodies from the "functional intercorporeality" that drives televised or otherwise digitally mediated Shi'i majalis (2022, 286–87; see also Ali 2022). We would add that the significance of the atmospheric in digitally mediated environments and interactions also rests on the basic fact that the felt-body exceeds the limits of the physical body and that therefore the intermingling of the atmospheric with felt-bodies can far exceed the latter's boundaries and also reach into digitally mediated worlds and situations.[12]

Mediatic production and reproduction of atmospheres shape the affordances for different dimensions of sensory experience in distinct ways. The visuality of azadari videos is constrained by the small screens of mobile devices on which they are most often watched in Mumbai. This is to say nothing of the elimination of the olfactory, which Hugo Tellenbach (1968) takes as the original dimension of atmospheres. To return to the earlier discussion of the reproducibility of the sonic, following Wolfgang Ernst (2012), the equally original quality *(Gleichursprüglichkeit)* of technically reproduced sonic events as always-already synesthetic also applies here. But, ultimately, atmospheres are a bundling mechanism that make religious discourse, iconographies, auditory dispositions, and memories resonate, generating an overarching feel pervading all these modes of experience.

Nevertheless, the lack of bodily copresence and spatial intercorporeality that often accompanies the watching of azadari videos does have consequences for the atmospheric register of resonance, entrainment, and attunement as a mutual process of "gearing" into the world (Merleau-Ponty [1945] 1962, 250). As argued by Carola Lorea, Aditi Mukherjee, and Dishani Roy (2023), digital religion may privilege a shift of sensory engagement toward the visual, while marginalizing the sonic and tactile dimensions of religious practice. In a related manner, video reproduction of azadari ritual events invite for uptake a constrained range of felt-bodily aesthesis, but in which the sonic continues to play a major role. In fact, several of Patrick's interlocutors stressed the sonic aspects of atmospheres when speaking about what their uses of azadari videos meant for them. Afsar told Patrick that when he listened to recorded recitations of mournful poetry in honor of the martyrs of Karbala of the *nauha* genre that it was not just the words but also and especially the sound of the poetry that made him cry, while for Baqer the sonic aspects of such poetry reminded him of his pilgrimage to holy shrines in Iraq and the feeling and overwhelming experience of finally reaching these places.

The balance between different sensory modalities may be shifted in digital religion. However, the attenuation and dampening of holistic felt-bodily gearing into the world together with others in a way that goes beyond any particular sensory modality often appears to be a consequence of this kind of mediatization of public ritual events. This mediatization offers fewer possibilities for felt-bodily incorporation in Schmitz's sense, the provisional merging of participants into a shared we-*Leib* through suggestions of motion and literal resonance. At the very least, participation shifts to a limited register of the visual and auditory, while synchronized sonic participation often proves impossible due to minimal time lags in digital networked interaction (Othman 2022). Given the relative malleability and spatial flexibility of the felt-body in comparison to physical bodies, a sense of felt-bodily presence and emplacement is not preempted per se but at least significantly altered in practice. Overall, it is also hard to overlook the parallels between atmospheric affection as forward-pointing phenomena in a temporality of latency and twenty-first-century digital media as "feed-forward" agents that anticipate and preempt through automated nudges, recommendations, and adjustments, constituting "tertiary protentions" (Hui 2021). Atmospheric suggestions of motion and the anticipatory processes of digital media that Mark B.N. Hansen (2015) has called "feed-forward" operate on the threshold of the "not yet," just before that which is latent becomes manifest. There is, of course, a difference between the felt-bodily motor projects of atmospheric affection and machine protentions. But if, as mentioned, the felt-body exceeds the boundaries of the physical body, sensing and intermingling with environments, this can also include digital ones, and therefore felt-bodily suggestion of motion and machine protentions may closely interact and share certain latencies.

The magnifying and publicizing of Karbala's latency through its mediatic production and reproduction therefore also includes atmospheric dimensions. Azadari videos are used mostly as a technique for shaping ethical selves through generating pious emotions and for establishing and reinforcing sociality among Twelver Shi'is. With respect to the felt aspects of belonging to the city, their role is different from Ashura processions as large-scale public events that also address non-Shi'is and non-Muslims more broadly. Azadari videos of such processions that are explicitly framed as taking place in the city, featuring recognizable streets and landmarks, are in turn more conducive for feeding the atmospheric dimensions of such ritual events into claims to the city. This recalls sensibilities among Twelver Shi'is in Lahore, for who recordings they classify as "live" have a more intense atmospheric presence (Cooper 2022). In terms of our Mumbai example, these are recordings of live azadari performances in recognizable urban settings. Such videos and their uses bring about a fusion of shaping ethical selves and making claims to the city.

In the end this is also an alternative to, and not just an extension, of established discursive strategies of Twelver Shi'i activists. Activists such as those at World Islamic Network have argued for a right to the city and inclusion into the nation on moral and ethical terms. In claiming the legacy of Gandhi and in presenting themselves as the world's first victims of terrorism in annual Muharram Awareness

Campaigns, these activists have in the past sought to portray Twelver Shiʿis as exemplary Indian citizens. The making of such claims in an atmospheric register that evades discursive critique and mobilizes somatic evidence for its claims offers advantages for those marginalized in mainstream discourses of citizenship, opening up an alternative and possibly more promising area for making such claims. The temporal category of latency not only is a fulcrum of Shiʿi ritual life but also cuts across the atmospheric and mediatic dimensions of Shiʿi claims to the city. Latency is the distinct temporality of atmospheres, a regime of time that supports inclusion in a body politic and in a territorialized community by mobilizing the felt dimensions of place making and belonging.

8

Atmospheres as Environmentality

Chanting Climate Change

Throughout this book we have approached the atmospheric as forces that intervene into the felt-body's spatial economy, thereby generating sensorially holistic forms of affectedness that at the same time manifest as nondiscursive ways of knowing. We have also argued that such atmospheric knowledge is environmental in several ways. At the most fundamental level, atmospheric forces, or "half-things" in Hermann Schmitz's parlance, can set in motion processes of individuation that bring about the emergence of feeling bodies out of a larger, diffuse whole (1978, 116–32). They thereby cocreate the difference between such bodies that feel as distinct entities and what simultaneously become their environments. Further, we have discussed atmospheres as always-already environmental because they stand for embodied relationality, or felt-bodies' entanglement and overlapping with the world, making accessible somatic kinds of knowledge. Such atmospheric environmentality is also deeply enmeshed in power and politics, because the atmospheric relations between felt-bodies, as well as between felt-bodies and their environments, are also subject to design, manipulation, and control.

In this chapter we finally bring this perspective of atmospheres as fundamentally environmental to bear on what, in an everyday sense, is referred to as "the environment," namely the currently most salient environmental issue of climate change. Micronesia has been deeply troubled by the interrelating effects of colonialism and climate change. Not coincidentally, Micronesian communities are leading both climate-awareness campaigns and adaptation strategies alongside other Pacific Islanders, "often combining traditional practices and cutting-edge science, to build the resilience of their communities and ecosystems in the face of increasing climate risk" (McLeod et al. 2019). Such approaches frequently rekindle Indigenous governance and traditional knowledge systems by harnessing the intimate knowledge of local ecosystems in these communities as well as their innate adaptive potential in the face of natural crises. At many climate-related official events, Pacific Islander climate advocates have opened their formal speeches with a traditional chant, which attests to the significance of the performing arts as Indigenous knowledge practices in this process. Resonating with this development, recent work in both music studies and Indigenous Pacific studies has called for an epistemology that accepts a plurality of knowledge systems rather than insisting on *one* authoritative way of knowing. After all, Pacific Indigenous knowledge has historically provided coping strategies for responding to irresolvable dilemmas.

To combat climate change such strategies are desperately needed right now, and it seems that, both intellectually and politically, the time has come to more seriously consider alternative epistemologies. Throughout the book we have argued—sometimes explicitly, sometimes implicitly—that such consideration should include the alternative epistemologies of the performing arts. The phenomenological analytic of atmospheres in some ways runs parallel to Pacific Indigenous knowledges of the environment. These resonances between a European philosophical approach to atmospheres and Pacific epistemologies of the environment and transoceanic connections indicate that neither is a provincial body of knowledge strictly confined to particular regions in their claims. Likewise, other fruitful comparisons between the phenomenology of atmospheres and other knowledge traditions around the globe have already been explored, highlighting, for example, resonances between neophenomenological approaches to atmospheres and the Japanese concept of ki and drawing on the Chinese intellectual tradition of qi (Hisayama 2014; Marinucci 2019; Wang 2024).

Owing to the specifics of their medium, sound-based epistemologies are by nature dynamic and ambivalent. When sound waves materially affect the felt-body, the latter transduces them into something else (Simondon [1964] 1992). In this way a sonic event becomes a recognizable musical structure, a familiar tune, a sentiment, or even a memory or sense of familiarity. Throughout this transductive process, the knowledge specific to the performing arts is not so much a knowledge of *what*; instead, it is a knowledge of *how*. As it mediates between various experiential orders beyond the felt-bodily and operates in their in-between (Abels 2018), the knowledge at stake here is the knowledge of how to bring the various trajectories of the human experience in connection with one another. This connection is forged in sound and, as such, is a fleeting phenomenon. The physical vibration of a sonic event is at the beginning of any such process. The vibration creates resonances, both materially and metaphorically: the sensation of a dance shout during a Micronesian men's dance, for instance, merges with the intense historicity it resounds in the Indigenous listener, and that person may not necessarily be able to separate this from the listening sensation itself. This is how the performing arts bring about multifaceted connections. As an epistemic register, the performing arts harbor the knowledge of how to build connections. This is the way in which chanting as a knowledge practice creates its efficacy.

While, at first glance, the fact that sonic transduction processes necessarily depend not on sound but on the experience of sound seems to be a general observation of mostly conceptual relevance, it also has deep methodological implications. Chanting as a knowledge practice is always a situated practice and deeply imbricated with its environment. This conceptualization of the knowledge inherent in sonic practices resonates well with recent critiques on the anthropology of sound (e.g., Eisenlohr 2018). This points again to the interstitial as a significant site of alternative knowledge generation based on understanding the world though chanting. As counter-knowledge practices are being increasingly acknowledged in postcolonial societies around the world—for instance, oral history and historical chants are being acknowledged as legal evidence in cases of land-rights disputes— we find ourselves in the middle of an epistemological shift (Babcock 2013). It is precisely here that the notion of sonic atmospheres as deeply environmental allows for an important shift of analytical perspective.

Atmospheres are important because they can set the terms on which environmental relations can unfold, which makes them one of the pivotal dimensions of a variety of forms of power, control, and appeal. Proceeding from this notion of atmospheric environmentality, we focus on a specific musical situation to illustrate this idea, through a close reading of "Obil ngesur," a traditional chant from Palau, Micronesia. This chant is regularly used to frame official statements by Palauan advocates for increased climate-protection measures. The lyrics of the chant detail particular rules for the sustainable use of natural resources. However, in keeping with the rationale of this book, rather than emphasizing the message of the lyrics, we focus on the atmospheric intensity of the chant. We examine some of the energetic forces specific to the chant's medium and sound and the nature of its atmospheric intensity, exploring them vis-à-vis the environmental relations from within which they emerge. We identify sonic suggestions of movement to explore the subtleties of the chant performance's rhythmicity, swirls of sonic intensities, and relevance to issues of sustainability and climate protection.

Our analysis is less concerned with the discursiveness and representational mechanics of the chant than with its felt-bodily affectivity. If chanting allows for access to a specific sonic type of environmental knowledge, then it is a potential resource in climate-crisis adaptation strategies and a possible potent cultural strategy for fostering resilience to climate change. This potential, we suggest, is rooted in the intimacy between the distinct atmospheres chants create, the felt-bodily experiences they enable, and the somatic knowledge of environmental relations that arises from the felt-bodily sensation of being connected in sound. This is how sonic suggestions of motion mark individual distinctiveness and, at the same time, interconnectedness: the environmentality of individuals, their historicity, and the relationality inscribed into their being-in-the-world. As a tempo-spatial practice, this is how sonic atmospheres create and prefigure the space in which environmental relations unfold.

"OBIL NGESUR"

In the words of chanter Faustina Rehuher-Marugg, "Obil ngesur" is a chant that "can never be chanted enough. It needs to be chanted often and often because it needs to remind us that . . . it's our responsibility to make sure that [this is] still Palau, forever."[1] Indeed, Rehuher-Marugg has chanted "Obil ngesur" on a number of official occasions.

> *Obil ngesur iiang*
> *Kom diul merrael e mei*
> *Meng kal beluad a ikang, meng kal chetemed a ikang*
> *Ng di bad ma ralm ma*
> *Badngeasek a merredel era a*
> *Chutem iiang.*[2]

Rehuher-Marugg summarizes the message of the chants as follows: "The conceptual translation of this chant is [that] we are transiting this earth; we are trespassers. We really don't own what's here; we don't own the land, the trees, the forest, the water. It's only the rocks and the water and the core of the earth [that] own the land. Therefore, it's our responsibility to ensure its continuity into the future." More literally, the *chesols*, across its variations, says, "We came to this place with nothing. The land and the rocks are not ours. We are not the rightful owners of them. It's only the water and the rocks that own the land" (Rehuher-Marugg 2016).

"Obil ngesur" is a chesols, a particular type of Palauan chant. The chesols genre is related to the notion of *kelulau* (whispered principles). *Kelulau* is a set of values drawing on "respect and honor, praise [and] appreciation, compassion, cooperation and communication, good conduct and character, and unity" as central principles of Palauan governance (Iechad 2014, 3). The Palauan gods had installed the *klobak*, a council of *rubak* (chiefs) to oversee and preserve these values; traditionally, chesols are an integral part of *klobak* negotiations. In today's coexistence of elected and traditional governments, they are also a preferred medium for a *rubak* to criticize the elected government. Many chesols were composed either by deities or by ancestors. Accordingly, their lyrics are often imbued with a sense of divine authority. But chesols also handle a complex, at times archaic language full of subtext, hidden meanings, and often arcane references. They are the sonic embodiment of a complex cultural history of making sense of one's surroundings both historically and spatially; at the same time, they encode political ideologies, value structures, and historiography in terms of both mythological stories and musical genres. In the effort to analytically tap into this knowledge that lingers on in chesols, the gradual emergence of sound

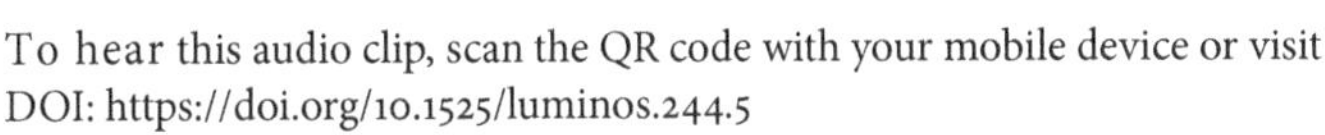

AUDIO CLIP 5. Faustina Rehuher-Marugg's "Obil ngesur" performance. Recorded by Barbara B. Smith.

To hear this audio clip, scan the QR code with your mobile device or visit DOI: https://doi.org/10.1525/luminos.244.5

knowledge along musical form, layered discursive formations, and emotional dispositions are key. Listen to Faustina Rehuher-Marugg chanting the first stanza of "Obil ngesur" in audio clip 5.

Chesols follow recognizable structural genre conventions both in musical form and in terms of melodic-rhythmic features, and so does this performance as well. Chesols are recitations that divide into verses, and their verses in turn subdivide into recitative lines and cadence. Verses are not necessarily identical in melodic and rhythmic details, but they always follow recognizable, genre-conventional melodic and rhythmic contours. Chesols usually have several verses, but today often only one or two are performed. Rehuher-Marugg's "Obil ngesur" performance, too, includes only one verse. Characteristic of chesols performance is the involvement of the audience: when opening the chant and after each verse, they respond to the chanter, *"hm . . . huei!"* This reply is the community's approval of both the chanter and the suitability of the chesols for the occasion. Without this chanter-audience interaction, any chesols is incomplete and therefore, void of meaning to the situation. In addition, the performance of a chesols has historically been preceded by the *okisel a chesols* (rising of chesols), and Rehuher-Marugg decided to open this "Obil ngesur" performance with an *okisel a chesols* as well. *Okisel a chesols* refers to the spoken preamble *"o-desuokl,"* exclaimed by the chanter; the audience, again, responds with *"huei!"* No longer an intelligible phrase to contemporary Palauans, *o-desuokl* is often taken to performatively signify to the audience the beginning of a chant performance. In current-day practice, it has become an optional introduction to the chant; if it is included in the performance, it evokes the chant's historicity and therefore adds gravity and seriousness to the performance.

The reply *"hm . . . huei!"* continues to be an integral part of chesols performance and is typically interpreted as an expression of approval and encouragement for the chanter. It has to be inserted at the end of each verse and is integral to the performance of a chant. It makes the audience active participants in a chesols performance. Both the *okisel a chesols* and the interpolation of *"hm . . . huei!"* gesture toward a category that is key to the meaningfulness of chesols in Palauan public life: the lived experience of relationality and the sensation of social configurations and how they matter in daily life. The degree of involvement with which the

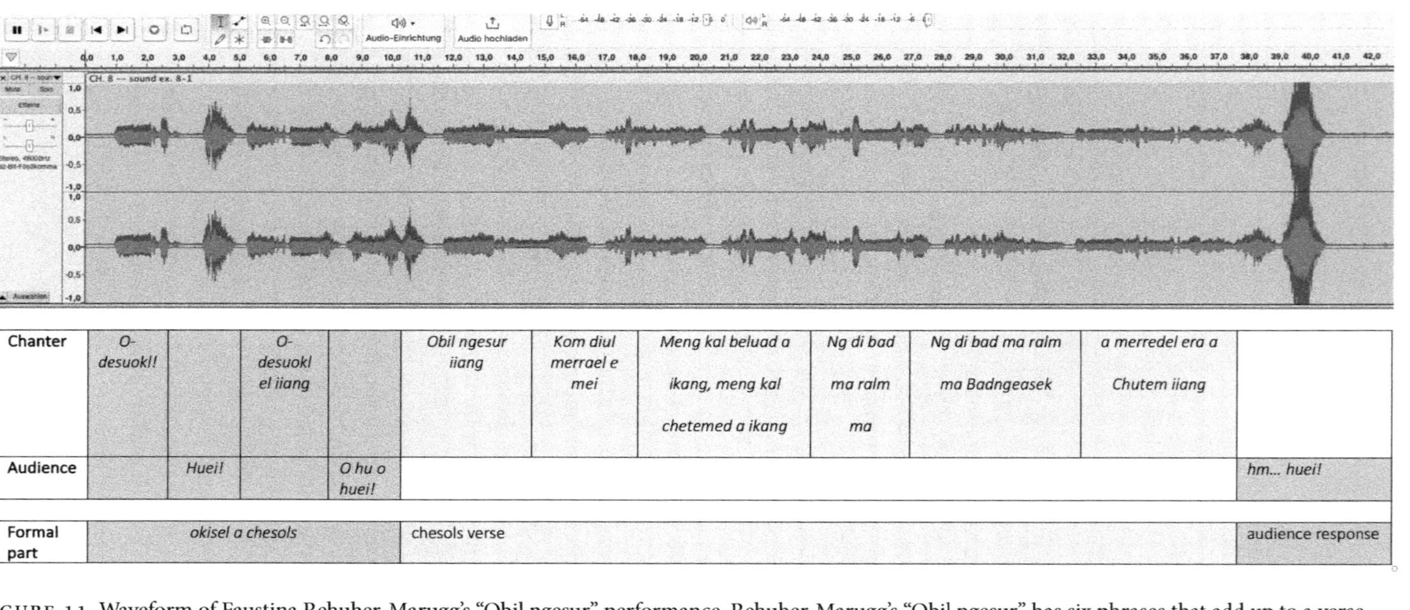

Chanter	O-desuokl!		O-desuokl el iiang		Obil ngesur iiang	Kom diul merrael e mei	Meng kal beluad a ikang, meng kal chetemed a ikang	Ng di bad ma ralm ma	Ng di bad ma ralm ma Badngeasek	a merredel era a Chutem iiang	
Audience		Huei!		O hu o huei!							hm... huei!
Formal part	okisel a chesols				chesols verse						audience response

FIGURE 11. Waveform of Faustina Rehuher-Marugg's "Obil ngesur" performance. Rehuher-Marugg's "Obil ngesur" has six phrases that add up to a verse.

audience responds both to the chanter's *okisel a chesols* and the verses matters: it can range from restrained approval to verve and enthusiasm, and the small audience on the "Obil ngesur" recording certainly displays the latter.

Like all chesols, the verse of "Obil ngesur" starts with a recitative line, a loose sequence of variations on the same melodic motif. The basic melodic contour of this motif is standardized and immediately signifies to the listener the genre of chesols, but it adapts to the rhythmic necessities of the lyrics. Melodic motifs are characterized by the repetition of one central tone in punctuated rhythm that bends up and down roughly a hundred cents before it reaches its final note. Depending on the rhythmic demands of the lyrics, the rough repetition of this motif results in phrases; Rehuher-Marugg's "Obil ngesur" has six phrases that add up to a verse.

The chanting voice performs the distinctive chesols rhythm, punctuated and recognizable across the entire genre's repertoire. Already upon hearing the rhythm of the first melodic motif, Palauan listeners identify the chant as unmistakably chesols. The rhythmic pattern, therefore, is imbued with the genre's historicity and deep imbrication with Palauan mythology and the sea and the land. The characteristic rhythm of chesols chanting, therefore, is always-already atmospherically charged with this connection. To Hermann Schmitz, rhythm is one of music's primary structural means to increase and indeed, play, with atmospheric intensity because it establishes a loop between suggestions of motion and actual acoustic motion. What is more, rhythm creates a pattern of acoustic events; it therefore structures the acoustic motion that interacts with the performance's suggestions of motion. Patterns create gravitational direction because they are carried by a pull toward balance and completion (2016, 89). Enveloping the felt-bodies of everyone involved in the musical situation, rhythmic suggestions of motion affect the felt-bodies they encounter sonically.

The melodic line develops across phrases and typically, like in Rehuher-Marugg's performance, develops a descending melodic line. The lowest melodic point marks the end of the final phrase, and therefore also of the chanted verse. Therefore, it also prompts the audience approval. The audience approval is the verse's, and in this case also the entire performance's, final conclusion: "*hm . . . huei!*" In the case of chesols performance in general, and in this performance of "Obil ngesur" in particular, the emergence of the musical chesols forms prompts but also requires the audience response. The audience response is nothing without the emergence of musical form, and the musical form is not complete and, indeed, valid, unless the audience responds. As the melodic line reaches its lowest pitch, it invites the audience's "*hm . . . huei!*"—not simply as another structural genre requirement but as a resounding of that which the emergence of musical chesols form has just given rise to: the sensation of a profound interconnectedness of Palauan mythology, the historicity of chesols, and present-day social configurations. Already visually, the audience's final approval stands out, owing to its acoustic loudness: it is by far the loudest component of the chant performance and, as such, a major suggestion of movement with significant felt-bodily affectivity.

These two acoustic parameters of the "Obil ngesur" performance illustrate how musical processes bring together, according to Schmitz, two types of felt-bodily intensity. First, the spatial intensity arising from motional dynamics affects the dynamics of felt-bodily space. As we have pointed out throughout this book, such sensing of motion and spatial location is a fundamental dimension of being-in-the-world. The second kind of felt-bodily intensity that musical processes draw on and manipulate is the temporal intensity of duration and the playful modulation of the rhythm of alternating expansion and contraction that governs the vital drive (2016, 87). Such musical interlacing of different types of acoustic intensity is provocative in nature; musical repetition such as recurrent rhythmic patterns, then, are not so much mild suggestions as "thrusts of provocative densification."[3] The provocative nature of musical atmosphere invites engagement, but its intrinsic ambivalence leaves it to the listener how to respond. Music, "in a very open and multi-faceted way, brings home to people the sensation of their fate: their exposedness to space and time and how they can be affected by it" (90).[4]

It is, then, not so much the lyrics and hence the discursive message of "Obil ngesur" that carries the performance's sonic intensity; it is the atmospheric affectivity of holistically engaging with a sonic event through felt-bodily expansion that turns a sober message ("climate protection matters") into an ethical mission ("climate protection matters TO US; we care!"). The reason for this is that, in a musical situation, the boundaries between one's temporospatial surroundings and oneself potentially blur. What affects my environment always potentially affects myself. For the fleeting moment of its performance, "Obil ngesur" makes this distinctly sonic insight felt-bodily and thus unmistakably experiencable. This is how the chant derives its efficacy and deep meaningfulness.

Deeply entangled with the cultural history of the genre as such, chesols actualize a number of discursive configurations, and they do so through their musical specificities. Often originating from the gods who created them, they extend, first, into the Palauan present from a mythological past, thus charging current performance situations with a deep sense of historicity. As chesols are often transmitted along family lineages and their history of use is often well known, this historicity concerns both individuals and the community's historiographies. Chesols evoke the individual as well as the community becoming up until the moment of the given performance. Second, they contain the cultural memory of the ethical configuration constitutive to the ideal Palauan society as devised by the gods when they created the Palauan islands. They are thus resoundings of a divine vision of the islands and, as such, scripts for another, ideal Palau. Chanting chesols, therefore, invariably evokes the idea that an ideal society is possible and that Palau was created to be one. Third, the musical form of chesols rests on the interaction between chanters, who chant by virtue of their social standing, and the audience, whose response affirms the chesols' message as well as the chanter and their legitimacy to present this chant in a given situation. The fact that chesols are incomplete without the group's response means that the genre of chesols requires an active involvement of all present persons: a conscious, performative "I too belong" that turns the experience of sound into the experience of one's own social relationality. Palauan historicity, ethics, and social fabric are emotionally charged discursive formations. But in chesols chanting, they resound with yet something else, and it is this *yet something else* that I refer to as sound knowledge. It gradually manifests as a felt-bodily certitude as the musical form unfolds, amplifying, complicating, and commingling discursive and emotional configurations.

Sonic events, from a single sound to a complex sonic texture, are sound waves moving through space; acoustically, sound waves are variations in air pressure. When sound waves hit the felt-body, the latter transforms the energy of the sound waves into nerve impulses. But beyond neural activity, there is also another, transductive process that takes place as sound moves. Process philosopher Erin Manning has referred to this process as "body-worlding." To her, movement "is one with the world, not body/world but body worlding" ([2009] 2012, 6). In movement the body brings about the world it experiences. Sonic motion, therefore, actualizes the interlacing of the felt-body with its surroundings both in material terms (i.e., referring to physical vibrations permeating both body and world) and in terms of discursive configurations (i.e., referring to cultural and social dispositions). In movement the human body comes about vis-à-vis the dynamics of its own relationality, actualizing itself along the divergent registers from which lived experience emerges. Seen this way, sound experience is centrally the experience of relational repositioning. Musical conventions including genres, then, are cultural techniques to actualize, stimulate, and transform the dynamics of human relationality. In the case of genres, musical genre conventions accentuate but also stimulate resonance across temporal, spatial, and social axes. Such resonance is necessarily always a resonance *of connection*, and this connection is where sound knowledge is located. Chanting chesols, then, sets resonance in motion and in this way actualizes sound knowledge as a relational resource. This, therefore, is also where the environmentality of "Obil ngesur" is located.

A CHANT AND ITS ENVIRONMENTALITY

Palauans have regularly told us they felt that chesols, as a genre, were "incredibly powerful" and "overwhelming," carrying a "deep meaning." For instance, "It's all there," said a member of the staff of the Palauan Ministry for Community and Cultural Affairs, a woman in her early thirties, during a project meeting on the ethnography of traditional land rights in Palau in 2006: "It's all there in traditional chesols; the chants spell it all out." She wasn't referring to the chant's lyrics—she was referring to the actual knowledge inherent to, and rendered experiencable by, chesols. To her the knowledge harbored by chesols includes issues of environmental sustainability, social acceptability, and potential avenues for future developments of various kinds, including social and economic ones (Abels 2018). But specifically, how does "Obil ngesur" render the knowledge inherent in the traditional performing arts in Palau experienceable, thus creating the atmospheric terms on which environmental relations can unfold?

In this book we have used the notion of environmentality in an inclusive sense, referring to the webs of relations atmospheric practices emerge from and impact. This includes the multilayered relations sonic practices have with their environment. In many Indigenous ontologies, including the Palauan one, the physical environment isn't a given. It is an "agential being . . . engaged in social relations that profoundly shape human lives," full of divine presence and breathing the entire history of its relationship with humans, deities, and spiritual beings (Tallbear 2015, 234). Paraphrasing global Indigenous literatures scholar Chadwick Allen (2020), the environment is "imbued with social, psychic, and spiritual power that humans encounter physically, socially, and spiritually, and through which humans encounter each other as well as other-than-human beings and forces." Such environmental vitality is pivotal also for the history of Palauan cultural engagement with the land and the sea. As Allen goes on to explain for Native American mound and earthwork construction, "Words were spoken and chanted, songs were sung, dances were danced *into* earth. . . . In these ways, layers of packed rocks and soils were imbued with the power of sacred discourse, the energy of rhythmic movement."

Far beyond both the metaphorical and the material, Allen's "energy of rhythmic movement" is particularly instructive here. It refers to the sociocultural history of human-environmental intermingling, evoking an alternative conception of the environment: one in which it is pivotal that over the time of human history, the particular rhythm of chesols has, time and again, ensounded the soil and the sea. Energy, and therefore suggestions of motion, never simply dissipate; they only transform. Accordingly, the Palauan environment today is also the archive of its own rhythmic reverberation with sound-based atmospheric practices such as chesols. Resounding this archive, every performance of "Obil ngesur" carries forth into the present moment an age-old yet new connection with the land that will only ever be owned by the rocks and the water—but for which, by virtue of this atmospheric connection, Palauans have stewardship.

Faustina Rehuher-Marugg's remark that the chant "needs to be chanted often and often" comes back to mind here. It needs to be chanted "often and often," not so much because the lyrics require repetition to convey a particular message. It requires repetition because the rhythmic movement specific both to chesols as a genre and to this particular chesols, "Obil ngesur," needs to continue going deep into the land and the sea, ensounding them with human presence and at the same time reassuring itself of its resonance with the natural environment. Only when they continue to reverberate with the soil and the ocean can felt-bodies attune to and experience the existential vitality of this connection. Rehuher-Marugg's remark also points to the normative potential of atmospheric knowledge as enviromentality. Her perspective does not neatly fit the Foucauldian paradigm of environmentality as a major form of contemporary governmentality that we have referred to on several occasions in this book. Nevertheless, her exhortation that this chant needs to be chanted "often and often" reminds us that atmospheres as environmentality can also be a matter of organized, active engagement and design rather than simply centered on a primordial being-with. Even though atmospheres are diffusely meaningful and therefore upstream from more specific political and ideological projects, such relative openness can also invite their drafting into the more qualified ethical and normative directions of the day. This is the case here, when Rehuher-Marugg makes the case for the cultivation and regular repetition of an atmospheric practice that is now geared not just to the carrying forth of Palauan traditions centered on ensounding the soil, the rocks, and the sea. In the current historical moment, this practice also becomes part of an existential Western Pacific struggle against climate change.

Repetition along with rhythmic movement as characteristics of chesols as a genre and performative practice highlight that "rhythm," in connection with the environmentality of "Obil ngesur," holds several meanings. On one hand, it does point to the familiar notion of rhythm as repetition and as akin to meter. On the other hand, rhythm is also a relational category of movement and emergence in which formal aspects of a phenomenon engender changes in perception or aesthetic experience that revolve around relationships of entrainment or attunement not necessarily tied to repetition or regular recurring patterns (Vara Sánchez 2023). In atmospheric terms the latter dimension of rhythm is especially evident in suggestions of motion, which are the central working mechanism of sonic atmospheres and to which felt-bodies respond in relationships of intermingling and attunement. In this sense rhythm also refers to the timbral qualities of the recitative voice and to the recognizable melodic contours that all chesols share and, not just in a more literal sense, to the genre's characteristic punctuated rhythm. As sound waves and qualities, they all come about in the temporal circularity that both shape and add meaningfulness to the cultural practice of chanting chesols, a never-ending circle of contraction and expansion. This experiential circularity sonically situates the present moment in a much grander historical framework, and it evokes an unequivocal aura of Pacific Islander deep knowledge, wisdom, and responsibility for the islands and the ocean. It is the felt-bodily experience of this sonicity that leaves no doubt: being a Palauan means to be ethically involved with the environment both in the literal and in the broad sense. This felt-bodily sensation of being connected, through a link that is as sound as it is subtle, becomes complicated within the complex postcolonial framework of contemporary Palau, but it remains a key register of the Palauan experience of the presence regardless. In resonating with the natural environment and human responsibility for it at the same time, "Obil ngesur" points to connection and relation, in all their complexity, because it invites felt-bodily expansion—expansion into one's surroundings.

CONCLUSION

Both the sound knowledge and the environmentality of "Obil ngesur," then, are not simply in the normative discourse and narrative put forth in the lyrics, which resonates strongly with the challenges posed by climate change in the Pacific Island world. Not a knowledge of absolute truth but one of relational situationality, the chant's sound knowledge and environmentality emerge in connection-with; what is more, they are about continuing to become in connection-with. Chesols in general and "Obil ngesur" in particular, then, can safely be considered a knowledge practice. When chanters pick this chant to perform on formal occasions, they use it to actualize age-old Oceanic wisdom and deep knowledge to urge toward the forging of ancient, yet new, sustainable relationships.

Conclusion

Atmospheric Knowledge as Embodied Futurity

The field of atmospheric studies involves a steadily growing number of disciplines. Despite the ever-increasing breadth and complexity of this field, there is widespread agreement that atmospheres are always already there. Accordingly, in any given situation, atmospheres are present, affording modulation, intermingling with, and even being redesigned by human actors. In some ways this is reminiscent of Martin Heidegger's notion of moods, which are the first and primary mode in which the world discloses itself to us. As we have shown in this book by way of a range of ethnographic contexts and settings, atmospheres differ from moods in the Heideggerian sense in that they are thoroughly spatial and situational and therefore shifting, with no existential constants. Nevertheless, our surroundings always already have atmospheric qualities, regardless of our paying attention to them, because we invariably find ourselves in situations along with their modalities of spatial emplacement. In other words, our being immersed in atmospheres is a fundamental condition of being-in-the-world.

Therefore the question is never whether there is an atmosphere to begin with, but only what kind of atmosphere or atmospheres there are and in what degree of intensity. However, this perspective on atmospheres is also limited. With the existence of atmospheres as temporal phenomena, it is striking that studies of atmospheres tend to focus only on atmospheres' preexistence and presence, while their inbuilt futurity is often overlooked. Much of the discussion on atmospheres has centered on what atmospheres are, along with the social and political implications of their presence, including those effects that are due to their staging and manufacturing. Still, we argue that this cross-disciplinary engagement with atmospheres has overlooked one of the key reasons why atmospheres are so important, namely that they underpin our sense of being in time, possibly the most central dimension of embodied existence. Our embodied sense of being in time is modal—that is, it revolves around the incessant interplay and coconstitution of past, present, and future. In the phenomenological terms originally coined by Edmund Husserl, this happens through the ongoing intersection of retentions of the past with protentions or anticipations. In chapter 1 we recall that Maurice Merleau-Ponty seeks to derive this phenomenology of time-consciousness from bodily motion in a bottom-up manner, with body memory and suggestions of motion as the embodied correlates of retentions and protentions, respectively, constituting a unified intentional arc.

Atmospheric research has so far sidelined the future- or protention-oriented dimension of atmospheres, which we suggest, adopting Hermann Schmitz's term, rests on suggestions of motion. A reason for this is that atmospheric research, in its concern with what atmospheres are and the sociopolitical implications of their qualities, has so far insufficiently focused on the concrete working mechanisms of atmospheres at the felt-bodily level. Following Schmitz on this point, throughout this book we have treated suggestions of motion as the most salient of such mechanisms. Whether in the cases of music or other sonic practices establishing transoceanic connections, sonic dimensions of urban religion generating felt dimensions of citizenship, or dance or other traditions of structured movement, the latent dimensions of atmospheres or sound knowledge as environmental knowledge turned out to be the chief manifestation of atmospheres' intermingling with sentient bodies. From our perspective suggestions of motion engender the momentary union of the feeler and the feeling poured out in space. This union obviates the separation between perceiving subjects and what they perceive and is a hallmark of the atmospheric. The crucial point to be stressed here is that atmospheres' power does not rest on motion but on *suggestions* of motion. One of the key conclusions of our investigation of atmospheric knowledge or atmospheres as epistemology is that atmospheres are forward-pointing phenomena, which suggest incipient situations or constellations that are not yet fully manifest.

The often-remarked vagueness and diffuse qualities of atmospheres are due to this fact of incipiency and futurity; atmospheres are about a "hunch" of something that is not yet manifestly present and subject to further qualification. Another way to put this is that suggestions of motion as the bodily mechanism of atmospheres are due to atmospheres' rhythmicity. Atmospheric half-things are made up of aesthetic rhythms that invite and suggest a range of degrees of bodily entrainment and attunement (see also Vara Sánchez [2023]). This is a point especially salient in the sonic phenomena we have investigated throughout this book. Our predilection for sonic wave phenomena in the analysis of atmospheres rests precisely on the centrality of aesthetic rhythms as suggestions of motion and not only on our respective disciplinary backgrounds as a musicologist and an anthropologist of sonic practices.

The upshot of all this is that atmospheric knowledge, the central theme of our book, is not just about knowing what is presently the case or what happened in the past. This knowledge, which is a multisensory kind of knowledge that primarily rests on modulations of the feeling of having and being a body, is also about suggestion and incipiency. In fact, these are frequently its primary role. Atmospheric knowledge is often especially about the sense of something that is not yet manifest and in need of further qualification to become present. In this sense atmospheres are threshold phenomena that enable knowledge of something or a situation before it is fully in place (Cooper 2024). In chapter 6 we analyze structured movement as a practice of dwelling on the threshold in this sense. This temporal understanding of the notion of the threshold as a continuum stretching from atmospheric latency to manifest presence also aligns with another continuum we have repeatedly pointed to in this book: the continuum between vague meaningfulness and more qualified cultural forms and discourses, which in the unfolding of practices also implies ontogenetic (micro)temporal progression. The figure of the threshold or the continuum is another way of thinking through suggestions of motion as the principal mechanism through which atmospheres function. Its forward pointing toward that which is not yet manifest is a firmly built-in feature of atmospheres' very mode of operation.

This futurity of the atmospheric will always remain obscure unless one takes seriously the centrality of embodied being-in-the-world—that is, the fact that humans, along with a broad range of nonhuman actors such as animals, do not just have but *are* felt-bodies. It is felt-bodily motion that allows us the feeling of having and being a body, more precisely the constant intersecting of body memory as kinetic memory with motor projects or suggestions of motion, integrated in intentional arcs. As Merleau-Ponty argues, this ever-shifting intersecting also allows us to have a sense of the temporal modalities of past, present, and future, in which the feeling of being a body and modal time as a key dimension of being-in-the-world fall together. Atmospheres' power in turn principally comes from its manipulation and modulation of motor projects through the suggestions of motion of its own and by extension also the modulation of futurity. This is also why, together with the figure of the threshold, the model of aesthetic rhythms is so useful for understanding the work suggestions of motion do. Atmospheric suggestions of motion contain a certain rhythmicity that can provoke at least partial alignment, entrainment, or even attunement by felt-bodies, not infrequently across a multitude of bodies simultaneously. The condition of possibility of such processes of at least partial rhythmic entrainment and attunement is in turn the anticipation and intuition of what likely comes next. In short, the anticipation of rhythmic patterns lies at the heart of atmospheric knowledge as a felt sense of the incipient and not yet manifest. Atmospheric half-things as sonic phenomena in turn provide particularly striking illustrations of suggestions of motion as enabling rhythmic entrainment and attunement.

Atmospheres' intimate relation with the incipient and the not-yet, should not be confused with a related figure of thought in affect theory. In his widely influential rendering of Baruch Spinoza's *affectus* through the work of Gilles Deleuze, Brian Massumi (2002) has argued for an "autonomy of affect." Such autonomy of affect from subjectivity and signification primarily rests on a "half-second delay" of consciousness catching up with affect. Conscious perception arrives in time only to perceive manifest phenomena resulting from affect but that are no longer affect. From this perspective affect belongs to the world of the virtual, the forces of difference and multiplicity that generate actual phenomena. In this reading, as radically unqualified intensity under the threshold of conscious perception on its way to manifest in actual phenomena, affect is precultural and prehistorical. Our discussion of atmospheric knowledge as incipient and sensing the not-yet qualified in some ways parallels affect's trajectory as an unqualified force on its way to generate the actual and perceivable entities and phenomena of the world.

Nevertheless, atmospheres differ from this understanding of affect in that they are multisensory phenomena at the threshold of, but in no way radically below, the limits of perception and attention. Rather than presupposing a binary between full conscious attention and the nonconscious, atmospheric theory points to a broad continuum between the nonconscious and full, focal attention, in which atmospheres often find themselves in zones of ambient, background, and semiconscious perception. Further, atmospheres, quite unlike precultural, prehistorical, and "autonomous" affect, are deeply meaningful and awash with sign phenomena. For example, in Peircean terms the relationships of at least partial entrainment and attunement that result in a momentary overlap of feeler and feeling and that atmospheric suggestions of motion can provoke contain combinations of iconicity (qualitative likeness) and indexicality (contiguity, co-occurrence and causality). In fact, in this book we have argued that atmospheres can be located on a continuum of meaningfulness between vaguely qualified felt-bodily stirrings and more qualified, often discursively elaborated cultural phenomena and traditions, such as sensory regimes, religious formations, and discourses of belonging. Far from being nonsignifying and unconscious forces, atmospheres are enmeshed with cultural and historical phenomena, often acting as a bundling mechanism that makes otherwise disparate discourses, memories, techniques of the body, and other strands of lived experience compatible by imbuing them with a shared feel.

Our book also has implications for the unease that the overwhelmingly European origins of most of the conceptual vocabulary of the social sciences and humanities provoke in contemporary academia. This is a problem that poses itself especially from our disciplinary perspectives in anthropology and cultural musicology. How can one defend the universal claims of phenomenology, the intellectual tradition that provides the theoretical underpinning for much of our book? How can the notion of atmospheres, as formulated in twentieth-century European, particularly Barly German, philosophy be a useful guide for understanding the range of ethnographic contexts we have treated in this book, extending from the Western Pacific to the Indian Ocean? Starting from the cue that atmospheric knowledge is perhaps first and foremost environmental or ambient knowledge, we have tried to set Indigenous Oceanic perspectives on environmental knowledge through music and dance in dialogue with neophenomenological approaches to atmospheres. The result of this juxtaposition and crossing of these different strands of knowledge is that considerable kinship and overlap obtains between such Indigenous Oceanic modes of knowing the environment and the terms of atmospheric philosophizing in a phenomenological tradition at home in Europe. Likewise, we found strong parallels between Mauritian Muslims' theorization of artful vocal recitation as felt-bodily motion and the idea that suggestions of motion are the central working mechanism of atmospheres from a phenomenological perspective. Furthermore, Patrick's Twelver Shi'i Muslim interlocutors in Mumbai spoke about the *mahaul,* or atmosphere, as a key dimension of the public religious processions that also have ramifications for urban belonging and citizenship.

While this may not be enough to conclusively establish the universality of phenomenology's claims, we believe it is sufficient evidence to show that similar forms of knowledge have long emerged in a range of non-European contexts. Our book does not attempt to prove the universality of the claims that come with phenomenological analytic of atmospheres; our combined research, however, provides support for the idea of atmospheres as a potentially universal category. On the basis of our investigation, we argue that the analytic of atmospheres is a useful and broad frame to get a better sense of ambient and environmental knowledge across an array of contexts in different world regions. The fact that, for example, Indigenous Oceanic epistemologies and the phenomenological language of atmospheric research resonate with each other gives us reason to assume that neither body of knowledge is a strictly provincial tradition whose claims hold true only in the respective areas in which they historically arose.

NOTES

1. INTRODUCING ATMOSPHERIC KNOWLEDGE

1. For more on the *Hōkūleʻa*, see Low (2013).

2. Anglophone scholars outside the discipline of philosophy who write on atmospheres sometimes appear unfamiliar with the pioneering and voluminous work of Hermann Schmitz, which stretches back to the 1960s, but see Philoppopoulos-Mihalopoulos (2015) and Gandy (2017).

3. There is now a substantial body of atmospheric theory dating back to the 1960s, and the expansion of atmosphere as a concept from philosophy to other academic fields has yielded a steadily growing literature. For example, for geography, see Ben Anderson (2009), Edensor (2012), and McCormack (2018); for anthropology, see Bille (2019), Cooper (2024), Eisenlohr (2018), Peterson (2021), Reinhardt (2020), Schnegg (2024), and Throop (2021); for anthropology and media studies, see Pink and Sumartojo (2019); for music studies, see Abels (2013, 2017, 2022), and Riedel and Torvinen (2020); for religious studies, see Gregersen (2021, 2024) and Radermacher (2021); and for law, see Philoppopoulos-Mihalopoulos (2015). For an overview, see also Riedel (2019).

4. With respect to atmospheres as knowledge, Sarah Pink and Shanti Sumartojo have distinguished between knowing in atmospheres as the sensory and affective dimension of our lives, knowing about atmospheres as the retroactive description and definition of atmospheres, and knowing through atmospheres as a way to investigate and intervene in the world through the concept of atmospheres (2019, 11–12). While we do not dispute the usefulness of this distinction, our exploration of atmospheric knowledge is concerned mainly with atmospheres' intervention in the felt-body, the ground for any kind of subjectivity and being in the world well beyond the human. As will become clear later on, we take atmospheres as playing a pivotal role in the very individuation of felt-bodies and modal time. In this sense our understanding of atmospheric knowledge points to a notion of knowledge that is also prior to Pink and Sumartojo's threefold distinction.

137

5. For phenomenologists Helmuth Plessner ([1925] 1982) is the main source for the distinction between *Leib* and *Körper*. Edmund Husserl (1973, 57) and Maurice Merleau-Ponty ([1945] 1962, 283) rely on Plessner's distinction, while Hermann Schmitz (1965) offers perhaps the most systematic explication of the *Leib*. The latter in turn provides the basis for Schmitz's theorizing of atmospheres that we draw on extensively in this book.

6. In contemporary India, connoisseurs of music and dance are often referred to and addressed as *rasika* (Ram 2011).

7. Rasa originated as a key concept in classical Indian aesthetics of performing arts and literature. "Theoretically . . . rasa can be regarded as a property of a text-object, a capacity of a reader-subject, and also as a transaction between the two. The whole process, in fact, exists as a totality even while its several moments can be analytically disaggregated. In this, rasa precisely resembles the 'taste' it metaphorically references, which may be regarded as existing at once in the food, the taster, and the act of tasting" (Pollock 2016, 26).

8. Having long transcended its origins in aesthetic theories of literature and drama, in South Asian settings, the spread of rasa can, more broadly, also be part of an overall trans-actionalist Indic aesthetics of coded, graded, and moral substances (Marriott 1976), which communities, castes, and selves partake in.

9. A similar effort toward global contextualization and diversification is also underway for the notion of affect as derived from Spinoza and Deleuze (Iskra 2023).

10. Beyond our specific interest in the phenomenology of atmospheres, Michael Schnegg has recently made a related argument with respect to the broader European phenomenological tradition and kindred traditions of thought elsewhere (2023, 92–93).

11. In addition to the two kinds of atmospheres described by Schmitz and Böhme, Tonino Griffero has distinguished a third type, which he calls spurious, subjective, and projective. The first of the three types of atmospheres, according to Griffero, is prototypical, objective, external, and unintentional and corresponds to Hermann Schmitz's original formulation of atmospheres. The second is derivative-relational, objective, and external but also often intentional and dependent on a subject-world relationship and largely corresponds to Böhme's aesthetics of atmospheres (2016, 144). Nevertheless, we find it difficult to uphold the distinction between Griffero's third type of atmospheres and the second kind of atmospheres outlined by Böhme, because Böhme's reintroduction of the subject-object and subject-world distinction in the study of atmospheres that Schmitz originally sought to overcome weakens any criteria of distinction according to which an intentionally designed atmosphere could be taken to be either spurious or realistic.

12. We thus take these practices as shaping what can be perceived and known in a manner consonant with other anthropological research, such as Greg Downey's work on capoeiristas and their training, which argues with respect to such training practices that "physiology and behaviour can be modified, affecting both what is 'known' and what is knowable" (2007, 236, cited in Gatt and Lembo 2022, 832). This is an insight that be easily extended to sonic practices as somatic forms of knowledge (see also Gatt and Lembo 2022).

13. An example for the latter would be Jurassic sediments depositing on Triassic geological layers in ways that are radically indifferent to the existence of humans, let alone their ways of apprehending time.

14. See also Kozak (2020, 169–78) on the significance of Merleau-Ponty's notion of the "flesh" for the enactive generation of musical time. By the "flesh" Merleau-Ponty means

the body's role as suspending the subject-object divide, because it is both perceiving and perceived at the same time, as in the well-known example of one hand touching the other. This kind of reversibility Merleau-Ponty calls flesh thus stands for the fundamental intermingling of body and world ([1964] 1968, 248).

15. Through the work of Indologist Heinrich Zimmer, Schmitz also draws on ancient Indic, more specifically Upanishadic, thought to conceptualize such a primal state of undifferentiated expansion. In explicating the felt-bodily dynamic of expansion and contraction, he makes reference to the deep sleep of Vishnu, himself the all-encompassing absolute and eternal. Vishnu's eon-long sleep here is, presupposing the Upanishadic identification of the self *(atman)* with the cosmic absolute *(brahman)*, equivalent to this self's state prior to any differentiation and individuation of entities and thus equivalent to a radical state of relaxation and expansion (1965, 83–84).

16. On the relationship between the relational capacities of sound-based cultural practices, notions of resonance, and the sound connection, see Abels (2020).

2. SENSING TRANSOCEANIC CONNECTIONS I: THE INDIAN OCEAN WORLD

1. In Pakistan the Ahl-e Sunnat's emblematic devotion to the figure of the Prophet has sometimes motivated followers of this tradition to level charges of blasphemy, a capital offense in Pakistan, against sectarian rivals as well as members of non-Muslim minorities (Ahmed 2009). In such a context, this kind of intense devotion can also feed into majoritarian politics, a scenario not relevant for Mauritius and India, where Muslims are a minority. That said, the atmosphere generated by a na't recital in a majoritarian Pakistani context may not just be about bringing about the presence of the Prophet but may also demonstrate the power of a religious majority. While, again, this aspect is irrelevant in the Mauritian Muslim context, the comparison points to the relative openness of atmospheres and their diffuse nature, which can be qualified in very different directions and thus be bundled with very different ethical and political stances.

2. See Kabir (2021) for a different approach to the role of movement and motion in the felt aspects of transoceanic links in the Goan Mando song-and-dance genre, whose practice summons body memories that link the Indian Ocean with the Atlantic world.

4. ATMOSPHERIC CITIZENSHIP

1. Mumbai is India's most populous city in terms of population within the boundaries of the respective municipal corporation. Counting the populations of the larger Indian urban agglomerations, the larger Delhi area is even more populous than the larger urban agglomeration of Mumbai.

2. The distinction between the sonic (traveling vibratory phenomena) and the acoustic (the limited range of the sonic that humans can perceive with the hearing apparatus) is crucial here. Writing of sonic rather than acoustic atmospheres, we emphasize the ways in which atmospheres can seize and intermingle with the felt-body in ways that exceed the sense of hearing. The notion of flesh also evokes the work of Maurice Merleau-Ponty, who used it to describe the body's doubling as both sentient and sensible and its consequent

intermingling with the world when, in the case of one hand touching the other, the body touches the body as an other and feels being touched by it or when the body utters vocal sound and senses one's own voice uttering. From this he draws the following conclusion: "That means that my body is made of the same flesh as the world (it is a perceived), and moreover that this flesh of my body is shared by the world . . . (the felt *[senti]* at the same time the culmination of subjectivity and the culmination of materiality), they are in a relation of transgression or of overlapping" ([1964] 1968, 148, 248). The flesh here stands for the fundamental overlap and entanglement of body and world, of which the perception of the sonic is a prime example.

3. Hermann Schmitz takes the felt-body to reach beyond the boundaries of the physical body, composing what is felt to pertain to the body beyond its conventional limits. The notion of the felt-body is useful for an understanding of how sonic phenomena intermingle with bodies (1965; 2016, 31–32, 83–84).

4. For a critique, see Eisenlohr (2018, 124–28). See also Maria Frederika Malmström's work on how sonic vibration provokes affective states in the recent political upheaval in Cairo (2019, 57–69).

5. Among the most significant actors of such activism in Mumbai is the Twelver Shi'i media center World Islamic Network; see Eisenlohr (2015a) and Mirza (2014).

6. We use the term *symbol* in a Peircean fashion, as a sign relationship established by social convention (distinct from icons and indices).

7. The sonic aspects of Shi'i ritual practice are of decisive importance not just for public processions. The same is true for Shi'i oration, where the sonic aspects of oratory performances as different from their strictly discursive dimensions are very consequential too (Jafri 2024).

8. It is important to keep in mind a diversity of ways of making social space. The creation of social space need not just unfold through such emotions poured into space that, among other things, operate through the temporary fusion of felt-bodies, relating them through suggestions of motion and subtle entrainment. Conversely, social space can also be produced through forms of attenuation of contact under conditions of relative spatial proximity of bodies (Russell 2020).

9. This resonates with Tim Cresswell's call for an integrated account of human mobilities ranging from long-distance migration and transport infrastructures to the politics of bodily mobility, which in his research also involve the regimentation and policing of dance steps traveling across the Atlantic. "My aim, then, is to provide a way of thinking that traces some of the processes that run through the different accounts of human mobility at different scales, and ties them into a single logic without negating the very important differences between them" (2006, 123–45, 7).

5. MULTISENSORIALITY

1. Just like atmospheres are related to yet different from affect, a similar relationship exists between atmosphere and mood, two terms often used interchangeably. In the phenomenological sense, atmospheres are thoroughly spatial and situational. This makes them different from, for example, the fundamental moods of existential thrownness Heidegger called *Stimmungen* or *Befindlichkeit*, which lack such context-bound qualities ([1927] 2010, 130–36). The spatiality of atmospheres is essential, because it is only by virtue of their

spatial extension that they can intermingle with felt-bodies, making themselves felt in a distinctively somatic way that does not apply to moods to the same extent.

2. Although our analysis is concerned with humans, this phenomenology of atmospheres focused on the felt-body is not to be taken as anthropocentric. Animals, like humans, certainly also have and are felt-bodies. For example, interaction between humans and other mammals that are important companions of humans such as horses, dogs, and cats and with whom linguistic interaction is impossible to a large extent unfolds through felt-bodily attunement and communication (e.g., Finkelstein 2022 on equine therapy). We would argue that, for example, in horse riding the human rider's safety and self-preservation even largely depends on it, given that linguistic interaction with horses is impossible and that horses' physical strength vastly exceeds that of humans. Thus, the phenomenology of atmospheres is part of a "transhuman sociology" that centers on felt-bodily interaction (Gugutzer 2017, 154).

3. See also Mikkel Bille and Kirsten Simonsen's recent observation: "Hence, one can also ask what the attention to the 'affective' in anglophone geography has contributed to, that the phenomenological notion of atmosphere did not have the potential to answer, and doing this without leaving us with the problem of transmission and distinction" (2021, 303–4). For a critique of equating atmospheres with affect, see also Eisenlohr (2018, 124–28).

4. Hermann Schmitz uses the term "internally diffuse meaningfulness *[binnendiffuse Bedeutsamkeit]*" (e.g., 2005, 341; 2016, 53–55) or "holistic internally diffuse meaningfulness *[ganzheitlich-binnendiffuse Bedeutsamkeit]*" (2016, 106).

5. Sarah Pink distinguishes sensory anthropology as a more interdisciplinary approach from the anthropology of the senses. Sensory anthropology nevertheless shares the overall cultural constructionist perspective on sensory perception that is characteristic of multisensory anthropology and the anthropology of the senses (Pink and Howes 2010; Pink 2011).

6. It might be argued that diffuseness can also be part of socioculturally framed sensory categories. There is, however, a fundamental difference between diffuseness as part of a sociocultural sensory regime and the diffuse qualities of prereflective felt-bodily sensation.

7. Drawing on early twentieth-century neurology, especially work conducted in Germany, Merleau-Ponty's phenomenology of the felt-body seeks to derive all intentional acts in a Husserlian sense from bodily motion in a bottom-up fashion. He is especially interested in how the intersection of motor projects *(Bewegungsentwürfe)* and kinetic memory *(kinetisches Gedächtnis)* (Liepmann 1905; Merleau-Ponty [1945] 1962, 138–39) constitute an "intentional arc" *(intentionaler Bogen)* (Beringer 1926, 190; Merleau-Ponty [1945] 1962, 136), emerging as the base of all human intentionality, including of course sensations. Merleau-Ponty is less concerned with atmospheres but uses this focus on bodily motion as basic intentionality to explain human temporality in terms of past, present, and future, in which the body "secretes time" (Merleau-Ponty [1945] 1962, 239–40), a theme we take up in chapter 7.

8. We have included these diagrams because a formal analysis of sound is indispensable to avoid the immediate reduction of sonic phenomena to language in the analysis. Taking sound seriously necessitates paying detailed attention to its qualities and features, and this cannot be done by verbal description alone. For this a formal analysis as visualized in the diagrams is necessary, following the model of other established scholarly writing practices that combine formal analysis with ethnography. For example, Patrick was trained

as a linguistic anthropologist, and scholars in this field engage in grammatical and other formal analyses of language used by their interlocutors in the field, even if the latter are not fully aware of such categories, which nevertheless may turn out to be very consequential. That said, these diagrams have their own limits, first because they reduce sonic movement to images and, second, because they represent such movement as unfolding in the three-dimensional space of the sciences, which is different from the nondimensional space of the felt-body in which atmospheric suggestions of motion occur as a manipulation of felt-bodies' spatial economies. Nevertheless, we consider such formal analysis in combination with more conventional ethnographic methods a very valuable tool for doing justice to the sonic as a phenomenon that goes beyond and often evades discourse.

9. As mentioned earlier, the union of the feeler and the feeling also evokes Maurice Merleau-Ponty's notion of the "flesh," pointing to the double character of the body as both sentient and sensible and the overlap of body and world ([1964] 1968).

10. The same is of course true for auditory perception, which also plays a pivotal role for spatial orientation and localization; see Don Ihde's classic explorations of the "auditory field" ([1976] 2007).

11. "Indeed, light or brightness is not just an optical quality, but also a stirring felt with one's own felt-body *[In der Tat ist ja Licht oder Helligkeit nicht bloß eine optische Qualität, sondern auch eine am eigenen Leib spürbare Regung]*" (Schmitz 1968, 57).

6. STRUCTURED MOVEMENT AS AISTHETIC LABOR

1. In the original German: "Der Leib, nicht der Geist des Künstlers, empfängt die Inspiration: Ein gedanklich oder gefühlshaft konzipiertes Motiv wächst im eigenleiblichen Spüren von Bewegungssuggestionen zu der Gestalt hin, als die es dann, beim Übergang in ein sicht-, hör- oder tastbares Medium, buchstäblich oder gleichsam das Licht der Welt erblicken kann. Das Kunstwerk ist also eine objektivierte, vom leiblichen Befinden inspirierte Gebärde, ein in feste Form geronnener Tanz" (Schmitz 1966, 77). All translations are our own.

2. Friedlind Riedel translates Schmitz's *Gestaltverlauf* as "gestalt-process" (2020, 22).

3. In the original German: "[Ästhetische Arbeit] wird allgemein bestimmt als Produktion von Atmosphären und reicht insofern von der Kosmetik über Werbung, Innenarchitektur, Bühnenbildnerei bis zur Kunst im engeren Sinne. Die autonome Kunst wird in diesem Rahmen nur als eine spezielle Form ästhetischer Arbeit verstanden, die auch als autonome ihre gesellschaftliche Funktion hat. Und zwar soll sie in handlungsentlastender Situation (Museum, Ausstellung etc.) die Bekanntschaft und den Umgang mit Atmosphären vermitteln" (Böhme [1995] 2013, 25).

4. In the original German: "Dabei wird Wahrnehmung verstanden als die Erfahrung der Präsenz von Menschen, Gegenständen und Umgebungen" (Böhme [1995] 2013, 25).

5. In the original German: "Körperräume des Klanges und Klangräume des Körpers treten miteinander in einen Austausch, um neue Körper-Klang-Räume entstehen zu lassen" (Schroedter 2012b, 48).

6. In the original German: "Teil der schwingenden Weltkörper alle" and "Kommunion mit dem Raum" (Wigman 1922, 864).

7. In the original German: "Auch der ekstatische Tanz vollendet sich in einem Rausch, bei dem die Gegenwart und das eigene Ich . . . an maßlose Weite preisgegeben wird" (Schmitz 1967, 173).

8. In the original German: "Erkennen blitzt in ihr auf. Der große unsichtbare, durchsichtige Raum breitet sich formlos wogend, ein Heben des Armes verändert, gestaltet ihn. Ornamente steigen auf, wuchtig, groß, tauchen unter; zierliche Arabesken tänzeln vorüber, versinken; ein Sprung mitten hinein: böse zischt es von zerplatzenden Formen; ein schnelles Drehen: die Wände weichen. Sie senkt die Arme, steht wieder still, schaut den leeren Raum, das Reich des Tänzers" (Wigman 1922).

7. LATENCY AS THE TEMPORALITY OF ATMOSPHERES

1. All names of interlocutors are pseudonyms to protect their identities.

2. The derogatory implications of Abbas's use of the term *duplicate* are not only evident from the context of the conversation but, in the Mumbai context, also reinforced in the evocation of a 1998 Hindi comedy film titled *Duplicate*, directed by Mahesh Bhatt and starring superstar Shah Rukh Khan in a double role as a hotel chef and a gangster who are two identical-looking men. One is a funny, good-hearted regular guy and the other a criminal hunted by the police, with the gangster playing a doppelgänger-like part in relation to the chef, underlining the moral opposition between the two characters played by the same famous actor. The comedy revolves around comical effects of mistaken identity as well as love and romance.

3. "Akut gegebene Ungegenwärtigkeit" is the original wording. Drawing on the metaphor of the stowaway, Hans Ulrich Gumbrecht has characterized situations of latency in the following terms: "We sense that something (or somebody) is there that we cannot grasp or touch—and that this 'something' (or somebody) has a material articulation, which means that it (or he, or she) occupies space. We are unable to say where, exactly, our certainty of the presence comes from, nor do we know where, precisely, what is latent is located now. And because we do not know the identity of the latent object or person, we have no guarantee that we would recognize this being if it ever showed itself. Moreover, what is latent may undergo changes while it remains hidden" (2013, 23).

4. Until the late nineteenth century, the Muharram processions in Bombay were a boisterous and widely shared public event, in which neighborhood associations under the control of informal strongmen competed for prestige and influence, leading to violence that prompted the colonial authorities to ban the processions for a number of years. The British subsequently enabled the Shi'i 'ulema to play a central role in running the ritual events, which then developed a more Islamic and eventually Shi'i character (Masselos 1982).

5. On Muslim ghettoization in Mumbai, see Gupta (2015).

6. Ernst Bloch has formulated a Marxist philosophy that takes utopia seriously and in which latency plays a key role. Latency indicates the not-yet; it is the material, energetic drive that underpins the utopian potential of history, what Bloch calls the "principle of hope." Latency ultimately drives and directs tendency or that which is becoming the future. "Latency is the quality that invests tendency with the strange preexistence of its direction and preemption; in other words: latency is the mode in which the final shape of the not-yet makes itself felt in tendency" (1975, 147–48). "The present, for Bloch, is characterized by latency and tendency: the unrealized potentialities that are latent in the present, and the signs and foreshadowings that indicate the tendency of the direction and movement of the present into the future . . . . Above all, Bloch's is a philosophy of hope and the future, a dreaming forward, a projection of a vision of a future kingdom of freedom" (Kellner and O'Hara 1976, 16).

7. Heidegger argues for the primacy of latency to the related notion of *Stimmung*, translatable as "mood" or "tuning." For Heidegger such moods offer a primary and privileged way of grasping existential conditions, especially our relationship to "Being" ([1927] 2010, 130–36). *Stimmungen* are often concealed and outside focused awareness but have an "ontological preeminence as primary mode of opening up Being-in-the-World *[In-der-Welt-Sein]*" (Wellbery 2011, 267; our translation). Atmospheres share the latency of *Stimmung* as obliquely present, underlying phenomena that are always already there in a concealed way. Unlike Heidegger's existential moods, atmospheres are thoroughly spatial and situational phenomena; they extend and expand in space, suffusing everything in a given setting. Because of their spatiality, they can exert suggestions of motion on felt-bodies. The latency we describe here relates to their incipient, suggested motion, adding another, different layer of latency to the kind that Heidegger already ascribed to existential moods and attunements.

8. See also Birgit Abels on the parallels between Manning's notion of preacceleration and atmospheric suggestions of motion: "Like the 'movement[s] of the not-yet that compose the more-than-one that is my body' . . . suggestions of movement, according to Schmitz, are key in the emergence of atmospheres. With this, sonic events are always atmospheric potential that is actualizing" (2020, 171–72).

9. In an evocative way, Timothy Cooper (2024) also treats atmospheres as threshold phenomena; his emphasis is on levels of intensity as moral thresholds. Our sense of atmospheres as threshold phenomena takes the threshold above all as pointing to temporal unfolding of the spatially extended emotion and its effects; this is why we argue that latency is the distinct temporality of atmospheres. In particular contexts these two senses of atmospheres as thresholds can overlap, such as when a vague feeling of right and wrong passes into something more qualified, such as a more defined moral stance and sensibility. Our use of the idea of atmospheres as threshold phenomena is also equivalent to what we throughout this book have described as a continuum between vague, diffuse meaningfulness and more strongly qualified sociocultural phenomena and discourses. Atmospheres are vaguely meaningful and operate along this continuum by bundling such more defined cultural phenomena with the vague but meaningful feel of a situation.

10. It is well known that Benjamin's understanding of aura is complex and shifting and not always conceived in simple opposition to technological reproduction; indeed, on some occasions "Benjamin suggests that aura as a medium of perception—or 'perceptibility'—becomes visible only on the basis of technological reproduction" (M. Hansen 2008, 342–43). Sometimes aura also seems to largely overlap with atmosphere in a phenomenological sense: "The aura is a medium that envelops and physically connects—and thus blurs the boundaries between—subject and object, suggesting a sensory, embodied mode of perception" (351). However, aura's principal remaining difference from atmosphere in all of Benjamin's uses of aura is the latter's clearly vision-centric analytic.

11. On the notion of affordance, see Gibson (1979) and Keane (2014). On the atmospheric affordances of Shi'i videos, see Cooper (2022).

12. See also Lucy Osler (2024), who points to the phenomenological distinction between the felt-body and the physical body to account for empathy in online interactions. In a parallel way, we point to the same classical distinction to argue for the significance of the atmospheric in online environments, even if its production and reproduction in digital worlds leads to significant shifts and alterations, not infrequently including its attenuation.

8. ATMOSPHERES AS ENVIRONMENTALITY

1. Faustina Rehuher-Marugg, ethnographic interview with Constanze Dupont, Koror, October 17, 2022.

2. I thank Kiblas Soaladaob for sharing her ideas on the various spelling variants of this chesols and additional discussion. Besebes and Tellames (2014) record this chesols as follows: "Obil meai iiang, a kededul di milrael el mei, ma beluu a diak el ngii aikang, ma chutem a diak el ngii aikang, leng di ralm ma bad el ngeasek a merreder ra chutem iiang."

3. In the original German: "Stöße herausfordernder Verdichtung."

4. In the original German: "Die Musik . . . bringt aber desto offener und vielseitiger dem Menschen sein Schicksal nahe, in Raum und Zeit ausgesetzt zu sein und betroffen werden zu können."

Abels, Birgit. 2008. *Sounds of Articulating Identity. Tradition and Transition in the Music of Palau, Micronesia*. Berlin: Logos.

Abels, Birgit. 2013. Hörgemeinschaften: Eine musikwissenschaftliche Annäherung an die Atmosphärenforschung. *Musikforschung* 66 (3): 220–31.

Abels, Birgit. 2017. Musical Atmospheres and Sea-Nomadic Movement among the Sama Dilaut: Sounding Out a Mobile World. *Mobile Culture Studies* 3 (3): 21–36. https://doi .org/10.25364/08.3:2017.1.2.

Abels, Birgit. 2018. Music, Affect and Atmospheres: Meaning and Meaningfulness in Palauan *Omengeredakl*. *International Journal of Traditional Arts* 2: 1–17.

Abels, Birgit. 2020. Bodies in Motion: Music, Dance and Atmospheres in Palauan *Ruk*. In Riedel and Torvinen 2020, 165–83.

Abels, Birgit. 2022. *Music Worlding in Palau: Chanting, Atmospheres, and Meaningfulness*. Amsterdam: Amsterdam University Press.

Adey, Peter. 2010. *Mobility*. New York: Routledge.

Agrawal, Arun. 2005. *Environmentality: Technologies of Government and the Making of Subjects*. Durham, NC: Duke University Press.

Ahmed, Asad Ali. 2009. Specters of Macaulay: Blasphemy, in Indian Penal Code, and Pakistan's Postcolonial Predicament. In *Censorship in South Asia: Cultural Regulation from Sedition to Seduction*, edited by Raminder Kaur and William Mazzarella, 172–205. Bloomington: Indiana University Press.

Ali, Aleeha Zahra. 2022. Conjuring Karbala Online and Offline: Experiences of the "Authentic" in Shiʿa majalis. *Journal of Muslims in Europe* 11: 124–45.

Allen, Chadwick. 2020. Vital Earth/Vibrant Earthworks/Living Earthworks Vocabularies. In *Routledge Handbook of Critical Indigenous Studies*, edited by Brendan Hokowhitu, Aileen Moreton-Robinson, Linda Tuhiwai Smith, Steve Larkin, and Chris Andersen, 215–28. London: Routledge.

Allen, Helen G. 1994. *Kalākaua: Renaissance King*. Honolulu: Mutual.

Alpers, Edward A. 2014. *The Indian Ocean in World History*. Oxford: Oxford University Press.

Aluli Meyer, Manulani. 2003. Our Own Liberation: Reflections on Hawaiian Epistemology. *Contemporary Pacific* 13 (1): 124–48. https://doi.org/10.1353/cp.2001.0024.

Anderson, Ben. 2009. Affective Atmospheres. *Emotion, Space and Society* 2: 77–81.

Anderson, Benedict. 1991. *Imagined Communities: Reflections on the Origin and Spread of Nationalism*. London: Verso.

Anderson, Kay, and Susan Smith. 2001. Emotional Geographies. *Transactions of the Institute of British Geographers*, n.s., 26 (1): 7–10.

Appadurai, Arjun. 2000. Spectral Housing and Urban Cleansing: Notes on Millennial Mumbai. *Public Culture* 12 (3): 627–51.

Babcock, Hope M. 2013 "[This] I Know from My Grandfather": The Battle for Admissibility of Indigenous Oral History as Proof of Tribal Land Claims. *American Indian Law Review* 37: 19–61. http://scholarship.law.georgetown.edu/facpub/1643.

Baldacchino, Godfrey. 2008. Studying Islands: On Whose Terms? Some Epistemological and Methodological Challenges to the Pursuit of Island Studies. *Island Studies Journal* 3 (1): 37–56.

Bear, Laura. 2014. Doubt, Conflict, and Mediation: The Anthropology of Modern Time. *Journal of the Royal Anthropological Institute* 20 (S1): 3–30.

Benjamin, Walter. 1968. *Illuminations*. New York: Harcourt, Brace and World.

Bergson, Henri. (1896) 1911. *Matter and Memory*. Translated by Nancy Margaret Paul and W. Scott Palmer. London: Allen and Unwin.

Beringer, Kurt. 1926. Denkstörung und Sprache bei Schizophrenen. *Zeitschrift für die gesamte Neurologie und Psychatrie* 103: 185–97.

Besebes, Meked, and Lynda Tellames. 2014. Preserving Traditional Place Names in Palau. In *Traditional Knowledge and Wisdom: Themes from the Pacific Islands*, edited by Samuel Lee, 30–45. Jeonju, South Korea: ICHCAP.

Bille, Mikkel. 2019. *Homely Atmospheres and Lighting Technologies in Denmark: Living with Light*. London: Bloomsbury.

Bille, Mikkel, and Kirsten Simonsen. 2021. Atmospheric Practices: On Affecting and Being Affected. *Space and Culture* 24 (2): 295–309.

Binder, Stefan. 2021. Feeling Religious—Feeling Secular? Emotional Style as a Diacritical Category. *South Asian History and Culture* 12 (2–3): 278–94.

Binswanger, Ludwig. (1932) 1953. Das Raumproblem in der Psychopathologie. In *Ausgewählte Vorträge und Aufsätze*, 2: 174–225. Bern: Francke.

Bloch, Ernst. 1968. Man as Possibility. *CrossCurrents* 18 (3): 273–83.

Bloch, Ernst. 1975. *Experimentum Mundi: Frage, Kategorien des Herausbringens, Praxis*. Frankfurt: Suhrkamp.

Böhme, Gernot. 1993. Atmosphere as the Fundamental Concept of a New Aesthetics. *Thesis Eleven* 36: 113–26.

Böhme, Gernot. (1995) 2013. *Atmosphäre: Essays zur neuen Ästhetik*. Berlin: Suhrkamp.

Böhme, Gernot. 2000. Acoustic Atmospheres: A Contribution to the Study of Ecological Aesthetics. *Soundscape* 1 (1): 14–18.

Böhme, Gernot. 2006. *Architektur und Atmosphäre*. Munich: Fink.

Böhme, Gernot. 2009. Die Stimme im leiblichen Raum. In *Stimm-Welten: Philosophische, medientheoretische und ästhetische Perspektiven*, edited by Doris Kolesch, Vito Pinto, and Jenny Schrödl, 23–32. Bielefeld: Transcript.

Böhme, Gernot. 2013. Synesthesia in a Phenomenology of Perception. *Wolkenkuckuck-sheim/Cloud-Cuckoo-Land: International Journal of Architectural Theory* 18 (31): 21–33.

Böhme, Gernot. 2017. *The Aesthetics of Atmospheres.* Edited by Jean-Paul Thibaud. London: Routledge.

Boos, Tobias, and Simon Runkel. 2018. Einführung: Die ungeheuerliche Raumphilosophie von Peter Sloterdijk. *Geographica Helvetica* 73: 261–72.

Bose, Sugata. 2006. *A Hundred Horizons: The Indian Ocean in the Age of Global Empire.* Cambridge, MA: Harvard University Press.

Brandstetter, Gabriele. 2012. "Listening"—Kinaesthetic Awareness im zeitgenössischen Tanz. In Schroedter 2012a, 113–27.

Bull, Cynthia Jean Cohen. (1997) 2018. Sense, Meaning and Perception in Three Dance Cultures. In *Senses and Sensation: Critical and Primary Sources.* Vol. 4, *Art and Design,* edited by David Howes, 263–76. London: Bloomsbury.

Bull, Michael, and Les Back, eds. 2003. *The Auditory Culture Reader.* Oxford: Berg.

Byl, Julia, and Jim Skyes. 2020. Ethnomusicology and the Indian Ocean: On the Politics of Area Studies. *Ethnomusicology* 64 (3): 394–421.

Carr, James R. 2014. *Hawaiian Music in Motion.* Urbana: University of Illinois Press.

Carter, Marina. 1995. *Servants, Sirdars, Settlers: Indians in Mauritius, 1834–1874.* Delhi: Oxford University Press.

Casey, Edward S. 1996. How to Get from Space to Place in a Fairly Short Stretch of Time: Phenomenological Prolegomena. In Feld and Basso 1996, 13–52.

Chady, Shareef. 2001. *Naaté-Rasool (SAW).* Vol. 8. Set of 2 audio CDs. Castel, Mauritius: Etoile Brilliant Sound.

Chady, Shareef. 2003. *Naaté-Rasool (SAW).* Vol 9. Set of 2 audio CDs. Castel, Mauritius: Etoile Brilliant Sound.

Chady, Shareef. n.d. *Naaté-Rasool (SAW).* Vol 7. Set of 2 audio CDs. Castel, Mauritius: Etoile Brilliant Sound.

Chaudhuri, Kirti N. 1985. *Trade and Civilization in the Indian Ocean: An Economic History from the Rise of Islam to 1750.* Cambridge: Cambridge University Press.

Chow, Evelyn T. 2018. The Sovereign Nation of Hawai'i: Resistance in the Legacy of "Aloha 'Oe." *Seattle University Undergraduate Research Journal* 2 (15): 104–17. https://scholar works.seattleu.edu/suurj/vol2/iss1/15.

Clarke, Bruce. 2017. Rethinking Gaia: Stengers, Latour, Margulis. *Theory, Culture and Society* 34 (4): 3–26.

Classen, Constance. 1993. *Worlds of Sense: Exploring the Senses in History and across Cultures.* London: Routledge.

Cooper, Timothy P.A. 2022. "Live Has an Atmosphere of Its Own": *Azadari,* Ethical Orientation, and Tuned Presence in Shi'i Media Praxis. *Journal of the Royal Anthropological Institute* 28 (2): 651–75.

Cooper, Timothy P.A. 2024. *Moral Atmospheres: Islam and Media in a Pakistani Marketplace.* New York: Columbia University Press.

Cox, Christoph. 2011. Beyond Representation and Signification: Toward a Sonic Materialism. *Journal of Visual Culture* 10: 145–61.

Cox, Christoph. 2018. *Sonic Flux: Sound, Art, and Metaphysics.* Chicago: University of Chicago Press.

Cresswell, Tim. 2006. *On the Move: Mobility in the Modern Western World.* New York: Routledge.

Csordas, Thomas J. 2008. Intersubjectivity and Intercorporeality. *Subjectivity* 22 (1): 110–21.

Darier, Eric. 1999. Foucault and the Environment: An Introduction. In *Discourses of the Environment*, edited by Eric Darier, 1–34. Oxford: Blackwell.

Das, Veena. 1984. For a Folk-Theology and Theological Anthropology of Islam. *Contributions to Indian Sociology*, n.s., 18 (2): 293–300.

Deeb, Lara. 2009. Emulating and/or Embodying the Ideal: The Gendering of Temporal Frameworks and Islamic Role Models in Shiʿi Lebanon. *American Ethnologist* 36 (2): 242–57.

Deleuze, Gilles. (1968) 1994. *Difference and Repetition*. Translated by Paul Patton. New York: Columbia University Press.

Diaz, Vicente M. 2011. Voyaging for Anti-colonial Recovery: Austronesian Seafaring, Archipelagic Rethinking, and the Re-mapping of Indigeneity. *Pacific Asia Inquiry* 2 (1): 21–32.

Diaz, Vicente M. Forthcoming. "Movement in the Flow of Seafaring's Intangible Cultural Heritage." *Proceedings of the International Symposium Negotiating Intangible Cultural Heritage*. Osaka: National Ethnology Museum.

Diettrich, Brian. 2016. Virtual Micronesia: Performance and Participation in a Pacific Facebook Community. *Perfect Beat* 17 (2): 52–70. https://doi.org/10.1558/prbt.v17i1.28841.

Diettrich, Brian. 2018a. A Sea of Voices: Performance, Relations, and Belonging in Saltwater Places. *Yearbook for Traditional Music* 50: 41–69.

Diettrich, Brian. 2018b. "Summoning Breadfruit" and "Opening Seas": Toward a Performative Ecology in Oceania. *Ethnomusicology* 62 (1): 1–27.

Diettrich, Brian, Jane Freeman Moulin, and Michael Webb. 2011. *Music in Pacific Island Cultures*. Oxford: Oxford University Press.

Downey, Greg. 2002. Listening to Capoeira: Phenomenology, Embodiment, and the Materiality of Music. *Ethnomusicology* 46 (3): 487–509.

Downey, Greg. 2007. Seeing with a "Sideways Glance": Visuomotor "Knowing" and the Plasticity of Perception. In *Ways of Knowing: New Approaches in the Anthropology of Knowledge and Learning*, edited by Mark Harris, 222–41. New York: Berghahn.

Edensor, Tim. 2012. Illuminated Atmospheres: Anticipating and Reproducing the Flow of an Affective Experience in Blackpool. *Environment and Planning D: Society and Space* 30 (6): 1103–12.

Eidsheim, Nina Sun. 2015. *Sensing Sound: Singing and Listening as Vibrational Practice*. Durham, NC: Duke University Press.

Eisenberg, Andrew. 2013. Islam, Sound, and Space: Acoustemology and Citizenship on the Kenyan Coast. In *Music, Sound, and Space: Transformations of Public and Private Experience*, edited by Georgia Born, 186–202. Cambridge: Cambridge University Press.

Eisenlohr, Patrick. 2006. As Makkah Is Sweet and Beloved, so Is Madina: Islam, Devotional Genres and Electronic Mediation in Mauritius. *American Ethnologist* 33 (2): 230–45.

Eisenlohr, Patrick. 2009. Technologies of the Spirit: Devotional Islam, Sound Reproduction, and the Dialectics of Mediation and Immediacy in Mauritius. *Anthropological Theory* 9 (3): 273–96.

Eisenlohr, Patrick. 2012. Cosmopolitanism, Globalization, and Islamic Piety Movements in Mauritius. *City and Society* 24 (1): 7–28.

Eisenlohr, Patrick. 2015a. Media, Citizenship, and Religious Mobilization: The Muharram Awareness Campaign in Mumbai. *Journal of Asian Studies* 74 (3): 687–710.

Eisenlohr, Patrick. 2015b. Media, Urban Aspirations, and Religious Mobilization among Twelver Shiʿite Muslims in Mumbai. In Van der Veer 2015, 415–31.

Eisenlohr, Patrick. 2015c. Mediating Disjunctures of Time: Ancestral Chronotopes in Ritual and Media Practices. *Anthropological Quarterly* 88 (2): 281–304.

Eisenlohr, Patrick. 2017. Reconsidering Mediatization of Religion: Islamic Televangelism in India. *Media, Culture and Society* 39 (6): 869–84.

Eisenlohr, Patrick. 2018. *Sounding Islam: Voice, Media, and Sonic Atmospheres in an Indian Ocean World.* Oakland: University of California Press.

Eisenlohr, Patrick. 2019. Sonic Privilege. The Holism of Religious Publics. *The Immanent Frame. Secularism, Religion, and the Public Sphere* (blog). Accessed February 25, 2021. https://tif.ssrc.org/2019/05/21/sonic-privilege/.

Eisenlohr, Patrick. 2022a. Atmospheric Resonance: Sonic Motion and the Question of Religious Mediation. *Journal of the Royal Anthropological Institute* 28 (2): 613–31.

Eisenlohr, Patrick. 2022b. From Race to Religion in a Creole Society: Mauritian Muslims, the Hindu-Muslim Interface, and the Question of Religion and Creolization. *Archives de Sciences Sociales des Religions* 197: 59–82.

Elbert, Samuel H., and Noelani K. Māhoe. 1970. *Nā mele o Hawaiʻi nei: 101 Hawaiian Songs.* Honolulu: University of Hawaiʻi Press.

Ernst, Wolfgang. 2012. *Gleichursprünglichkeit: Zeitwesen und Zeitgegebenheit technischer Medien.* Berlin: Kadmos.

Escobar, Arturo. 2020. *Pluriversal Politics: The Real and the Possible.* Durham, NC: Duke University Press.

Fa, Stefan Williamson. 2022. Voices of Sorrow and Joy: Cultivating Relations with the Unseen in Muslim Devotion. *Cultural Anthropology* 37 (4): 625–52.

Fa, Stefan Williamson. 2024. Mediated Devotion: Sound and Media in Transnational Azeri-Turkish Twelver Shiʻism. In *Shiʻi Materiality beyond Karbala: Religion That Matters*, edited by Fouad Gehad Marei, Yafa Shanneik, and Christian Funke, 76–97. Leiden: Brill.

Fahl, Karoline. 2016. *Atmosphäre am Werk: Gernot Böhmes Neue Ästhetik als Architekturästhetik.* Technical University Berlin. Accessed February 26, 2021. www.bda-bund.de/wp-content/uploads/2017/09/Fahl-Atmosph%C3%A4re-am-Werk-DGB-2016.pdf.

Farnell, Brenda, ed. 1995. *Human Action Signs in Cultural Context: The Visible and the Invisible in Movement and Dance.* Metuchen: Scarecrow.

Fazal, Tanweer. 2012. Minorities and Their Nationalism(s): The Terms of a Discourse in South Asia. *South Asian History and Culture* 3 (2): 163–76.

Feld, Steven. 1996. Waterfalls of Song: An Acoustemology of Place Resounding in Bosavi, Papua New Guinea. In Feld and Basso 1996, 91–135.

Feld, Steven. 2017. On Post-ethnomusicology Alternatives: Acoustemology. In *Ethnomusicology or Transcultural Musicology*, edited by Francesco Giannattasio and Giovanni Guiriati, 82–98. Udine: Nota.

Feld, Steven, and Keith Basso, eds. 1996. *Senses of Place.* Santa Fe, NM: School of American Research Press.

Feld, Steven, Aaron A. Fox, Thomas Porcello, and David Samuels. 2004. Vocal Anthropology: from the Music of Language to the Language of Song. In *A Companion to Linguistic Anthropology*, edited by Alessandro Duranti, 321–45. Malden: Blackwell.

Finkelstein, Maura. 2022. The Art of Therapeutic Horsemanship: Communication, Choreography, and Collaboration in Equine Therapy. *Anthropological Quarterly* 95 (3): 621–48.

Fischer, Franz. 1930. Raum-Zeit-Struktur und Denkstörung in der Schizophrenie. *Zeitschrift für die gesamte Neurologie und Psychatrie* 124: 241–56.

Fischer, Michael M.J. 1980. *Iran: From Religious Dispute to Revolution*. Cambridge, MA: Harvard University Press.

Fischer, Michael M.J. 2010. The Rhythmic Beat of the Revolution in Iran. *Cultural Anthropology* 25 (3): 497–543.

Förster-Beuthan, Yvonne. 2012. *Zeiterfahrung und Ontologie. Perspektiven moderner Zeitphilosophie*. Munich: Fink.

Foucault, Michel. 1991. Governmentality. In *The Foucault Effect: Studies in Governmentality*, edited by Graham Burchell, Colin Gordon, and Peter Miller, 87–104. Chicago: University of Chicago Press.

Gandy, Matthew. 2017. Urban Atmospheres. *Cultural Geographies* 24 (3): 353–74.

Gatt, Caroline, and Valeria Lembo. 2022. Introduction: Knowing by Singing. *American Anthropologist* 124 (4): 830–40.

Geselbracht, Jim. 2022. *Adidil er a Klechibelau: Songs of Palau, 1915–1970*. Oakland, CA: Kereomel Conservancy.

Geselbracht, Jim. n.d. Adidil er aw Klechibelau. *Ouchacha* (blog). https://ouchacha.word press.com/category/friday-night-club/.

Gibson, James J. 1979. *The Ecological Approach to Visual Perception*. Boston: Houghton Mifflin.

Gillespie, Kirsty. 2009. Behind Every Tree? Ethnomusicology in Papua New Guinea. In *Musical Islands: Exploring Connections between Music, Place and Research*, edited by Elizabeth Mackinlay, Brydie-Leigh Bartleet, and Katelyn Barney, 20–32. Cambridge: Cambridge Scholars Press.

Goldie, Matthew Boyd, and Sebastian Sobecki. 2016. Our Seas of Islands. *Postmedieval: A Journal of Medieval Cultural Studies* 7 (4): 471–83.

Goodman, Steve. 2010. *Sonic Warfare: Sound, Affect, and the Ecology of Fear*. Cambridge, MA: MIT Press.

Grant, Stuart. 2013. Performing an Aesthetics of Atmospheres. *Aesthetics* 23 (1): 12–32.

Gregersen, Andreas Melson. 2021. Exploring the Atmosphere Inside a Liturgical Laboratory. *Material Religion* 17: 627–50.

Gregersen, Andreas Melson. 2024. Religion as Atmosphere: The Material Mediation and Aesthetic Ambiguity of a Contemporary Night Church Atmosphere. *Anthropological Forum* 34 (3): 348–72. https://doi.org/10.1080/00664677.2024.2371112.

Griffero, Tonino. 2014. *Atmospheres: Aesthetics of Emotional Spaces*. Farnham: Ashgate.

Griffero, Tonino. 2017. *Quasi-Things: The Paradigm of Atmospheres*. Translated by Sarah De Sanctis. Albany: State University of New York Press.

Großmann, Rolf. 2014. Sensory Engineering: Affects and Mechanics of Musical Time. In *Timing of Affect: Epistemologies, Aesthetics, Politics*, edited by Marie-Luise Angerer, Bernd Bösel, and Michaela Ott, 191–205. Zurich: Diaphanes.

Grydehøj, Adam. 2017. A Future of Island Studies. *Island Studies Journal* 12 (1): 3–16.

Gugutzer, Robert. 2017. Leib und Situation. Zum Theorie- und Forschungsproramm der Neophänomenologischen Soziologie. *Zeitschrift für Soziologie* 46 (3): 147–66.

Gumbrecht, Hans Ulrich. 2013. *After 1945: Latency as Origin of the Present*. Stanford, CA: Stanford University Press.

Gupta, Radhika. 2015. "There Must Be Some Way Out of Here": Beyond a Spatial Conception of Muslim Ghettoization in Mumbai? *Ethnography* 16 (3): 352–70.

Guyer, Jane. 2007. Prophecy and the Near Future: Thoughts and Macroeconomic, Evangelical, and Punctuated Time. *American Ethnologist* 34 (3): 409–21.

Halder, Epsita. 2019. Shia Women and Their "Place-Making": Gendered Agency in the Muharram Gatherings in Kolkata. In *Women Speak Nation: Gender, Culture, and Politics*, edited by Panchali Ray, 59–78. London: Routledge.

Halder, Epsita. 2022. Mourning over Karbala: Rethinking Ritual Actions of Shia Women in Kolkata. In *Psychoanalytical and Socio-cultural Perspectives on Women in India: Violence, Safety, and Survival*, edited by Paula L. Ellman, Jhuma Basak, and Gertraud Schlesinger-Kipp, 60–72. New York: Routledge.

Hansen, Mark B.N. 2015. *Feed-Forward: On the Future of 21st Century Media*. Durham, NC: Duke University Press.

Hansen, Miriam Bratu. 2008. Benjamin's Aura. *Critical Inquiry* 34 (2): 336–75.

Hansen, Thomas B. 2001. Bridging the Gulf: Migration, Modernity, and Identity among Muslims in Mumbai. In *Community, Empire, and Migration: South Asians in Diaspora*, edited by Crispin Bates, 261–85. Delhi: Orient Longman.

Hansen, Thomas B., and Oskar Verkaaik. 2009. Urban Charisma: On Everyday Mythologies in the City. *Critique of Anthropology* 29 (1): 5–26.

Haraway, Donna. 2016. Tentacular Thinking: Anthropocene, Capitalocene, Chthulucene. In *Staying with the Trouble: Making Kin in the Chthulucene*, 30–57. Durham, NC: Duke University Press.

Harkness, Nicholas. 2014. *Songs of Seoul: An Ethnography of Voice and Voicing in Christian South Korea*. Berkeley: University of California Press.

Hasse, Jürgen. 2012. *Atmosphären der Stadt: Aufgespürte Räume*. Berlin: Jovis.

Hasse, Jürgen. 2013. Synästhesie: Eine Grundform der Wahrnehmung-zum Beispiel von Architektur. *Wolkenkuckucksheim/Cloud-Cuckoo-Land: International Journal of Architectural Theory* 18 (31): 37–65.

Hasse, Jürgen. 2014. *Was Räume mit uns machen- und wir mit ihnen: Kritische Phänomenologie des Raumes*. Freiburg: Alber.

Hauʻofa, Epeli. 1993. Our Sea of Islands. In *A New Oceania: Rediscovering Our Sea of Islands*, edited by Eric Waddell, Vijay Naidu, and Epeli Hauʻofa, 2–16. Suva: University of the South Pacific.

Hauʻofa, Epeli. 2008. *"We Are the Ocean": Selected Works*. Honolulu: University of Hawaiʻi Press.

Hayward, Philip. 2012. Aquapelagos and Aquapelagic Assemblages: Towards an Integrated Study of Island Societies and Marine Environments. *Shima: The International Journal of Research into Island Cultures* 6 (1): 1–11.

Heidegger, Martin. (1927) 2010. *Being and Time*. Translated by Joan Stambaugh. Albany: State University of New York Press.

Henriques, Julian. 2011. *Sonic Bodies: Reggae Sound Systems, Performance Techniques, and Ways of Knowing*. London: Bloomsbury.

Herder, Johann Gottfried. 1772. *Abhandlung über den Ursprung der Sprache, welche den von der Königl: Academie der Wissenschaften für das Jahr 1770 gesetzten Preis erhalten hat; Auf Befehl der Akademie herausgegeben*. Berlin: Voß.

Hereniko, Vilsoni. 2000. Indigenous Knowledge and Academic Imperialism. In *Remembrance of Pacific Pasts: An Invitation to Remake History*, edited by Robert Borofsky, 78–91. Honolulu: University of Hawaiʻi Press.

Hirschkind, Charles. 2006. *The Ethical Soundscape: Cassette Sermons and Islamic Counterpublics*. New York: Columbia University Press.

Hisayama, Yuho. 2014. *Erfahrungen des Ki: Leibessphäre, Atmosphäre, Pansphäre*. Freiburg: Alber.

Ho, Engseng. 2006. *The Graves of Tarim: Genealogy and Mobility across the Indian Ocean*. Berkeley: University of California Press.

Ho, Engseng. 2017. Inter-Asian Concepts for Mobile Societies. *Journal of Asian Studies* 76 (4): 907–28.

Holston, James, and Arjun Appadurai. 1996. Cities and Citizenship. *Public Culture* 8 (2): 187–204.

Hörl, Erich, ed. 2017. *General Ecology: The New Ecological Paradigm*. With James Burton. London: Bloomsbury.

Howes, David. 2019. Multisensory Anthropology. *Annual Review of Anthropology* 48: 17–28.

Howes, David. 2022. The Misperception of the Environment: A Critical Evaluation of the Work of Tim Ingold and an Alternative Guide to the Use of the Senses in Anthropological Theory. *Anthropological Theory* 22 (4): 443–66.

Hui, Yuk. 2021. Problems of Time in the Digital Epoch. In Volmar and Stine 2021, 77–87.

Husserl, Edmund. 1964. *The Phenomenology of Internal Time-Consciousness*. Edited by Martin Heidegger. Translated by James S. Churchill. Bloomington: Indiana University Press.

Husserl, Edmund. 1973. *Zur Phänomenologie der Intersubjektivität I*. Husserliana XIII. Den Haag: Nijhoff.

Hyder, Syed Akbar. 2006. *Reliving Karbala: Martyrdom in South Asian Memory*. Oxford: Oxford University Press.

Iechad, Kora Mechelins. 2014. "The Whispered Memories of Belau's Bais: A cherechar a lokelii." Master's thesis, University of Hawai'i at Manoa.

Ihde, Don. (1976) 2007. *Listening and Voice: Phenomenologies of Sound*. Albany: State University of New York Press.

Ingersoll, Karin Amimoto. 2016. *Waves of Knowing: A Seascape Epistemology*. Durham, NC: Duke University Press.

Ingold, Tim. 2000. *The Perception of the Environment: Essays on Livelihood, Dwelling and Skill*. London: Routledge.

Ingold, Tim. 2011. *Being Alive: Essays on Movement, Knowledge and Description*. New York: Routledge.

Ingold, Tim, and David Howes. 2011. Worlds of Sense and Sensing the World. *Social Anthropology* 19 (3): 314–31.

Iskra, Anna. 2023. Decolonizing Affect: Resonance as an Ethnographic Technique. *Ethos* 51 (1): 130–45.

Ismaiel-Wendt, Johannes. 2011. *Tracksínítreks: Populäre Musik und Postkoloniale Analyse*. Münster: Unrast.

Jafri, Mohammad Nabeel. 2024. The Somatic and the Sonic in Contemporary Urdu Shi'i Khiṭābat. In *Practices of Islamic Preaching: Text, Performativity and Materiality of Islamic Religious Speech*, edited by Ayşe Amıla Akca, Mona Feise-Nasr, Leonie Stenske, and Aydın Süer, 23–39. Berlin: De Gruyter.

Jairazbhoy, Nazir Ali. 1971. *The Rāgs of North Indian Music: Their Structure and Evolution*. London: Faber and Faber.

Jameson, Frederic. 2003. The End of Temporality. *Critical Inquiry* 29 (4): 695–718.

Jolly, Margaret. 2001. On the Edge? Deserts, Oceans, Islands. *Contemporary Pacific* 13 (2): 417–66.

Jordan, Stephanie. 2007. Structural Categories for Relating Music and Dance: Towards an Analytical Method. In *Die Beziehung von Musik und Choreographie im Ballett*, edited by Michael Malkiewicz and Jörg Rothkamm, 27–34. Berlin: Vorwerk 8.

Kabir, Ananya Jahanara. 2021. Rapsodia Ibero-Indiana: Transoceanic Creolization and the Mando of Goa. *Modern Asian Studies* 55 (5): 1581–636.

Kaeppler, Adrienne. 1985. Structured Movement Systems in Tonga. In *Society and the Dance*, edited by Paul Spencer, 92–118. Cambridge: Cambridge University Press.

Kaeppler, Adrienne. 1995. Visible and Invisible in Hawaiian Dance. In Farnell 1995, 31–43.

Kaeppler, Adrienne. 1998. Understanding Dance. In Kaeppler and Love 1998, 311–18.

Kaeppler, Adrienne L., Peter R. Crowe, David Goldsworthy, Don Niles, Kim Poole, Jay W. Junker, Robin Ryan, et al. 1998. *Popular Music*. In Kaeppler and Love 1998, 126–71.

Kaeppler, Adrienne L., and Jacob W. Love, eds. 1998. *The Garland Encyclopedia of World Music. Vol. 9, Australia and the Pacific Islands. New York: Garland.*

Ka‘ili, Tēvita O. 2008. "Tauhi Vā: Creating Beauty through the Art of Sociospatial Relations." PhD diss., University of Washington.

Kame‘leihiwa, Lilikala. 2009. Hawai‘i-nui-akea Cousins: Ancestral Gods and Bodies of Knowledge Are Treasures for the Descendants. *Te Kaharoa: The eJournal on Indigenous Pacific Issues* 2 (1): 42–63.

Kane, Brian. 2015. Sound Studies without Auditory Culture: A Critique of the Ontological Turn. *Sound Studies* 1: 2–21.

Kaufmann, Walter. 1965. Rasa, Rāga-Mālā and Performance Times in North Indian Rāgas. *Ethnomusicology* 9 (3): 272–91.

Kaur, Inderjit N. 2024. Toward a Phenomenology of Rasa: Theorizing from Ras in Sikh Sabad Kīrtan Practice. In *The Oxford Handbook of Phenomenological Ethnomusicology*, edited by Harris Berger, Friedlind Riedel, and David Vanderhamm, 491–520. Oxford: Oxford University Press.

Kaur, Raminder. 2003. *Performative Politics and the Cultures of Hinduism: Public Uses of Religion in Western India.* London: Anthem.

Keane, Webb. 2014. Affordances and Reflexivity in Ethical Life: An Ethnographic Stance. *Anthropological Theory* 14 (1): 3–26.

Kellner, Douglas, and Harry O'Hara. 1976. Utopia and Marxism in Ernst Bloch. *New German Critique* 9 (Autumn): 11–34.

KETC (Krämer Ethnography Translation Committee). 2017. *Palau by Prof. Dr. Augustin Krämer.* Vol. 3. Koror: Belau National Museum/Etpison Museum.

Khan Barelwi, Ahmad Riza. n.d. *Hada‘iq-e bakhshish.* Mumbai: Raza Academy.

Khurana, Thomas. 2007. Latenzzeit: Unvordenkliche Nachwirkung; Anmerkungen zur Zeitlichkeit der Latenz. In *Latenz: 40 Annäherungen an einen Begriff*, edited by Thomas Khurana and Stefanie Diekmann, 142–47. Berlin: Kadmos.

King, John. 2007. Aloha ‘Oe. Nalu Music. www.nalu-music.com/?page_id=93.

Konishi, Junko, ed. 2014. *Utahong: 50 Selected Derrebechesiil; Japanese-Influenced Palauan Songs.* Naha: Okinawa Prefectural University of Arts.

Korom, Frank. 2002. *Hosay Trinidad: Muharram Performances in an Indo-Caribbean Diaspora.* Philadelphia: University of Pennsylvania Press.

Kovach, Margaret. 2009. *Indigenous Methodologies: Characteristics, Conversations, and Contexts*. Toronto: University of Toronto Press.

Kovach, Margaret. 2010. Conversational method in Indigenous research. *First Peoples Child and Family Review: An Interdisciplinary Journal Honoring the Voices, Perspectives and Knowledges of First Peoples through Research, Critical Analyses, Stories, Standpoints and Media Reviews* 5 (1): 40–48.

Kozak, Mariuz. 2020. *Enacting Musical Time: The Bodily Experience of New Music*. Oxford: Oxford University Press.

Krämer, Augustin. 1926. *Ergebnisse der Südsee-Expedition, 1908–1910*. Hamburg: Friederichsen.

Kramer, Lawrence. 2016. *The Thought of Music*. Oakland: University of California Press.

Labelle, Brandon. 2010. *Acoustic Territories: Sound Culture and Everyday Life*. New York: Continuum.

Larkin, Brian. 2014. Techniques of Inattention: The Mediality of Loudspeakers in Nigeria. *Anthropological Quarterly* 87 (4): 989–1016.

Latour, Bruno. 2007. *Reassembling the Social: An Introduction to Actor-Network-Theory*. Oxford: Oxford University Press.

Latour, Bruno. 2017. Why Gaia Is Not a God of Totality. *Theory, Culture and Society* 34 (2–3): 61–81.

Lear, Adriana. 2018. "A Study of Traditional Tongan Music Using the Tā-Vā (Time-Space) Theory of Art." Bachelor's thesis, University of Wollongong.

Lee, Tong Song. 1999. Technology and the Production of Islamic Space: The Call to Prayer in Singapore. *Ethnomusicology* 43 (1): 86–10.

Lefebvre, Henri. 1968. *Le droit à la ville*. Paris: Anthropos.

Lefebvre, Henri. 2004. *Rhythmanalysis: Space, Time, and Everyday Life*. London: Continuum.

Leys, Ruth. 2011. The Turn to Affect: A Critique. *Critical Inquiry* 37 (3): 434–72.

Liepmann, Hugo. 1905. *Über Störungen des Handelns bei Gehirnkranken*. Berlin: Karger.

Lorea, Carola E. Forthcoming. *Communities of Sound: Religion, Displacement and Caste in the Bay of Bengal*. Middletown, CT: Wesleyan University Press.

Lorea, Carola E., Aditi Mukherjee, and Dishani Roy. 2023. A Dalit Religion Online: Clashing Sensoryscapes and Remote Ethnographies behind the Screen. *Dialectical Anthropology* 48: 83–112. https://doi.org/10.1007/s10624-023-09708-6.

Lovelock, James. 1979. *Gaia: A New Look at Life on Earth*. New York: Oxford University Press.

Low, Sam. 2013. *Hawaiki Rising: Hōkūleʻa, Nainao Thompson, and the Hawaiian Renaissance*. Honolulu: University of Hawaiʻi Press.

Lynch, Julian Anthony. 2019. Festival "Noise" and Soundscape Politics in Mumbai, India. *Sound Studies* 5 (1): 37–51.

Māhina, Hūfanga ʻŌkusitino. 2010. *Tā, Vā*, and *Moana*: Temporality, Spatiality, and Indigeneity. *Pacific Studies* 33 (2–3): 168–202.

Malmström, Maria Frederika. 2019. *The Streets Are Talking to Me: Affective Fragments in Sisi's Egypt*. Oakland: University of California Press.

Manning, Erin. (2009) 2012. *Relationscapes: Movement, Art, Philosophy*. Cambridge, MA: MIT Press.

Manning, Erin. 2014. Wondering the World Directly, or How Movement Outruns the Subject. *Body and Society* 20 (3–4): 162–88.

Marinucci, Lorenzo. 2019. Mood, Ki, Humors: Elements and Atmospheres between Europe and Japan. *Studi di estetica* 14: 169–92.

Markovits, Claude. 1999. Indian Merchant Networks Outside India in the Nineteenth and Twentieth Centuries: A Preliminary Survey. *Modern Asian Studies* 33 (4): 883–911.

Marks, Laura U. 2010. *Enfoldment and Infinity: An Islamic Genealogy of New Media Art*. Cambridge, MA: MIT Press.

Marriott, McKim. 1976. Hindu Transactions: Diversity without Dualism. In *Transaction and Meaning: Directions in the Anthropology of Exchange and Symbolic Behavior*, edited by Bruce Kapferer, 109–42. Philadelphia: Institute for the Study of Human Issues.

Masoudi Nejad, Reza. 2015. The Muharram Procession of Mumbai: From Seafront to Cemetery. In Van der Veer 2015, 89–109. Masselos, Jim. 1982. Change and Custom in the Format of the Bombay Mohurrum in the Nineteenth and Twentieth Centuries. *South Asia* 5 (2): 47–67.

Massumi, Brian. 2002. *Parables for the Virtual: Movement, Affect, Sensation*. Durham, NC: Duke University Press.

McCormack, Derek P. 2018. *Atmospheric Things: On the Allure of Elemental Envelopment*. Durham, NC: Duke University Press.

Mcleod Elizabeth, Bruton-Adams Mae, Förster Johannes, Franco Chiara, Gaines Graham, Gorong Berna, James Robyn, Posing-Kulwaum Gabriel, Tara Magdalene, and Terk Eliza. 2019. Lessons from the Pacific Islands: Adapting to Climate Change by Supporting Social and Ecological Resilience. *Frontiers in Marine Science*, June 18, 2019. https://doi.rg/10.3389/fmars.2019.00289.

McTaggart, John M.E. 1908. The Unreality of Time. *Mind* 17 (68): 457–74.

Menon, Nandagopal R. 2015. Communal Harmony as Governmentality: Reciprocity, Peace-Keeping, State Legitimacy, and Citizenship in Contemporary India. *Modern Asian Studies* 49 (2): 393–429.

Merleau-Ponty, Maurice. (1945) 1962. *Phenomenology of Perception*. Translated by Colin Smith. London: Routledge.

Merleau-Ponty, Maurice. (1964) 1968. *The Visible and the Invisible*. Evanston: Northwestern University Press.

Meyer, Birgit, and Annelies Moors, eds. 2006. *Religion, Media, and the Public Sphere*. Bloomington: Indiana University Press.

Mignolo, Walter. 2009. Geopolitics of Sensing and Knowing: On (De)Coloniality, Border Thinking, and Epistemic Disobedience. *Transversal* 8. http://eipcp.net/transversal/0112/mignolo/en.

Mirza, Shireen. 2014. Travelling Leaders and Connecting Print Cultures: Two Conceptions of Twelver Shiʿi Reformism in the Indian Ocean. *Journal of the Royal Asiatic Society* 24 (3): 455–75.

Moorthy, Shanti, and Ashraf Jamal. 2010. Introduction: New Conjunctures in Maritime Conjunctures. In *Indian Ocean Studies: Cultural Social and Political Perspectives*, edited by Shanti Moorthy and Ashraf Jamal, 1–31. New York: Routledge.

Nadarajah, Yaso, and Adam Grydehøj. 2016. Island Studies as a Decolonial Project. *Island Studies Journal* 11 (2): 437–46.

Nero, Karen L. 1992. The Breadfruit Tree Story: Mythological Transformations in Palauan Politics. *Pacific Studies* 15 (4): 235–60.

Neyrat, Frédéric. 2017. Elements for an Ecology of Separation: Beyond Ecological Constructivism. In Hörl 2017, 101–27.

Nietzsche, Friedrich. 1883. *Also sprach Zarathustra*. Chemnitz: Schmeitzner.

Osler, Lucy. 2024. Taking Empathy Online. *Inquiry* 67 (1): 302–29.

Othman, Muhammad Lutfi Bin. 2022. Listening for/as Presence: Religious Mediation of a Sufi Ritual in the Time of COVID-19. *Religion* 52 (2): 265–83.

Palau Society of Historians. 2008. *Entertainment: Sports and Games, Dances and Songs*. Accessed January 29, 2025. https://ministryofhrctd.pw/wp-content/uploads/2020/07/Palau-Soc-Hist-Entertainment-2002-English.pdf.

Parmentier, Richard J. 1987. *The Sacred Remains. Myth, History, and Polity in Belau*. Chicago: University of Chicago Press.

Parmentier, Richard J. 1994. *Signs in Society: Studies in Semiotic Anthropology*. Bloomington: Indiana University Press.

Peirce, Charles Sanders. 1932. *Collected Papers of Charles Sanders Peirce*. Vol. 2, *Elements of Logic*. Cambridge, MA: Harvard University Press.

Perez, Craig Santos. 2016. New Pacific Islander Poetry. *Poetry* 208 (4): 373–77.

Peters, John Durham. 2001. Witnessing. *Media, Culture and Society* 23 (6): 707–23.

Peterson, Marina. 2021. *Atmospheric Noise: The Indefinite Urbanism of Los Angeles*. Durham, NC: Duke University Press.

Philoppopoulos-Mihalopoulos, Andreas. 2015. *Spatial Justice: Body, Lawscape, Atmosphere*. London: Routledge.

Pink, Sarah. 2011. Multimodality, Multisensoriality and Ethnographic Knowing: Social Semiotics and the Phenomenology of Perception. *Qualitative Research* 11 (3): 261–76.

Pink, Sarah, and David Howes. 2010. The Future of Sensory Anthropology/the Anthropology of the Senses. *Social Anthropology* 18 (3): 331–40.

Pink, Sarah, and Shanti Sumartojo. 2019. *Atmospheres and the Experiential World: Theory and Methods*. New York: Routledge.

Plessner, Helmuth. (1925) 1982. Die Deutung des mimischen Ausdrucks: Ein Beitrag zur Lehre vom Bewusstsein des anderen Ichs. In *Gesammelte Schriften*. Vol. 7, *Ausdruck und menschliche Natur*, edited by Günter Dux, Odo Marquard, and Elisabeth Ströker, with Frederik J. Buytendijk, 67–129. Frankfurt: Suhrkamp.

Pollock, Sheldon. 2016. Introduction: An Intellectual History of Rasa. In *A Rasa Reader: Classical Indian Aesthetics*, edited by Sheldon Pollock, 1–45. New York: Columbia University Press.

Pugh, Jonathan. 2013. Island Movements: Thinking with the Archipelago. *Island Studies Journal* 8 (1): 9–24.

Radermacher, Martin. 2021. "Not a Church Anymore": The Deconsecration and Conversion of the Dominican Church in Münster (Westphalia, Germany). *Material Religion* 17 (1): 1–28.

Rahnema, Ali. 1998. *An Islamic Utopian: A Political Biography of Ali Shari'ati*. London: Tauris.

Ram, Kalpana. 2011. Being "Rasikas": The Affective Pleasures of Music and Dance Spectatorship and Nationhood in Indian Middle-Class Modernity. *Journal of the Royal Anthropological Institute*, n.s., 17:S159–75.

Rasmussen, Anne. 2016. Performing Islam around the Indian Ocean Basin: Musical Ritual and Recreation in Indonesia and the Arabian Gulf. In *Islam and Popular Culture*, edited by Karin van Nieuwkerk, Mark Levine, and Martin Stokes, 300–322. Austin: University of Texas Press.

Rehuher-Marugg, Faustina. 2016. Explanatory remarks for the "Obil ngesur" performance. USAID-PACAM-PCS-HOPE Joint Project Launch, Koror, Palau, September 2016.

Reinhardt, Bruno. 2020. Atmospheric Presence: Reflections on "Mediation" in the Anthropology of Religion and Technology. *Anthropological Quarterly* 93 (1): 1523–54.

Reinhardt, Bruno, and Diogo Silva Corrêa. 2024. *In medias res*: Pensando com as atmosferas. *Revista Antropolítica* 56 (2). https://periodicos.uff.br/antropolitica/article/view/63407/37252.

Ricci, Ronit. 2011. *Islam Translated: Literature, Conversion, and the Arabic Cosmopolis of South and Southeast Asia*. Chicago: University of Chicago Press.

Riedel, Friedlind. 2015. Music as Atmosphere: Lines of Becoming in Congregational Worship. *Lebenswelt*, no. 6, 80–111.

Riedel, Friedlind. 2019. Atmosphere. In *Affective Societies: Key Concepts*, edited by Jan Slaby and Christian von Scheve, 85–95. New York: Routledge.

Riedel, Friedlind. 2020. Atmospheric Relations: Theorising Music and Sound as Atmosphere. In Riedel and Torvinen 2020, 1–42.

Riedel, Friedlind, and Juha Torvinen, eds. 2020. *Music as Atmosphere: Collective Feelings and Affective Sounds*. New York: Routledge.

Ringel, Felix. 2016. Can Time Be Tricked? A Theoretical Introduction. *Cambridge Journal of Anthropology* 34 (1): 17–21.

Robinson, Francis. 1983. Islam and Muslim Society in South Asia. *Contributions to Indian Sociology*, n.s., 17 (2): 185–203.

Roquet, Paul. 2016. *Ambient Media: Japanese Atmospheres of Self*. Minneapolis: University of Minnesota Press.

Rosaldo, Renato. 1994. Cultural Citizenship in San Jose, California. *PoLAR* 17 (2): 57–64.

Ruffle, Karen G. 2017. Presence in Absence: The Formation of Reliquary Shiʿism in Qutb Shahi Hyderabad. *Material Religion* 13 (3): 329–53.

Russell, Kamala. 2020. Facing Another: The Attenuation of Contact as Space in Dhofar, Oman. *Signs in Society* 8 (2): 290–318.

Salesa, Damon. 2014. The Pacific in Indigenous Time. In *Pacific Histories: Ocean, Land, People*, edited by David Armitage and Alison Bashford, 31–52. New York: Palgrave MacMillan.

Santos, Boaventura De Sousa. 2008. *Another Knowledge Is Possible: Beyond Northern Epistemologies*. London: Verso.

Santos, Boaventura De Sousa. 2014. *Epistemologies of the South: Justice against Epistemicide*. New York: Routledge.

Santos, Boaventura De Sousa. 2018. *The End of the Cognitive Empire: The Coming of Age of Epistemologies of the South*. Durham, NC: Duke University Press.

Sanyal, Usha. 1996. *Devotional Islam and Politics in British India: Ahmad Riza Khan Barelwi and His Movement (1870–1920)*. Oxford: Oxford University Press.

Schmitz, Hermann. 1965. *System der Philosophie*. Vol. 2, *Part 1: Der Leib*. Bonn: Bouvier.

Schmitz, Hermann. 1966. *System der Philosophie*. Vol. 2, *Part 2: Der Leib im Spiegel der Kunst*. Bonn: Bouvier.

Schmitz, Hermann. 1967. *System der Philosophie*. Vol. 3, *Part 1: Der leibliche Raum*. Bonn: Bouvier.

Schmitz, Hermann. 1968. *Subjektivität: Beiträge zur Phänomenologie und Logik*. Bonn: Bouvier.

Schmitz, Hermann. 1969. *System der Philosophie*. Vol. 3, *Part 2: Der Gefühlsraum*. Bonn: Bouvier.

Schmitz, Hermann. 1978. *System der Philosophie*. Vol. 3, *Part 5: Die Wahrnehmung*. Bonn: Bouvier.

Schmitz, Hermann. 1992. Zeit als leibliche Dynamik und ihre Entfaltung in der Gegenwart. In *Zeiterfahrung und Personalität*, edited by Forum für Philosophie Bad Homburg, 231–46. Frankfurt: Suhrkamp.

Schmitz, Hermann. 2005. Hermeneutik leiblicher Expressivität. *Zeitschrift für Philosophie* 53 (3): 339–47.

Schmitz, Hermann. 2007. Leibliche Bewegung auf dem Grund der Zeit. *Interdisziplinäre Phänomenologie* 4: 1–12.

Schmitz, Hermann. 2009. *Der Leib, der Raum und die Gefühle*. Bielefeld: Aisthesis.

Schmitz, Hermann. 2016. *Atmosphären*. Freiburg: Alber.

Schmitz, Hermann, Rudolf Owen Müllan, and Jan Slaby. 2011. Emotions Outside the Box: The New Phenomenology of Feeling and Corporeality. *Phenomenology and the Cognitive Sciences* 10 (2): 241–59.

Schnegg, Michael. 2023. Phenomenological Anthropology: Philosophical Concepts for Ethnographic Use. *Zeitschrift für Ethnologie/Journal of Social and Cultural Anthropology* 148: 59–102.

Schnegg, Michael. 2024. Rural Boredom: Atmospheres of Blocked Promises. *Journal of the Royal Anthropological Institute*, January 24, 2024. https://doi.org/10.1111/1467-9655.14095.

Schroedter, Stephanie, ed. 2012a. *Bewegungen zwischen Hören und Sehen: Denkbewegungen über Bewegungskünste*. Würzburg: Königshausen und Neumann.

Schroedter, Stephanie. 2012b. Neues Hören für ein neues Sehen von Bewegungen: Von der Geburt eines zeitgenössischen Balletts aus dem Körper der Musik; Annäherungen an Martin Schläpfers musikchoreographische Arbeit. In Schroedter 2012a, 43–104.

Schroedter, Stephanie. 2018. Listening in Motion and Listening to Motion: The Concept of Kinaesthetic Listening Exemplified by Dance Compositions of the Meyerbeer Era. In *Bild und Bewegung im Musiktheater: Interdisziplinäre Studien im Umfeld der Grand opéra/Image and Movement in Music Theatre: Interdisciplinary Studies around Grand Opéra*, edited by Roman Brotbeck, Laura Moeckli, Anette Schaffer, and Stephanie Schroedter, 13–42. Schliengen: Argus.

Schubel, Vernon James. 1993. *Religious Performance in Contemporary Islam: Shiʿi Devotional Rituals in South Asia*. Columbia: University of South Carolina Press.

Schulz, Dorothea E. 2012. *Muslims and New Media in West Africa: Pathways to God*. Bloomington: Indiana University Press.

Schwarz, Renate. 2015. Applied Embodiment und das Konzept der Leiblichkeit in Beratung, Supervision und Coaching. *Resonanzen: E-Journal für biopsychosoziale Dialoge in Psychotherapie, Supervision und Beratung* 3 (1): 52–64. www.resonanzen-journal.org.

Servan-Schreiber, Catherine. 2010. *Historie d'une musique métisse à l'île Maurice: Chutney indien et séga Bollywood*. Paris: Riveneuve.

Shani, Ornit. 2010. Conceptions of Citizenship in India and the "Muslim Question." *Modern Asian Studies* 44 (1): 145–73.

Shaw, Wendy M.K. 2019. Seeing with the Ear, Recognizing with the Heart: Rethinking the Ontology of the Mimetic Arts in Islam. In *Figurations and Sensations of the Unseen in Judaism, Christianity and Islam: Contested Desires*, edited by Birgit Meyer and Terje Stordalen, 37–56. London: Bloomsbury.

Shehabi, Fadlou. 1995. *Philosophies of Music in Medieval Islam*. Leiden: Brill.

Sheller, Mimi, and John Urry. 2006. The New Mobilities Paradigm. *Environment and Planning A: Economy and Space* 38 (2): 207–26.

Sheriff, Abdul. 2010. *Dhow Cultures and the Indian Ocean: Cosmopolitanism, Commerce, and Islam*. New York: Oxford University Press.

Sherman, Taylor C. 2015. *Muslim Belonging in Secular India: Negotiating Citizenship in Postcolonial Hyderabad*. Cambridge: Cambridge University Press.

Shouse, Eric. 2005. Feeling, Emotion, Affect. *M/C Journal* 8 (6). https://journal.media-culture.org.au/0512/03-shouse.php.

Simon, Ralf. 2020. Latenzzeit. In *Ästhetische Eigenzeiten: Ein Wörterbuch*, edited by Michael Bies, Michael Gamper, and Steffen Richter, 218–25. Hannover: Wehrhahn.

Simondon, Gilbert. (1964) 1992. The Genesis of the Individual. In *Incorporations*, edited by Jonathan Crary and Sanford Kwinter, 297–319. New York: Zone.

Simpson, Edward. 2006. *Muslim Society and the Western Indian Ocean: The Seafarers of Kachchh*. London: Routledge.

Sloterdijk, Peter. (1998) 2011. *Bubbles: Spheres I; Microspherology*. Cambridge, MA: MIT Press.

Sparey, Rhys Thomas. 2022. #IAMHUSSAINI: Television and Mourning during the COVID-19 Pandemic. *Religion* 52 (2): 284–305.

Staley, Andrea. 2017. "Identifying the Vā: Space in Contemporary Pasifika Creative Writing." Master's thesis, University of Hawai'i at Manoa. Accessed December 14, 2020. https://scholarspace.manoa.hawaii.edu/bitstream/10125/62661/2017-05-ma-staley.pdf.

Stengers, Isabelle. 2015. *In Catastrophic Times: Resisting the Coming Barbarism*. Ann Arbor, MI: Open Humanities.

Stepputat, Kendra, and Elina Seye. 2020. Introduction: Choremusical Perspectives. In Choremusicology. Special issue, *World of Music*, n.s., 9 (1): 7–24.

Sterne, Jonathan. 2003. *The Audible Past: Cultural Origins of Sound Reproduction*. Durham, NC: Duke University Press.

Stewart, Kathleen. 2011. Atmospheric Attunements. *Environment and Planning D: Society and Space* 29 (3): 445–53.

Stoller, Paul. 1989. *The Taste of Ethnographic Things: The Senses in Anthropology*. Philadelphia: University of Pennsylvania Press.

Stolow, Jeremy. 2005. Religion and/as media. *Theory, Culture and Society* 22 (4): 119–45.

Stratford, Elaine, Godfrey Baldacchino, Elizabeth McMahon, Carol Farbotko, and Andrew Harwood. 2011. Envisioning the Archipelago. *Island Studies Journal* (6) 2: 113–30.

Sundaram, Ravi. 2009. *Pirate Modernity: Delhi's Media Urbanism*. London: Routledge.

Sundberg, Johan. 1974. Articulatory Interpretation of the "Singing Formant." *Journal of the Acoustical Society of America* 55: 838–44.

Sykes, Jim. 2018. *The Musical Gift: Sonic Generosity in Post-war Sri Lanka*. Oxford: Oxford University Press.

Tallbear, Kim. 2015. An Indigenous Reflection on Working beyond the Human/Not Human. *GLQ: A Journal of Lesbian and Gay Studies* 21 (2–3): 230–35.

Tamimi Arab, Pooyan. 2017. *Amplifying Islam in the European Soundscape: Religious Pluralism and Secularism in the Netherlands*. London: Bloomsbury.

Tanabe, Hisao. 1978. *The Music of Micronesia, the Kao-shan Tribes of Taiwan, and Sakhalin (1934, 1922, 1923)*. Toshiba Records TW-80011.

Tatar, Elizabeth. 1985. *Call of the Morning Bird: Chants and Songs of Palau, Yap, and Ponape, Collected by Iwakichi Muranushi, 1936.* Honolulu: Pauahi Bishop Museum.

Teaiwa, Katerina. 2020. On Decoloniality: A View from Oceania. *Postcolonial Studies* 23 (4): 601–3. https://doi.org/10.1080/13688790.2020.1751429.

Tellenbach, Hugo. 1968. *Geschmack und Atmosphäre: Medien menschlichen Elementarkontaktes.* Salzburg: Müller.

Thibaud, Jean-Paul. 2011. A Sonic Paradigm of Urban Ambiances. *Journal of Sonic Studies* 1 (1): 1–14.

Thomas, Allan, Peter Russell Crowe, Allan Marett, Lamont Lindstrom, Steven Knopoff, Mary E. Lawson Burke, Vida Chenoweth, Adrienne L. Kaeppler, John D. Waiko, and Vereara Teariki Monga Maeva. 1998. Compositional Processes. In Kaeppler and Love 1998, 353–70.

Throop, Jason C. 2021. Meterological Moods and Atmospheric Attunements. In *Vulnerability and the Politics of Care,* edited by Victoria Brown, Jason Danely, and Doerthe Rosenow, 60–77. Oxford: Oxford University Press.

Titon, Jeff Todd. 2017. Interview with Jeff Todd Titon re *The Sound of Climate Change. Whole Terrain* 22. www.academia.edu/37366485/Interview_with_Jeff_Todd_Titon_re _The_Sound_of_Climate_Change_2017_.

Trnka, Susanna, Christine Dureau, and Julie Park, eds. 2013. *Senses and Citizenships: Embodying Political Life.* London: Routledge.

Urry, John. 2007. *Mobilities.* Cambridge, MA: Polity.

Van der Ryn, Fepulea'i Micah. 2007. *The Measina of Architecture in Samoa: An Examination of the VĀ in Samoan Architecture and Socio-cultural Implications of Architectural Changes.* Apia, Samoa: Institute of Samoan Studies, National University of Samoa.

Van der Veer, Peter, ed. 2015. *Handbook of Religion and the Asian City: Aspiration and Urbanization in the Twenty-First Century.* Oakland: University of California Press.

Vara Sánchez, Carlos. 2023. *Aesthetic Rhythms.* Sesto San Giovanni: Aesthetica.

Verne, Julia, and Markus Verne. 2017. Introduction: The Indian Ocean as Aesthetic Space. *Comparative Studies of South Asia, Africa, and the Middle East* 34 (2): 314–20.

Volmar, Axel, and Kyle Stine, eds. 2021. *Media Infrastructures and the Politics of Digital Time: Essays on Hardwired Temporalities.* Amsterdam: Amsterdam University Press.

Von Laban, Rudolf. 1920. *Die Welt des Tänzers.* Stuttgart: Seifert.

Wang, Zhoufei. 2024. *Atmosphären-Ästhetik: Die Verflochtenheit von Natur, Kunst und Kultur.* Freiburg: Alber.

Weiner, Isaac A. 2014. Calling Everyone to Pray: Pluralism, Secularism, and the Adhān in Hamtramck, Michigan. *Anthropological Quarterly* 87 (4): 1049–77.

Wellbery, David E. 2011. Latenz und Stimmung. In *Latenz: Blinde Passagiere in den Geisteswissenschaften,* edited by Hans Ulrich Gumbrecht and Florian Klinger, 265–76. Göttingen: Vandenhoek und Ruprecht.

Wesley-Smith, Terence, ed. 2010. Epeli's Quest: Essays in Honor of Epeli Hau'ofa. Special issue, *Contemporary Pacific* 22 (1).

Western, Tom. 2020. Listening with Displacement: Sound, Citizenship, and Disruptive Representations of Migration. *Migration and Society: Advances in Research* 3 (1): 294–309.

Westmoreland, Mark R. 2022. Multimodality: Reshaping Anthropology. *Annual Review of Anthropology* 51: 173–94.

Wigman, Mary [Karoline Sofie Marie Wiegmann]. 1922. Tanz. *Die Tat* 13 (2): 863–65.

Williams, Philippa. 2012. India's Muslims, Lived Secularism, and Realising Citizenship. *Citizenship Studies* 16 (8): 979–95.

Willke, Elke. 2020. *Tanztherapie: Theoretische Kontexte und Grundlagen der Intervention.* Wiesbaden: Reichert.

Wilson, Oli T. 2014. Ples and Popular Music Production: A Typology of Home-Based Recording Studios in Port Moresby, Papua New Guinea. *Ethnomusicology Forum* 23 (3): 425–44. https://doi.org/10.1080/17411912.2014.975142.

Wolf, Richard K. 2000. Embodiment and Ambivalence: Emotion in South Asian Muharram Drumming. *Yearbook for Traditional Music* 32: 81–116.

Wolfe, Patrick, and Adria Imada. 2013. "Aloha 'Oe": Settler-Colonial Nostalgia and the Genealogy of a Love Song. *American Indian Culture and Research Journal* 37 (2): 35–52. https://doi.org/10.17953/aicr.37.2.c4x497167lx48183.

"Year 2017 Ashura in Mumbai." Jawadia TV. Accessed February 10, 2025. www.youtube.com/watch?v=qsbhkPk7Woo.

Yunkaporta, Tyson. 2019. *Sand Talk: How Indigenous Thinking Can Save the World.* Melbourne: Text.

INDEX

power: of atmospheres, 12, 31, 36, 79, 107, 133; of chesols, 127; colonial powers, 42; environmentality and, 11–12, 119, 121, 128, 132; latency and, 106, 107, 115; of na't recitals, 85, 86; power-knowledge, 6; of religious majority, 139n1; of sonic atmospheres, 71, 73–74; sonic suggestions of motion and, 85; of sound, 36, 38, 45, 51–52, 59, 78. *See also* environmentality; governmentality

predimensional space, 30–31, 70, 96

primitive present, 14, 15

principium individuationis, 9, 14–15. *See also* individuation

projections of motion, 13, 14, 15, 141n7

protentions, 13, 21, 132

Pugh, Jonathan, 46

Qi concept, 6

rasa aesthetics, 5, 138nn7–8

Rehuher-Marugg, Faustina, 122–25, 128–29

religion: boundaries, 32, 35; religious forms of belonging, 25, 37, 56–59, 63, 66, 67, 71–73; religious knowledge, 3–4, 25, 32, 36, 38; ritual remembrance, 4; traditions, 25–39, 27, 28, 58, 61–62, 70, 139n1. *See also* Islam

religious networks: Indian Ocean world and, 3–4, 31–35, 82; Mauritius and, 31–35, 82; na't devotional poetry and, 31–35, 82; politics and, 25

retentions, 13, 21, 132

Roquet, Paul, 11

Roy, Dishani, 116

ruk (dance), 94, 97, 99–100

Salafis, 38

Samoa, 98

Santos, Boaventura De Santos, 54

Schmitz, Hermann: on ancient Indic thought, 139n15; approach to atmospheres, 4, 6–7, 8, 77, 137n2, 138n5, 138n11; on atmospheres as half-things, 4, 67, 77, 79, 87, 119; Böhme and, 96; conception of dance, 101; decentering of subjectivity, 77, 87; on emotions as atmospheres, 31, 60; encorporation and, 70; environmentality and, 9, 10, 60–61; individuation and, 14–15, 119; on meaningfulness, 141n4; on musical processes, 126; notion of felt-body, 140n3; notion of space, 97–98; objectivity discourse, 20; on observation of atmospheres, 38; on rhythm, 125; sociocultural phenomena and, 18; structured movement, 100–101; suggestions of motion and, 70, 77, 78, 88, 91–94, 100, 110, 117, 132; surfaceless space concept, 94, 96, 99; synesthesia and, 15, 16, 17, 79, 89

Schnegg, Michael, 138n10

Schroedter, Stephanie, 96

sensory holism, 79–82

Shariati, Ali, 113

Shi'i Muslims: character of, 60, 61, 67, 69, 70, 73, 107, 110, 114, 143n4; media and, 104, 108, 111, 114–17, 140n5; messianic time and, 112; in Mumbai, 4, 58, 59, 61, 63–64, 71–72, 73–74, 106; oration of, 140n7; ritual life, 70, 72, 104, 108, 109, 110–11, 118; suggestions of motion/movement and, 71; World Islamic Network, 62, 111. *See also* Ashura processions; Karbala, Battle of; Karbala paradigm; Muhammad, Prophet; Muharram processions; Twelver Shi'i Muslims

Simondon, Gilbert, 9

Simonsen, Kirsten, 141n3

Sloterdijk, Peter, 12

Smith, Barbara B., 47

sociocultural phenomena, 9, 15, 46, 58, 144n9

sonic atmospheres: citizenship and, 73–74; environmentality and, 23, 121–22; as feelings, 67; meaningfulness continuum and, 81; in Mumbai, 22, 56, 57; recitation and, 30–31; ritual contexts and, 32, 70, 73; suggestions of motion/movement, 67, 70, 71, 81–82, 88–89, 129; synesthetic characters and, 90. *See also* Muharram processions; Mumbai; na't devotional poetry

sonic multimodality. *See* multimodality

sonic practices: atmospheric knowledge and, 4, 18; environmentality and, 2, 21, 24, 39, 121, 128; felt-bodies and, 24; multisensoriality and, 76, 88; religious knowledge and, 3–4, 25, 32, 36, 38; sound as medium and, 19; suggestions of motion/movement and, 38, 39. *See also* Muharram processions; na't devotional poetry; sound knowledge; transoceanic connections; Twelver Shi'i Muslims

sonic privilege, 15–18, 18, 20–21, 52, 54, 56, 59, 74, 88. *See also* holisms

sound knowledge, 2, 5, 18–21, 40, 127, 130, 132. *See also* sonic practices

sound ties, 43, 46, 51–54, 55

Founded in 1893,
UNIVERSITY OF CALIFORNIA PRESS
publishes bold, progressive books and journals
on topics in the arts, humanities, social sciences,
and natural sciences—with a focus on social
justice issues—that inspire thought and action
among readers worldwide.

The UC PRESS FOUNDATION
raises funds to uphold the press's vital role
as an independent, nonprofit publisher, and
receives philanthropic support from a wide
range of individuals and institutions—and from
committed readers like you. To learn more, visit
ucpress.edu/supportus.